Compliance Officer's Handbook

by

John Virgo
Barrister
Guildhall Chambers

Philip Ryley
Solicitor and Head of Financial Services Regulation
TLT Solicitors

Members of the LexisNexis Group worldwide

United Kingdom	LexisNexis UK, a Division of Reed Elsevier (UK) Ltd, 2 Addiscombe Road, CROYDON CR9 5AF
Argentina	LexisNexis Argentina, BUENOS AIRES
Australia	LexisNexis Butterworths, CHATSWOOD, New South Wales
Austria	LexisNexis Verlag ARD Orac GmbH & Co KG, VIENNA
Canada	LexisNexis Butterworths, MARKHAM, Ontario
Chile	LexisNexis Chile Ltda, SANTIAGO DE CHILE
Czech Republic	Nakladatelství Orac sro, PRAGUE
France	Editions du Juris-Classeur SA, PARIS
Germany	LexisNexis Deutschland GmbH, FRANKFURT and MUNSTER
Hong Kong	LexisNexis Butterworths, HONG KONG
Hungary	HVG-Orac, BUDAPEST
India	LexisNexis Butterworths, NEW DELHI
Ireland	LexisNexis, DUBLIN
Italy	Giuffrè Editore, MILAN
Malaysia	Malayan Law Journal Sdn Bhd, KUALA LUMPUR
New Zealand	LexisNexis Butterworths, WELLINGTON
Poland	Wydawnictwo Prawnicze LexisNexis, WARSAW
Singapore	LexisNexis Butterworths, SINGAPORE
South Africa	LexisNexis Butterworths, Durban
Switzerland	Stämpfli Verlag AG, BERNE
USA	LexisNexis, DAYTON, Ohio

© Reed Elsevier (UK) Ltd 2004

Published by LexisNexis UK

First published 2004
Reprinted 2005

All rights reserved. No part of this publication may be reproduced in any material form (including photocopying or storing it in any medium by electronic means and whether or not transiently or incidentally to some other use of this publication) without the written permission of the copyright owner except in accordance with the provisions of the Copyright, Designs and Patents Act 1988 or under the terms of a licence issued by the Copyright Licensing Agency Ltd, 90 Tottenham Court Road, London, England W1T 4LP. Applications for the copyright owner's written permission to reproduce any part of this publication should be addressed to the publisher.

Warning: The doing of an unauthorised act in relation to a copyright work may result in both a civil claim for damages and criminal prosecution.

Crown copyright material is reproduced with the permission of the Controller of HMSO and the Queen's Printer for Scotland. Any European material in this work which has been reproduced from EUR-lex, the official European Communities legislation website, is European Communities copyright.

A CIP Catalogue record for this book is available from the British Library.

ISBN 0 7545 25708

Typeset by Kerrypress Ltd, Luton, Beds, http://www.kerrypress.co.uk
Printed and bound in Great Britain by Hobbs the Printers Ltd, Totton, Hampshire
Visit LexisNexis UK at www.lexisnexis.co.uk

About the Authors

John Virgo is a Barrister of 20 years' experience and an arbitrator with the Centre for Business Arbitration. He has wide experience of claims arising from mis-selling of endowment policies, home income plans, permanent health insurance policies and personal pension plans. John lectures widely on Financial Services Law and Regulation and is the author of or contributor to several books and numerous articles on aspects of the subject, including *Financial Advice and Financial Products* (Oxford University Press) and *Mortgage Regulation for Intermediaries* (LexisNexis), with Philip Ryley.

Philip Ryley, Solicitor and Head of Financial Services Regulation, TLT Solicitors, specialises in regulatory issues that affect financial services product providers, mortgage lenders, general insurers, networks and intermediaries. Philip is a founder member of the board of the Association of Mortgage Intermediaries (AMI) and also advises the National Association of Commercial Finance Brokers (NACFB) on FSA regulatory issues. Philip is an Associate of the Institute of Financial Planning and has the Financial Planning Certificate. He is also an Associate of the Compliance Institute (Vice-Chairman: South West Region), a Member of the Chartered Insurance Institute and the Life Insurance Association. He is also a Member of the Association of Regulatory and Disciplinary Lawyers. He is a contributor to *Mortgage Regulation for Intermediaries* (LexisNexis), writes regularly for compliance journals and other publications and is a frequent speaker at compliance and training conferences.

Foreword

For the busy compliance practitioner change is truly the only constant, as the regulatory system continues to expand into new areas and standards steadily rise.

The increased focus on senior management responsibility is also changing the role of the compliance function. From being essentially a monitor of compliance performance, the modern Compliance Officer is increasingly an adviser and catalyst in helping drive the compliance culture within the organisation. Compliance specialists are thus expected to marry strong personal skills with increasingly sophisticated regulatory tools, whilst at the same time analysing the impact of ever-changing rules and regulations.

Against this background of change it is easy to lose sight of the wider regulatory picture in which we operate. The *Compliance Officer's Handbook* is a welcome aid to both the experienced practitioner and the newcomer to compliance, providing a comprehensive yet practical overview of the new regulatory world, explaining how to get it right and avoid the pitfalls into which others have fallen.

Ken Davies
BA (Law) MBA ACII FCoI MSI
President of the Compliance Institute

The Compliance Institute (www.complianceinstitute.co.uk) is a non-profit making body dedicated to promoting the interests, development and training of compliance professionals.

Preface

No one attempting to write on the subject of financial services can be other than daunted by the scope of the material and the extent to which it evolves and mutates: the mass of common law and statutory provisions which go to make up the law of financial services, the detailed rules and regulations promulgated by the FSA, the Guidance regularly issued by the Regulator, the range of financial products and services increasingly falling under FSA regulatory control – to anyone new to the subject it is difficult to know where to begin.

The purpose and aim of this book is to offer a broad overview by way of introduction to the main topics which combine to make up this subject. One of the difficulties for anyone working in financial services is 'seeing the big picture'; the specialised nature of unique markets and practices often means that individuals acquire pockets of detailed knowledge necessarily relevant to their particular areas of activity; consequently they are not fully aware of how their work fits into the regulatory picture as a whole. In a professional world governed by an unusually high number of acronyms the abbreviated language so prevalent in this area can often seem mysterious and uninformative. It is hoped that this book will serve to de-mystify the topic and enable as much the newcomer as the experienced more specialised hand to see the essential framework within which financial services are delivered.

Consistent with the above aims, a conscious decision has been taken to keep to a minimum any overt reference to or citation of FSA rules, Guidance and legal authority. The approach is to set out an understanding of the core material without becoming enmeshed in the minutiae of the wording of particular provisions. In doing so, arguably precision is sacrificed in the interests of simple explication. The book should accordingly be seen as a 'first steps' reference source for the enquirer, who will then need to consider as appropriate whatever section of the *Financial Services and Markets Act 2000*, the secondary legislation made thereunder and parts of the FSA Handbook provide a detailed answer to any specific problem. It is hoped in this respect the work will also be useful to both seasoned compliance professionals and apprentices. It should be borne in mind that given the speed with which any aspect of financial regulation can change as a result of amendments to existing and/or future rules and regulations any commentary is almost inevitably at once out of date. Nonetheless, we have attempted to describe the framework governing compliance as it presents at October 2004.

Embracing the challenges implicit in the above has been a task greatly aided by the patient encouragement and helpful comments of our development editor,

Preface

Cara Annett, and the editorial team at LexisNexis (in particular Vicki Hillyard who has made numerous suggestions to simplify the text). We are very grateful for their support.

John Virgo
Guildhall Chambers

Philip Ryley
TLT Solicitors
October 2004

Contents

Abbreviations	xi
Table of Cases	xiii
Table of Statutes	xiv
Table of Statutory Instruments	xv

1. Market Regulation — 1
   Pre-1986: A Brief Background — 1
   The Changing Landscape — 1
   Regulation under the Financial Services Act 1986 Regime — 1
   Growth of Compliance — 4

2. The New Landscape — 7
   Regulated Products and Regulated Activities — 7
   Regulated Products — 8
   Regulated Activities — 9
   General Exclusions — 19

3. Applying for Authorisation — 23
   Introduction — 23
   Three Routes to Authorisation — 23
   The Principles for Business — 26
   Threshold Conditions — 30
   Approved Persons — 32
   The Statements of Principle for Approved Persons — 36
   Application and Determination — 39
   Limitations and Requirements — 42

4. Risk Based Compliance — 53
   Risk Assessment Framework — 53

5. Enforcement Action — 63
   Introduction — 63
   Uncovering non-compliance — 63
   Obtaining Information — 63
   Skilled Person's Report — 65
   General Investigations — 65
   Specific Investigations — 66

Search and Seizure 67
Supervisory Powers 68
Disciplining Firms and Approved Persons 72
Procedural Issues in respect of Enforcement and Disciplinary Action 74
Insolvency Orders 75
Administration Orders 76
Winding up by the Court 77
Voluntary winding up 77
Bankruptcy Orders 77
FSA Powers in relation to Voluntary Arrangements 78
Transactions at an Undervalue 79
The Financial Services and Markets Tribunal 79

6. **Compliance Models** **81**
Introduction 81
Compliance Output Supervision 81
Compliance Input Supervision 82
Dealing with Professional Indemnity Insurers 87

7. **Training and Competence** **95**
Core Standards 95
High Level Standards 95
Recruitment 96
Competence Levels 96
'Employee' and 'Activities' 97
Further Controls on Training and Competence 99
Maintaining Competence 100
Supervising Employees 101
Record Keeping 101

8. **Money Laundering** **103**
The FSA's Objectives 103
The Money Laundering Regulations 2003 108
The Proceeds of Crime Act 2002 109

9. **Complaints Handling, the Financial Ombudsman Service and the Financial Services Compensation Scheme** **111**
Complaints Handling 111
The Financial Ombudsman Service 117
The Financial Services Compensation Scheme 122

10. **Lessons from Past Failures** **129**
Introduction 129
Lessons from Equitable Life 129

Particular Case Study Examples	141
11. Conduct Of Business	**159**
Introduction	159
Designated Investment Business	159
Principal Obligations	162
Conduct of Business and Mortgage Sales	170
Insurance: Conduct Of Business	177
12. Financial Promotions	**183**
Background	183
General restriction	183
General requirements	195
Index	**197**

List of Abbreviations

AAE	ABM AMRO Equities (UK) Limited
AAI	ABM AMRO Inc
AVCs	Additional Voluntary Contributions
BAT	Business Assessment Team
BoS	Bank of Scotland
COB	Conduct of Business
CIS	Collective Investment Schemes
CPD	Continuing Professional Development
CVA	Corporate Voluntary Arrangement
DEC	Decision Making Manual
DISP	Dispute resolution: Complaints (FSA Handbook)
DTI	Department of Trade and Industry
DTWM	Deloitte & Touche Wealth Management Limited
E&O	Errors and Omissions (insurance)
EEA	European Economic Area
EIGP	Extra Income and Growth Plans
FIMBRA	Financial Intermediaries and Brokers Regulatory Association
FOS	Financial Ombudsman Services
FSA	Financial Services Authority
FSAVCs	Free-Standing AVCs
FSMA 2000	Financial Services and Markets Act 2000
GAO	Guaranteed Annuity Option
GAR	Guaranteed Annuity Rate
GIA	Group Internal Audit
HC	Holding Co Plc
ICOB	Insurance Mediation Services
IDD	Initial Disclosure Document
IMRO	Investment Management Organisation
IRECO	Irish European Reinsurance Company Limited
KFI	Key Features Illustration
LAUTRO	Life Assurance and Unit Trust Regulatory Organisation
LTSB	Lloyds TSB Bank Plc

List of Abbreviations

MBS	Mortgage Broker Subsidiary
MCOB	Regulated mortgages
MFL	Mortgage Funding Ltd
ML	Mortgage Loans Ltd
MLRO	Money Laundering Reporting Officer
NAS	New Account Sanctioner
NCIS	National Criminal Intelligence Service
OEIC	Open-Ended Investment Company
OPS	Occupational Pension Scheme
PI	Professional Indemnity
PIA	Personal Investment Authority
PSV	Professional Standards Visits Team
RAC	Retirement Annuity Contract
RAO	Financial Services and Markets Act 2000 (Regulated Activities) Order 2001 (SI 2001 No 544)
RDC	Regulatory Decisions Committee
RMC	Regulated Mortgage Contract
RPB	Recognised Professional Body
RTO	Risk to Objective
RTOGs	Risk to Objective Groups
SARs	Suspicious Activity Reports
SCARPs	Structured Capital At Risk Products
SIB	Securities and Investment Board
SFA	Securities and Futures Association
SFO	Serious Fraud Office
SGP	Secure Growth Portfolio
SROs	Self-Regulatory Organisations
SVD	Sales Verification Department
SYSC	Senior Management Arrangements, Systems and Controls
UCITS	Undertakings for Collective Investment in Transferable Securities
VJ	Voluntary Jurisdiction

Table of Cases

Alexander Forbes v SBJ Ltd [2003] Lloyd's Rep IR 432...................... 6.13
Barings Plc (No 5), Re [2000] 1 BCLC 523....................................... 3.43
Equitable Life Assurance Society v Hyman [2000] 4 WLR 529... 10.7, 10.10, 10.11
J Rothschild Assurance Plc v Collyear et al, 29.09.1998........... 6.8, 6.9, 6.14

Table of Statutes

Banking Act 1979..................... 1.2
Building Societies Act 1986........ 1.2
Companies Act 1985
  s 71 .... 3.42
  s 425 .... 5.19
Companies Act 1989................. 1.2
Company Directors
  Disqualification Act 1986 ...... 5.15
Consumer Credit Act 1974....... 3.48
Data Protection Act 1998........... 9.5
Financial Services Act 1986........ 1.3
  s 62 .... 10.10
Financial Services and Markets
  Act 2000 .... 1.4, 2.1, 3.7, 3.54,
                       4.1, 5.12, 5.16,
                     5.22, 10.28, 12.1,
                           12.2, 12.9
  Part IV 2.2, 2.4, 2.14, 2.15, 3.2,
                      3.6, 3.25, 3.30,
                     3.38, 3.45, 3.46,
                      5.6, 5.9, 5.17,
                        10.26, 10.30

Financial Services and Markets Act
  2000 – *contd*
  Part XXIV 5.18
Friendly Societies Act 1846........ 1.2
Friendly Societies Act 1875........ 1.2
Friendly Societies Acts
  1974–1992 .... 1.2
Insolvency Act 1986
  s 214(4) 3.40
Insurance Brokers
  (Registration) Act 1977 ...... 11.36
Insurance Companies Acts
  1958–1982 .... 1.2
Limitation Act 1980............... 11.20
National Loans Act 1968.......... 12.6
Prevention of Fraud
  Investment Act 1939 .... 1.2
Prevention of Fraud
  Investment Act 1958 .... 1.2
Proceeds of Crime Act 2002...... 8.1,
                            8.10–8.13

Table of Statutory Instruments

Financial Services and Markets Act 2000 (Exemption) Order 2001 (SI 2001 No 1201) 3.4

Financial Services and Markets Act 2000 (Financial Promotion) Order 2001 (SI 2001 No 2633) 12.6, 12.7, 12.9, 12.11, 12.14, 12.15

Parts V, VI 12.12

Financial Services and Markets Act 2000 (Regulated Activities) Order 2001 (SI 2001 No 544) ... 2.2, 2.5, 2.22

Part 3 .... 2.3
art 6 .... 2.6
art 9C 2.7
art 9K 2.7

Financial Services and Markets Act 2000 (Regulated Activities by Way of Business) Order 2001 (SI 2001 No 1177) 2.5

Insurance Brokers Registration Council (Code of Conduct) Approval Order 1994 (SI 1994 No 2569) 11.36

Insurance Companies Regulations 1981 (SI 1981 No 1654) 10.11

Insurer's (Winding up) Rules 2001 (SI 2001 No 3635) 9.31

Judgments Enforcements (Northern Ireland) Order 1981 (SI 1981 No 226) 9.19

Money Laundering Regulations 2003 (SI 2003 No 3075) 8.1, 8.3, 8.9
reg 3 .... 8.10

Third Parties (Rights Against Insurers) Act 1930 .... 9.23

Uncertificated Securities Regulations 2001 (SI 2001 No 3755) 2.16

Chapter 1
Market Regulation

Pre-1986: A Brief Background 1.1

The need for and role of the modern day Compliance Officer developed out of the gradual increase in market regulation and statutory control exerted over financial services. Historically, the same general law that applied to all domestic and business transactions governed the delivery of financial products to the market. The provision of financial advice and the arranging of product sales required almost no more than that the product provider or financial adviser comply with the laws of contract, the common law of negligence and avoid falling foul of a handful of criminal statutes outlawing fraud. In as much as anything was bought and sold without paying any conscious regard to any of these areas of law, so it was with financial service products. There was accordingly no identified need for a 'Compliance Officer'.

The Changing Landscape 1.2

The landscape began to change in response to the impact of large-scale market failures. Speculative investment and spectacular losses in the infamous South Sea Company led to the first ever attempt at statutory regulation by the enactment of the *Bubble Act* in the 18th century. This was the forerunner of the later *Prevention of Fraud Investment Acts* of 1939 and 1958. Legislation was introduced in a piecemeal fashion, addressing different sectors of the market, and included:

- the *Insurance Companies Acts 1958–1982*;
- the *Banking Act 1979*;
- the *Friendly Societies Acts 1846, 1875* and *1974–1992*; and
- the *Building Societies Act 1986*.

The concept of 'compliance' as we understand it today, however, remained undeveloped.

Regulation under the Financial Services Act 1986 Regime

There was by the early 1980s at least a perception that these evolving measures of financial regulation did not secure adequate investor protection. The Gower Report, *A Review of Investor Protection*, was published in 1984 with sweeping recommendations for a new model of regulatory control for the delivery of investment services. The aim was to devise a system that offered (as the Report put it) 'no greater protection than necessary to protect reasonable people from being made fools of.'

These proposals were largely adopted and resulted in the *Financial Services Act 1986* ('the 1986 Act'). The scheme of protection began from the premise that only authorised persons should be able to advise on and sell investment products. Submitting to regulatory control by the Securities and Investment Board (SIB) would confer authorisation, as would membership of bodies approved for the purpose by the SIB.

The approved bodies were the self-regulatory organisations (SROs) such as the Life Assurance and Unit Trust Regulatory Organisation (LAUTRO), the Financial Intermediaries and Brokers Regulatory Association (FIMBRA), the Investment Management Organisation (IMRO), the Securities and Futures Association (the SFA) and later the Personal Investment Authority (PIA), together with certain recognised professional bodies (RPBs) such as the Law Society in the case of solicitors and the Institute of Actuaries (again to name but a few).

Authorisation could also be granted directly by the Secretary of State. The SIB provided a template in the form of detailed sets of rules to be followed in advising upon and arranging investments (the SIB rulebook). The SRO rulebooks were modelled on this draft.

Central to the regime was the ability of the authorised firm to demonstrate compliance with the rulebooks issued by the self-regulatory bodies. To begin with the rulebooks were required to provide a level of protection equivalent to the SIB rulebook. The result in practice was a detailed, prescriptive and unworkable mass of regulations and rules, which rendered compliance with the regime difficult if not impossible to manage. Infringements of the rules attracted a right to compensation and so exposed those concerned with advising on and arranging investments at risk of claims from both private investors and sophisticated market counterparties. The balance was not right.

In 1989 the framework thus devised was loosened up by amendments to the 1986 Act introduced through the *Companies Act 1989*. This was achieved first by giving the SIB power to issue 'Statements of Principle' which defined the underlying principles behind regulation and acted as a guide to interpreting and implementing the new core rules.

There were ten Principles set out as cornerstones to regulation defining in broad terms high aspirational standards in respect of:

1. Integrity
2. Skill, care and diligence
3. Market practice
4. Information about customers
5. Information for customers
6. Conflicts of interest
7. Customer assets
8. Financial resources
9. Internal organisation
10. Relations with regulators

Although superseded by the now 'Principles for Businesses' discussed at 1.4 below, the SIB Statements of Principle were similar in scope and identical in aim to the new overarching provisions which now define the essential requirements for all financial service market operators.

Any requirement for virtual replication of and compliance with the detail of the SIB rulebook was diluted. Instead the SIB was given power to designate certain core rules in its rulebook, which the SROs and RPBs would need to reproduce in effect in their own member rulebooks. These are now of historic interest. There were 40 core Conduct of Business rules, covering key issues such as advertising and marketing, customer relations and dealing with customers, market integrity and administration. There were also five financial supervision core rules addressing such matters as financial resources, records and reporting, internal controls and systems, and relations with the regulator.

Rule breaches became actionable only in the main at the instance of private investors. Market counterparties and non-private (ie business investors) were considered able to look after themselves. This revised approach became known as 'the new settlement'.

The regime, however, depended for enforcement largely on a contractual model. In other words the authorised firm 'agreed' in exchange for membership of the SRO or RPB to abide by its regulator's rules (including therefore the designated core rules and the Statements of Principle). The SROs and RPBs were obliged to have in place adequate systems for monitoring compliance by its members with the rules. Thus, 'compliance' became a key issue for self-regulated firms. The focus was on ensuring observance of the rules relating to the delivery of financial transactions and being able to demonstrate that the rules had been followed.

Growth of Compliance

The origins of 'compliance' can be traced back to these early attempts at self-regulation. SIB Statement of Principle 9 required that:

> 'a firm should organise and control its internal affairs in a responsible manner, keeping proper records, and where the firm employs staff or is responsible for the conduct of investment business by others, should have adequate arrangements to ensure that they are suitable, adequately trained and properly supervised and that it has well defined compliance procedures.'

Included within core Conduct of Business rule 34 was a requirement that:

> 'a firm must take reasonable steps, including the establishment and maintenance of procedures, to ensure that its officers and employees and officers and employees of its appointed representatives act in conformity with ... their own and their employer's relevant responsibilities under the regulatory system.'

Further this core rule stipulated that:

> 'a firm must take reasonable steps, including the establishment and maintenance of procedures, to ensure that sufficient information is recorded and retained about its regulated business and compliance with the regulatory system.'

These provisions brought to the fore the 'office of compliance' as a distinct and necessary adjunct to any properly run financial services business. The ethos can be seen in the international context of Conduct of Business principles devised and adopted in 1990 by the International Organisation of Securities Commissions which included the following (Principle 7):

> 'A firm should comply with all regulatory requirements applicable to the conduct of its business activities so as to promote the best interests of customers and the integrity of the market.'

The ensuing history, however, was one of ineffective self-regulation in which the adoption of these high standards proved difficult to implement and enforce. Scandals such as the mass mis-selling of personal pension plans in the late 1980s and early 1990s; Additional Voluntary Contributions (AVCs) mis-sales over a similar period; and mis-selling and mis-marketing of home income plans and endowment-linked mortgage products all revealed weaknesses in the ability of the self-regulatory structure governing investment products to secure compliant sales transactions. Further scandals such as the Maxwell affair, the collapse of Barings Bank, BCCI, the 'Peter Young' affair at Morgan Grenfell and the demise of Equitable Life each raised concern at the extent to which financial institutions and corporations could be relied upon to manage their businesses without posing a threat to the market.

Likewise, such scandals posed questions as to the efficacy of prudential and supervisory control exerted by their regulators. Outside the investment and long-term insurance market, the picture of regulatory control was fragmented with a proliferation of different regulatory bodies exerting varying degrees of control and influence over its members – the Building Societies Commission, the General Insurance Standards Council, the Mortgage Code Compliance Board, and the Registrar of Friendly Societies to name but a few.

The result was a move away from self-regulation to a unified system of statutory control implemented by the *Financial Services and Markets Act 2000* (*FSMA 2000*). The philosophy of the new regime is very different from that which immediately preceded it: 'compliance' is no longer based on submitting by agreement to the SRO and RPB rules as an incident of membership – it is now a matter of statutory duty enforceable by the Financial Services Authority (the FSA) as statutory regulator.

Much more than a shift in the basis of power and enforcement rights, the new regime embraces a different approach to the concept of 'compliance'. The FSA Handbook (a more comprehensive and user-friendly version of the old rule books) sets out new Conduct of Business rules and lays down other prudential and supervisory requirements. Whilst adherence to these new rules governing promotions and sales is both necessary and important, compliance is not just about demonstrating adherence but establishing systems and controls for identifying risk areas of likely default. Further, the responsibility for managing and ensuring that a business is efficiently and compliantly operated is placed firmly on the shoulders of those in charge of firms: the chief executive, managing directors and partners. These key personnel are now personally accountable for the way in which a business is run. In the new landscape the 'Compliance Officer' and his role has accordingly assumed a hitherto unparalleled significance.

The aim of this book is to examine in outline the scheme of the new regime and look particularly at the role of compliance in it. It is unrealistic in a book of this size to attempt to distil the detailed content of the FSA Handbook. Compliance Officers working in different sectors of the industry may be expected to have a detailed knowledge of those regulations, rules and requirements relevant to their particular sector. Often, however, because of the necessary focus of their attention on a limited area of the market the Compliance Officer does not see the broad picture; new recruits to the work of compliance may also be unfamiliar with the broad scheme of the UK market regulation. It is hoped that this book will accordingly paint, albeit with a broad brush, the main features of the landscape. The book is accordingly offered as a navigational guide which it is hoped will be of value to anyone seeking to find their way around the main landmarks of the regulatory canvas.

Chapter 2
The New Landscape

Regulated Products and Regulated Activities 2.1

In outline, the basic regulatory framework of the *Financial Services and Markets Act 2000* (*FSMA 2000* or 'the 2000 Act') involves categorising certain products as falling within the scope of intended regulatory control ('regulated products') but only in respect of particular activities (as described) carried out in relation thereto ('regulated activities'). The 2000 Act then provides that no person may carry on a regulated activity in the United Kingdom, or purport to do so, unless he is an authorised person or an exempt person. This is known as the general prohibition.

The general prohibition 2.2

The consequences of a breach of the general prohibition are:

- the commission of a criminal offence carrying a risk of imprisonment or a fine or both. It is a defence for the accused to show that he took all reasonable precautions and exercised all due diligence to avoid committing the offence;

- agreements made by or through unauthorised persons are prima facie unenforceable and damages may be recovered by the other party for losses caused by entering into an agreement with or through an unauthorised firm (along with a return of any money or property parted with under the agreement).

To become 'authorised' to carry out particular activities in relation to regulated products, the firm in question will require a Part IV (of the *FSMA 2000*) permission from the Financial Services Authority (FSA) (unless it is treated as authorised already under a number of other provisions in the Act discussed at 3.3 below). The Part IV permission will specify the scope of activities the firm may perform relative to particular products. The process of obtaining a Part IV permission is discussed in CHAPTER 3.

2.3 *The New Landscape*

It follows that it is necessary and appropriate to identify *firstly* the products falling within the scope of regulatory control and *secondly* the activities which, if performed in respect of such products, also attract an authorisation requirement.

Regulated Products 2.3

This section identifies the 'regulated products'. These were first defined by *SI 2001 No 544* (The *Financial Services and Markets Act 2000 (Regulated Activities) Order 2001* ('the RAO'). The RAO has been amended on a number of occasions but the scheme of the original remains pretty much intact. The relevant list of regulated products is set out in Part 3 of the RAO as follows:

- deposits;
- electric money;
- rights under a contract of insurance;
- stocks and shares;
- debentures, debenture and loan stock, bonds, certificates of deposit and 'any other instrument creating or acknowledging indebtedness';
- certain government and public securities;
- warrants and other instruments entitling the holder to subscribe for stocks, shares, debentures, debenture and loan stock, bonds, certificates of deposit and any other instrument creating or acknowledging indebtedness;
- units in collective investment schemes;
- rights under stakeholder pension schemes;
- futures and options;
- contracts for differences;
- the underwriting capacity/membership of a Lloyd's Syndicate;
- rights under a funeral plan contract;
- rights under a regulated mortgage contract; and
- rights to or interests in any of the above categories of investment (save interests under the trusts of an occupational pension scheme and any investment otherwise falling specifically within any of the above definitions).

Understanding the nature of the product 2.4

Clearly an understanding of the instrument comprising the 'investment' in any particular instance is critically important, both for the purpose of ensuring that the firm is entitled to perform any of the (below) 'regulated activities' in respect of it under the terms of its Part IV permission and also for taking steps to avoid breaches of the general prohibition.

This issue can be of particular importance where the authorised firm carries on business through appointed representatives. Take, as an example, an authorised firm with a Part IV permission to advise on and arrange pension transfers, pension opt-outs and other typical life assurance investments which trade through an appointed representative. The appointed representative will only be able to carry out activities on behalf of its principal for which the latter has a relevant Part IV permission.

The writers are familiar with one recent example involving threatened enforcement action for carrying on an unregulated activity in the following circumstances: the appointed representative wished to raise capital for the purpose of business development. It accordingly solicited 'investments' taking the form of unsecured interest bearing loans made by established clients of the business. On one view it was possible to regard the receipt of such loan money as involving accepting 'deposits'. The intention was for the appointed representative business to be funded to an extent which could not be disregarded as immaterial out of the capital provided by way of deposit. Although the appointed representative firm was not holding itself out as accepting deposits on a day-to-day business (and did not carry on business as a deposit taker in a conventional sense) the deposits solicited were not limited to ones requested on particular occasions but were solicited as part of a wider 'investment' marketing opportunity.

It was also, on one view, possible to regard the arrangements as apt to create a collective investment scheme (for which the principal also lacked a discrete Part IV permission).

The risks of breaches of regulatory control accordingly facing the principal and the appointed representative firm were serious: carrying on an unauthorised regulated activity and failure properly to supervise the activities by the principal of its appointed representative. The importance of defining 'investment activity' by reference to the above list of 'regulated products' accordingly cannot be overestimated.

Regulated Activities 2.5

The *Financial Services and Markets Act 2000 (Regulated Activities) Order 2001 (SI 2001 No 544)* ('the RAO') also defines the type(s) of activity carried on in relation to 'regulated products' which bring matters within the scope of regulatory control. In each instance the activity in question must be carried on by way of business. The latter requirement is developed in the *Financial Services and Markets Act 2000 (Carrying on Regulated Activities by Way of Business) Order 2001 (SI 2001 No 1177)*.

2.6 The New Landscape

This 'by way of Business Order' deals with three particular types of business: deposit taking business, investment business and managing investments of occupational pension schemes.

So far as 'deposit taking business' is concerned, the carrying on of such an activity will not be regarded as 'by way of business' if the person concerned does not hold himself out as accepting deposits on a day-to-day basis and any deposits accepted are taken on particular occasions only. In deciding whether deposits are accepted only on particular occasions, regard is to be had to the frequency of those occasions and to any characteristics distinguishing them from each other.

So far as carrying on investment business 'by way of business' is concerned, the Regulations bite only in respect of the following activities:

- dealing in investments as principal or agent;
- arranging deals in investments;
- managing investments;
- safeguarding and administering investments;
- sending dematerialised instructions;
- establishing and performing certain functions in relation to collective investment schemes or stakeholder pension schemes;
- advising on investments; and
- agreeing to do any of the above.

Although the above refers to 'investments', the scope of the Regulations extends to many general insurance contracts and certain types of mortgage advances which might be thought of conventionally as 'investments'.

So far as managing the investments of an occupational pension scheme are concerned, detailed provisions are set out in the RAO, the gist of which is to catch professional investment managers.

The scheme of the RAO is to define particular types of 'activity' and then specify (in most instances) exclusions to particular activities. Given the breadth of many of the regulated activities it is appropriate to spend some time looking at each.

Accepting deposits 2.6

Accepting deposits is a regulated activity if the money received by way of deposit is lent to others or any other activity of the person accepting the deposit is financed wholly or to a material extent out of the capital of or interest on money received by way of deposit. The money maybe repayable with or without interest either on demand or at a time or in circumstances agreed between the parties to the transaction, provided the sum of money advanced is not referable to the provision of property (other than currency) or services or the giving of security.

Deposits by certain categories of person are excluded, eg payments made by the Bank of England, the Central Bank of an EEA State other than the United Kingdom, or the European Central Bank. A list of relevant institutions is set out in Article 6 of the RAO. Sums received by practising solicitors in the course of their profession likewise are excluded from the definition of 'accepting deposits'. Similarly, a sum is not a deposit for the purpose of the activity of 'deposit taking' if it is received by a person who is authorised to carry on certain other specified activities (notably dealing in investments as principal, dealing in investments as agents, arranging deals in investments, managing investments and establishing collective investment schemes or stakeholder pension schemes). Also, a sum of money is not a deposit if it is immediately exchanged for electric money.

Electric money 2.7

The issuing of electric money is a specified regulated activity subject to exclusions in respect of persons certified as small issuers. Articles 9C and 9K of the RAO provide a detailed regime for such issuers to obtain certificates in respect of the excluded activity.

Insurance 2.8

Effecting or carrying out a contract of insurance as principal is a regulated activity. Principal exclusions relate to community co-insurers, provision of breakdown insurance and special arrangements made in relation to Lloyd's Underwriting.

Dealing in investments as principal 2.9

Buying, selling, subscribing for or underwriting securities or contractually based investments (other than funeral plans and regulated mortgage contracts) as principal is a regulated activity. Such dealing is, however, excluded unless the firm:

- holds itself out as willing, as principal, to buy, sell or subscribe for investments of the kind to which the transaction relates at prices determined by it generally and continuously rather than in respect of each particular transaction;

2.9 The New Landscape

- holds itself out as engaging in the business of buying investments of the kind to which the transaction relates, with a view to selling them;
- holds itself out as engaging in the business of underwriting investments of the kind to which the transaction relates; or
- regularly solicits members of the public with the purpose of inducing them, as principals or agents, to enter into transactions constituting relevant dealings and the transaction is entered into as a result of the member of the public having been solicited.

For the above purpose 'members of the public' include any persons other than:

- authorised or exempt persons in relation to the activity of dealing;
- members of the same group as the firm;
- persons who are or who propose to become participators with the firm in a joint enterprise;
- any person solicited by the firm with a view to the acquisition by it of 20% or more of the voting shares in a limited company;
- if the firm (either alone or with members of the same group) holds more than 20% of the voting shares in the limited company concerned, any person solicited by it with a view to the acquisition by the firm of further shares in the same company or the disposal of shares to the person solicited (or to a member of the same group as the person solicited);
- any person who is solicited by the firm with a view to the disposal by it of shares in a limited company to the person solicited or to a member of the same group as that person provided the person (alone or with members of the same group) holds 20% or more of the voting shares in the company; and
- any person whose head office is outside the UK, who is solicited by an approach made or directed to him at a place outside the UK and whose ordinary business involves him in carrying on activities comprising dealing in investments as principal, dealing in investments as agents, arranging deals in investments, managing investments, safeguarding and administering investments, sending dematerialised instructions, establishing collective investment schemes and the stakeholder pension schemes and/or advising on investments.

Further, a person who is not an authorised person does not 'deal in investments as principal' in respect of contractually based investments by effecting a transaction with or through an authorised or exempt person or through an office outside the UK maintained by a party to the transaction whose ordinary business involves dealing in, arranging, managing and advising on investments.

Further, a person does not carry on the activity of dealing in investments as principal but accepting an instrument created or acknowledging indebtedness in respect of any loan, credit, guarantee or other similar financial accommodation or assurance which *he* has made, granted or provided. Likewise, the issue by a company of its own shares, share warrants or debentures or debenture warrants does not involve the activity of 'dealing as principal'.

A number of 'other exclusions' apply to this activity which, insofar as they relate to a number of other regulated activities are described at 2.24 and 2.30 below.

Dealing in investments as agent 2.10

With the exception of funeral plans and regulated mortgage contracts, buying, selling, subscribing for or underwriting securities or relevant instruments as agent is specified as a regulated activity.

A person is not treated as 'dealing in investments as agent' where, being unauthorised, he enters into a transaction as agent for another with or through an authorised person, provided either the transaction is entered into on advice given to the 'other person' by an authorised person or it is clear in all the circumstances that the 'other person', in his capacity as an investor, is not seeking and has not sought advice from the agent as to the merits of entering into the particular transaction.

This exclusion, however, does not apply to contracts of insurance or where the agent receives from any person other than his principal any pecuniary reward or other advantage for which he does not account to his principal arising out of his entering into the transaction.

Arranging deals and investments 2.11

There are two aspects to 'arranging deals and investments'. First, it is a regulated activity for a firm to make arrangements for another person (whether as principal or agent) to buy, sell, subscribe for or underwrite a particular investment which is a security, a relevant investment or an interest in a relevant investment. This activity contemplates a person entering into a transaction in respect of a particular investment.

Secondly, it is a regulated activity to make arrangements with a view to a person who participates in them buying, selling, subscribing for or underwriting any of the above types of investment. Here, it is sufficient if the person participating in the arrangements does so with a view to any relevant investment coming about rather than any particular investment. Either type of arranging undertaken in respect of regulated mortgage contracts and in relation to persons acting as borrower are similarly caught.

Arrangements made in respect of particular investments are excluded from the activity of arranging deals and investments where they do not or would not bring around the transaction to which they relate. Likewise, there are excluded from the definitions any arrangements for transactions into which the person making the arrangements enters or is to enter as principal or as agent for some other person. In those circumstances the activities of 'dealing as principal' or 'dealing as agent' would arise.

Deals arranged for a person with or through an authorised firm are also not caught provided the transaction is to be entered into on advice given by the authorised person alone or it is clear in all the circumstances that no reliance is placed on the intermediary in respect of the merits of the proposed transaction.

Arrangements made by a money lender to advance sums on the security of an investment contract are also outside the definition of arranging deals and investments provided (in particular) the person who is intending to borrow money is introduced by the authorised person (or someone acting on his behalf) who either entered into or is about to enter into the relevant transaction over which security will be taken.

Excluded from the definition of 'arranging deals and investments' are also arrangements under which a person accepts or is to accept (whether as principal or agent) an instrument creating or acknowledging indebtedness in respect of any loan, credit, guarantee or other similar financial accommodation or assurance which is (or is to be) made, granted or provided by that person or his principal. This therefore excludes the acceptance of debentures in connection with loans.

Arrangements having as their sole purpose the provision of finance to enable a person to buy, sell, subscribe or underwrite investments likewise fall outside the definition of making arrangements with a view to those participating in them buying, selling, subscribing for or underwriting investments.

Introducers 2.12

There is an important exception for 'introducers' save where the regulated product is a contract of insurance. Under this exclusion, arrangements under which a client will be introduced to an authorised or exempt person are taken out of the definition of 'arranging deals and investments' where the introduction is made with a view to the provision of independent advice or the independent exercise of discretion in relation to investments generally or any class of investments to which the arrangements relate. Plainly, this would not apply therefore to introductions to a particular life office which would be unable to provide independent advice.

Arrangements made by a company for the purposes of issuing its own shares, share warrants, debentures or debenture warrants are also excluded from the activity of arranging deals and investments (see 2.11).

Managing investments 2.13

The activity of managing assets belonging to another person in circumstances involving the exercise of discretion is a regulated activity where the assets consist of or include investments which are securities or contractually based investments.

An exclusion applies, however, in relation to a person appointed to manage the assets in question under a power of attorney provided all routine or day-to-day decisions in respect of investments are taken by an authorised person with permission to carry on the activity of managing investments or is otherwise an exempt or overseas person.

This activity also benefits from certain generic exclusions discussed at 2.24 and 2.26 below.

Assisting in the administration and performance of a contract of insurance 2.14

Performing and/or assisting in the administration of a contract of insurance is a regulated activity.

In addition to generic exclusions discussed at 2.24 to 2.30 below, the activities of certain categories of individual are also taken outside this particular regulated activity, namely those providing an expert appraisal, loss adjusters and claims managers on behalf of relevant insurers. For these purposes 'relevant insurer' means a person with a Part IV permission to effect or carry out a contract of insurance, members of the society of Lloyd's, certain EEA firms and relevant reinsurers.

Safeguarding and administering investments 2.15

Subject to general and specific exclusions discussed at 2.24 to 2.30 below, the 'safeguarding and/or administering' of investments is a regulated activity provided the assets consist of or include any investment which is either a security or a contractually based investment. For these purposes a 'security' means stocks and shares, debentures, debenture and loan stock, bonds, certificates of deposit and any other instrument creating or acknowledging indebtedness, along with certain Government and public securities, warrants and other instruments relating to the foregoing, certificates representing certain securities, units in collective investment schemes and rights under stakeholder pension schemes.

'Contractually based' investments means options, futures, contracts for differences and rights under funeral plan contracts along with rights under qualifying contracts of insurance. 'Qualifying contracts of insurance' means contracts of long-term insurance which are not reinsurance contracts nor ones in respect of which certain conditions are met (ie where the benefits under the contract are payable only on death or in respect of incapacity due to injury, sickness or infirmity and the benefits (where payable on death) are only due in the event of death occurring within ten years of the date on which the life of the person in question was first insured or where the death occurs before that person attains a specified age not exceeding 70 years).

Excluded from the above activity are arrangements under which the assets are entrusted to a 'qualifying custodian' with a Part IV permission in respect of safeguarding and administering investments. Further, certain activities are taken outside the definition of asset administration, being the provision of information as to the number of units or the value of any assets safeguarded, converting currency and receiving documents relating to investments solely for the purpose of onward transmission to, from or at the direction of the person to whom the investment in question belongs.

This particular activity also benefits from general exclusions discussed at 2.24 to 2.30 below.

Sending de-materialised instructions 2.16

The sending on behalf of another person of dematerialised instructions relating to a security or a contractually based investment is also a specified regulated activity. The instructions must be sent by means of a relevant system in respect of which the operator is approved under the *Uncertificated Securities Regulations 2001 (SI 2001 No 3755)*.

Excluded from the scope of this regulated activity are instructions sent by or on behalf of a participating issuer, a settlement bank and/or an offer or making a takeover. There is also an exclusion in respect of the act of sending or causing to be sent a dematerialised instruction as a necessary part of providing a network, the purpose of which is to carry dematerialised instructions which are at all times properly authenticated.

As with other activities discussed in this section certain generic exclusions discussed at 2.24 to 2.30 below also apply.

Collective investment scheme activities 2.17

Establishing, operating or winding up a collective investment scheme is a regulated activity; so too is the activity of anyone acting as Trustee of an authorised unit trust scheme and/or anyone acting as the depository or sole Director of an open-ended investment company (OEIC).

Stakeholder pension schemes 2.18

Activities comprising the establishing, operating or winding up of a stakeholder pension scheme are also specified as regulated activities.

Advising on investments 2.19

This is an important area of regulated activity. Advice given on the merits of buying, selling, subscribing for or underwriting a particular investment given to a person in his capacity as an investor or potential investor is a regulated activity. It follows that the provision of information or generic advice about investments is not caught since it would not involve the provision of advice in respect of 'a particular investment'. In practice, however, it is not difficult for general advice to turn into a specific recommendation.

The regulated activity includes providing advice to a borrower or potential borrower as to the merits of entering into or varying the terms of a particular regulated mortgage contract.

Specific exclusions are set out in respect of general advice given in newspapers, journals and other periodicals along with advice offered in the course of the broadcast or transmission of television or radio programmes. In these instances, however, the 'advice' must be generic and not designed to lead or enable investors to deal or take steps in respect of any particular product.

Again, the activity benefits from a number of generic exclusions discussed at 2.24 to 2.30 below.

Lloyd's activities 2.20

Advising in respect of Lloyd's Syndicate Membership and the activities of Lloyd's Managing Agents are all regulated activities. So also is the arranging of deals in contracts of insurance written at Lloyd's.

Funeral plan contracts 2.21

Entering as provider into a funeral plan contract is a regulated activity. The following arrangements are then excluded from this regulated activity:

- plans entered into in circumstances where the customer and the provider intend or expect a funeral to occur within one month;
- plans covered by a whole of life insurance policy effected and carried out by an authorised person with a permission to effect and carry out such contracts of insurance for the purpose of providing the funeral; and

- certain trust schemes under which sums paid by the customer are independently managed for the relevant purpose.

Regulated mortgage contracts 2.22

The entering into a regulated mortgage contract as lender is a regulated activity; so to are the activities involved in administering such contracts. A mortgage contract is regulated for these purposes if it satisfies all of the following conditions:

- the contract is one under which a lender provides credit to an individual or Trustee ('the borrower');
- the obligation of the borrower to repay is secured by first legal mortgage on land (other than time share accommodation) in the UK; and
- at least 40% of that land is used or intended to be used as or in connection with a dwelling by the borrower (or in the case of Trustees by an individual who is a beneficiary of the Trust) or by a related person. A related person means:
    (i) that person's spouse;
    (ii) a person whose relationship has the characteristics of that between husband and wife (whether or not of the opposite sex); or
    (iii) that person's parent, brother, sister, child, grandparent or grandchild.
  Administering a regulated mortgage contract includes notifying the borrower of changes in interest rates or payments due under the contract and taking any necessary steps for the purposes of collecting or recovering payments from the borrower. Administering does not, however, extend to the act of simply taking steps to enforce the contract where a right to do so has arisen.

In addition to certain generic exclusions the RAO also provides for the specific exclusion of activities comprising:

- arranging for another authorised person to administer the contract;
- administering the contract for a period of not more than one month after an arrangement of the kind mentioned above comes to an end; and
- providing an administration service to a person who is appropriately authorised.

Agreeing to carry on activities 2.23

With the exception of accepting deposits, issuing electronic money, effecting and carrying out contracts of insurance and regulated activities in respect of collective investment schemes and stakeholder pension schemes, agreements to carry on any of the other prescribed activities discussed at 2.6 to 2.11 and 2.13 to 2.22 above are also caught as involving the carrying on of a regulated activity.

General Exclusions

Trustees, nominees and personal representatives 2.24

The first generic exclusion seeks to protect activities of certain Trustees, nominees and personal representatives from a need which would otherwise arise to become authorised to carry out particular activities. The first generic exclusion is relevant to activities concerned with:

- dealing in investments;
- managing investments;
- assisting in the administration and performance of a contract of insurance;
- safeguarding and administering investments;
- advising on investments and regulated mortgage contracts;
- entering into and/or administering regulated mortgage contracts.

In general, trustees, nominees and personal representatives acting on behalf beneficiaries, certain third parties and estates do not need to be authorised in respect of the above activities where they are provided otherwise than as part of a business concerned with the provision of such services and provided they do not receive any remuneration for the work in addition to that which would be received for acting as Trustee or personal representative.

Activities carried on in the course of the profession or non-investment business 2.25

By definition, this will not apply to firms carrying on regulated investment business activity. It is mentioned here as a general exclusion for completeness only. It arises in respect of the following activities which would otherwise be caught:

- dealing in investments as agent;
- arranging and making arrangements with a view to investments/ regulated mortgage contracts;
- assisting in the administration or performance of contracts of insurance;
- safeguarding and administering investments; and

- advising on investments and regulated mortgage contracts.

Where the above activities are undertaken in the course of carrying on any professional business which does not otherwise consist of carrying on regulated activities a need for authorisation does not arise provided the particular activity in question may reasonably be regarded as a necessary part of the provision of other services provided in the course of the particular professional business. It is also a requirement that the activity in question is not separately remunerated from other services. It is an exclusion which will be of most use to (for example) accountants and lawyers providing advice on tax implications of investments and/or legal advice in respect of investment transactions.

Activities carried on in connection with the sale of goods or supply of services 2.26

The following generic exclusion is relevant to particular activities of:

- dealing in investments as principal and agent;
- arranging investments;
- managing investments;
- assisting in the administration and performance of contracts of insurance;
- safeguarding and administering investments;
- sending dematerialised instructions;
- establishing collective investment schemes and stakeholder pension schemes; and
- advising on investments.

In general, where the above activities are carried on for the purposes of or in connection with the sale of goods or the supply of other services to a customer a discrete need for authorisation is avoided. The exclusions do not, however, extend to insurance contracts and units in collective investment schemes. Again, by definition this generic exclusion will not be relevant to mainstream financial service businesses.

Groups and joint enterprises 2.27

In broad terms dealing in investments as principal or agent and arranging investments are excluded from the scope of regulation where these are undertaken as between members of the same group or passed between participators in a joint enterprise. Here, 'joint enterprise' means an enterprise in which two or more persons (the 'participators') enter for commercial purposes related to a business other than that of engaging in a regulated activity. The exclusion does not extend to advice relating to and/or the sale or purchase of a contract of insurance.

Activities carried on in connection with the sale of a body corporate   2.28

For completeness it may be mentioned that the activities of dealing in investments, advising and arranging where the investments comprise shares in a company (other than an open-ended investment company) are excluded from the regime where the transaction in question involves the acquisition or disposal of (in effect) 50% or more of the floating shares or sufficient of the holding with a view to acquiring day-to-day control of the affairs of the company.

Miscellaneous further exclusions   2.29

We mention finally a collection of further general exclusions particularly relevant to activities involving dealing in, arranging and advising on investments. These provide exclusions in respect of such activities carried on in connection with employee share schemes; they further avail overseas persons dealing with authorised businesses in the UK. A further exclusion deals with the provision of an information society service from any EEA State other than the UK.

Further exclusions in respect of insurance contracts   2.30

Certain types of 'connected contracts of insurance' benefit from exclusions from the regulated activity regime in respect of dealing as agent, arranging, assisting in the administration, and performance and advising. The contracts of insurance are ones providing breakdown, loss of or damage to non-motor goods and damage to or loss of baggage and other risks linked to travel. The insurance contract must be for a total duration of five years or less and involve an annual premium of 500 euro or less. Further, the insurance contract must be of such a kind that the only information a person requires in order to (for example) arrange or advise on it is detail in respect of the cover provided. The exclusion avails 'providers', meaning any person who supplies non-motor goods or provides services related to travel in the course of carrying on a professional business which does not otherwise consist of carrying on regulated activities.

A further discrete set of exclusions arises in respect of (in particular) arranging insurance where the following conditions are satisfied: the activity must consist of the provision of information to the policyholder or potential policyholder; it must be carried on by a person in the course of a professional business which does not otherwise consist of the carrying on of regulated activities and is such that it may reasonably be regarded as incidental to the professional business otherwise being undertaken.

Finally, excluded from the activities of dealing as agent, arranging, assisting in the administration and performance of a contract and advising on an insurance contract are cases concerned with large, risks not situated in an EEA State. A 'large risks contract of insurance' is one in which the principal object is covered in respect of risks in relation to railway rolling stock, aircraft, ships, goods in transit, aircraft or ship liability along with certain credit or surety ship risks relating to a business carried on by the policyholder. The exclusion also extends to risks in respect of land vehicles, fire and natural forces, damage to property, motor vehicle liability, general liability and certain examples of miscellaneous financial loss. In the last set of examples the business in respect of which cover is provided must satisfy certain financial criteria involving (in respect of the most recent financial year for which information is available) a balance sheet total exceeding 6.2m euro, a net turnover exceeding 12.8m euro and an employee population exceeding 250.

Chapter 3
Applying for Authorisation

Introduction 3.1

CHAPTER TWO discussed the need for authorisation for a firm lawfully to carry on any regulated activity in respect of any regulated product(s). It also pointed out the criminal and civil law consequences of trading (or purporting to trade) without authorisation. This chapter looks at the process of obtaining authorisation. Further, the preservation of authorisation depends upon maintaining to the satisfaction of the FSA those factors discussed at 3.19 to 3.24 below which the FSA will consider in granting a permission or otherwise treating a firm as authorised. Those responsible for a firm's compliance have therefore as much interest in identifying factors relevant to obtaining and sustaining authorised person status in seeking permission for any new trading entity (whether part of an existing authorised firm or not) as they will have in being aware of the firm's ability to continue to satisfy the basic requirements for authorisation.

Three Routes to Authorisation 3.2

In considering the application of the general prohibition to the conduct of regulated business in respect of regulated products, there are broadly three routes by which lawful trading is permitted. These are where the firm:

- is treated as 'authorised' without the need for a specific Part IV permission;
- is 'exempt' from a need for authorisation;
- has a Part IV permission.

Deemed authorised 3.3

The following firms/persons are 'deemed authorised':

- The Society of Lloyd's.

3.4 *Applying for Authorisation*

- The operator, trustee or depository for the time being of a recognised collective investment scheme constituted in another EEA state (a UCITS (undertakings for collective investment in transferable securities) qualifier).
- Certain financial services providers authorised in another home EEA state seeking to establish a branch in or provide cross-border services into the UK under the single market directives or the Treaty of Rome.

Paragraphs 3.47 to 3.49 below consider in a little more detail the conditions which will need to be satisfied to attract deemed authorised status in respect of passport and treaty firms.

Exempt persons 3.4

In outline the following persons are exempt from the requirement to be authorised:

- appointed representatives of authorised firms;
- a recognised investment exchange or recognised clearing house;
- certain persons or classes of person exempted under the *Financial Services and Markets Act 2000 (Exemption) Order 2001 (SI 2001 No 1201)*, for example, the Bank of England, the European Central Bank, the European Community and the European Investment Bank.

Members of the professions 3.5

Although neither treated as deemed authorised nor exempt, members and firms under the control of designated professional bodies (eg solicitors, accountants and actuaries carrying on non mainstream investment business incidental to the exercise of their profession and regulated by their own professional bodies such as the Law Society, Institute of Chartered Accountants and Institute of Actuaries) are permitted to undertake activities which would otherwise be regulated if performed on an incidental basis to the provision of other professional services. This is of value to firms of accountants, solicitors and actuaries.

Applicants for Part IV permission 3.6

Where a firm is neither deemed authorised nor exempt, it will require a Part IV permission. There is a single process for such applications to the FSA. Any permission granted will (so far as is possible) be tailored to the regulated activities the firm wishes to undertake. The scope of the permission will be set in practice by one or more of the following 22 standard permission descriptions:

Applying for Authorisation **3.6**

- Accepting deposits.
- Issuing electronic money.
- Effecting contracts of insurance.
- Carrying out contracts of insurance.
- Dealing in investments as principal.
- Dealing in investments as agent.
- Arranging (bringing about) deals in investments.
- Making arrangements with a view to transactions in investments.
- Managing investments.
- Safeguarding and administering investments (divided into safeguarding and administration of assets (without arranging) and arranging, safeguarding and administration of assets).
- Advising on investments (divided as between advising on investments (except pension transfers and pension opt-outs) and advising on pension transfers and pension opt-outs).
- Sending dematerialised instructions.
- Causing dematerialised instructions to be sent.
- Establishing, operating or winding up a collective investment scheme (divided between establishing, operating, or winding up a regulated collective investment scheme and establish, operating or winding up an unregulated collective investment scheme).
- Acting as trustee of an authorised unit trust scheme.
- Acting as the depository or sole director of an open-ended investment company.
- Establishing, operating or winding up a stakeholder pension scheme.
- Advising on syndicate participation at Lloyd's.
- Managing the underwriting capacity of a Lloyd's syndicate as a managing agent at Lloyd's.
- Arranging (bringing about) deals in investments in respect of the Lloyd's market.
- Making arrangements with a view to transactions in investments in respect of the Lloyd's market.
- Entering as provider into a funeral plan contract.

To the above list will of course be added the activities of entering into, arranging and advising on regulated mortgage contracts when these fall within the scope of full regulatory control.

3.7 *Applying for Authorisation*

Insofar as permission to carry on the activity of agreeing to carry on a regulated activity is itself a regulated activity, permission will be given automatically by the FSA in relation to those regulated activities for which an applicant is given permission by reference to the 22 permission scope descriptions set out immediately above.

In the FSA's guidance in respect of applications for Part IV permissions, it is indicated that an applicant 'will be expected to demonstrate to the FSA that it is ready, willing and organised to comply, and to continue to comply, with the regulatory obligations that are relevant to the regulated activities' for which it seeks a relevant permission. This will involve the firm demonstrating an ability to comply with certain relevant 'threshold conditions' and with such of the principles and other rules and guidance promulgated by the FSA relevant to the regulated activities in question. The applicant will accordingly need to demonstrate not only familiarity with but ability and commitment to maintain compliance with:

- prudential requirements (both high level and detailed) relevant to the business in question;

- the provision and operation of appropriate systems, controls and internal arrangements to facilitate compliance with the FSA's principles, guidance and rules (relevant to the business in question);

- the operation of the intended business through suitable 'approved persons' (described at 3.25 to 3.37 below); and

- the detailed regulatory obligations relating to the business in question in respect of the conduct of business and regulatory obligations imposed in respect of dispute resolution, participation in the compensation scheme and (where appropriate) the detailed requirements of specialist sourcebooks comprising part of the FSA Handbook.

The Principles for Business 3.7

Taking a lead from the SIB Statements of Principle the statutorily based regime for market regulation under *FSMA 2000* is underpinned by the identification of eleven high level Principles for Businesses. These impose requirements on all firms as set out at 3.8 et seq below.

There are three key purposes behind the Principles as they apply to all authorised firms. Firstly, the ability of the firm to implement and abide by the Principles for Businesses will be a key factor in assessing the firm's suitability to be authorised to conduct regulated investment business.

Secondly, due compliance with the Principles for Businesses will be important in avoiding liability to disciplinary sanctions. A breach of a Principle exposes firms (and possibly those responsible for its management) to disciplinary action by the FSA. This reflects the importance attached to these high level standards by the FSA.

Thirdly, the Principles are relevant to the FSA's powers of information gathering with a view to the FSA not only considering disciplinary action but also exercising supervisory control over a firm eg by varying the scope of its authorisation and/or requiring it to make restitution for losses occasioned to clients caused by other rule breaches. The Principles themselves, however (as with the former SIB Statements of Principle), are not directly enforceable by customers of the firm.

Given the importance of the Principles for Businesses it is appropriate to spend a few moments looking at each.

1. Integrity 3.8

A firm must ' ... conduct its business with integrity.'

This imports notions of honesty, fairness and openness. The Principle must, however, be understood in the context of the other high-level standards set out. For example, Principle 5 obliges the firm to 'observe proper standards of market conduct.' Principle 8 requires a firm to 'manage conflicts of interest fairly'. The requirement for integrity is unlikely therefore to require more of the firm than is implied by adherence to 'proper standards of market conduct' and of a 'fair' approach to managing conflicts of interest between itself and its customers.

2. Skill, care and diligence 3.9

A firm must ' ... conduct its business with due skill, care and diligence.'

This implies a duty of timely compliance with the rules set out the FSA's Handbook as they apply to the authorised firm in question. A firm will only exercise 'due skill, care and diligence' by measuring up to the standards and requirements set by the rules. Many of the individual rules, however, involve an obligation to take no more than 'reasonable steps'. It suffices here to note that the Compliance Officer will have an important responsibility in qualitative terms in assessing whether the steps taken by a firm are reasonably sufficient to comply with the rules.

3. Management and control 3.10

A firm must ' ... take reasonable care to organise and control its affairs responsibly and effectively, with adequate risk management systems.'

3.11 *Applying for Authorisation*

This third Principle is of key importance and underpins the firm's obligations in respect of 'systems and control' discussed at 3.50 to 3.52 below. The FSA expects all firms to have adequate arrangements in place to enable compliance with the Handbook requirements – (for example) systems to ensure that staff are 'suitable' ie fit and proper persons to undertake their particular role in the business; that they are adequately trained and will be properly and effectively supervised in their work. These are key areas for the Compliance Office and will be the focus of developed consideration in CHAPTER 7.

4. Financial prudence 3.11

A firm must ' ... maintain adequate financial resources.'

This is a relative concept; capital adequacy requirements are determined by the FSA according to the nature of the business undertaken. That said, this Principle imposes a strict standard and is not confined to the taking of reasonable steps to maintain adequate financial resources. The question of 'adequacy' in this context reflects the need for the firm to be able to meet its business commitments and withstand the risk to which it is subject.

5. Market conduct 3.12

A firm must ' ... observe proper standards of market conduct.'

In imposing this obligation, firms will be constrained to accept the FSA Handbook rules as setting the standards for proper market conduct. Practices which may have been regarded as acceptable in the past will not be regarded as 'proper' if they conflict with the specific requirements of the rules. The Compliance Officer will accordingly be expected to have a sound working knowledge of those sections of the rule book relevant to the business in question.

6. Customer interests 3.13

A firm must ' ... pay due regard to the interests of its customers and treat them fairly.'

This Principle is an exhortation against (in particular) high-pressure sales eg selling practices that commit customers (or lead customers to believe that they are committed) to an investment product before they have been able to consider an illustration document. Such conduct would also involve a departure from the observance of proper standards of market conduct and involve an infringement of Principle 1 (integrity).

The overarching nature of Principle 6 is apparent from the fact it would require an adviser (for example) to desist from an execution-only sale where the particular product was obviously unsuitable for the customer. The selling and arranging of an inappropriate product would involve a breach of this Principle in that it would involve a regulated activity being conducted without due regard to the customer's interests. Compliance with the Principle would require the firm to tell the customer to seek advice before proceeding.

7. Communication with clients   3.14

A firm must ' … pay due regard to the information needs of its clients, and communicate information to them in a way which is clear, fair and not misleading.'

This Principle focuses particular attention on the information needs of the firm's clients and the duty to communicate information to them in a way which is clear, fair and not misleading. It will be very much part of the Compliance Officer's role to be involved in the preparation and issue of the firm's financial promotions.

8. Conflicts of interest   3.15

A firm shall ' … manage conflicts of interest fairly, both between itself and its customers and between a customer and another client.'

This Principle recognises that (inevitably) a conflict of interest may arise between a firm and its customers. The duty is to then ensure that any conflict is managed 'fairly'. One conflict management strategy involves simple conflict avoidance. A less extreme strategy of conflict management is reflected in the rules about disclosure in respect of charges. This Principle recognises that, if a customer is fully aware of the financial benefit accruing to the firm recommending or selling a particular product and consents to it, such disclosure ensures any perceived conflict of interest is thereby fairly managed.

9. Customers: relationship of trust   3.16

A firm must ' … take reasonable care to ensure the suitability of its advice and discretionary decisions for any customer who is entitled to rely upon its judgment.'

Customers inevitably place considerable trust and confidence in their financial advisers. The duty therefore to take reasonable care to ensure the suitability of advice to a customer is a cornerstone obligation of the Principles. For a firm to be able to take such care it must naturally measure up to the requirements of the Principles for Businesses as a whole and have in place adequate systems and controls for ensuring compliance with the detailed stipulations of Conduct of Business Rules in the FSA Handbook as they apply to the transaction in question.

10. Client's assets 3.17

A firm must ' … arrange adequate protection for clients' assets when it is responsible for them.'

This Principle identifies the need to ensure client assets are protected eg by segregation and identification. The extent to which the Compliance Officer will need to address this issue will of course depend on the nature of the firm's business and whether it holds client assets at all.

11. Relations with the regulator 3.18

A firm must ' … deal with its regulators in an open and co-operative way, and [to] disclose to the FSA appropriately anything relating to the firm of which the FSA would reasonably expect notice.'

The relations between the firm and the FSA must be evidenced by openness and co-operation. The firm must report to the FSA anything relating to its business of which the FSA would reasonably expect notice. Thus breaches of the capital adequacy requirements and fraudulent mis-selling of any particular product line will be obvious candidates for reporting. Timely replies to requests for information about the business and its personnel raised by the FSA will satisfy the requirement of open co-operation. Regulatory reporting issues are considered in CHAPTER 5. It is an area of utmost responsibility so far as the firm's Compliance Officer is concerned and one apt to give rise to the greatest tensions between management and compliance.

Threshold Conditions 3.19

There are five material threshold conditions representing pre-conditions to any successful application for authorisation. They are (in brief) as follows:

1. Legal status 3.20

Where the regulated activity concerned involves the effecting or carrying out of contracts of insurance the applicant must be a limited company (other than a limited liability partnership), a registered friendly society or a member of Lloyd's. If the activity concerned involves accepting deposits the applicant must be a limited company or a partnership.

2. Location of head office 3.21

Where the applicant is a limited company it must have its head office and registered office located in the UK; in considering where a firm's head office is located the FSA will take into account the location of the directors and other senior managers responsible for making decisions in respect of the firm's central direction and look to the place where the central administrative functions of the firm (eg central compliance) are carried out. Where the regulated activity is concerned with motor vehicle insurance the applicant must also have a claims representative in each EEA state other than the UK.

3. Close links 3.22

Where the applicant has close links with another person, the FSA must also be satisfied that those links are not likely to prevent its effective supervision of the applicant (which includes being satisfied that if the closely linked person is subject to the laws, regulations or administrative provisions of a territory outside the EEA that those foreign provisions will not prevent effective supervision of the applicant). For these purposes, a person has close links with the applicant if either a parent undertaking or subsidiary undertaking of the applicant for permission or a parent undertaking of a subsidiary or a subsidiary undertaking of a parent of the applicant; a person also has close links if he owns or controls 20% or more of the voting rights or capital of the applicant.

4. Adequate resources 3.23

The FSA must also be satisfied that the resources of the applicant will be adequate in relation to the regulated activities proposed to be carried on. The relevant FSA guidance indicates that 'resources' for these purposes includes both financial and non-financial resources and the firm's means of managing its resources; 'adequate' means 'sufficient' in terms of quantity, quality and availability. Thus of particular relevance will be any of the following:

- Whether there are indications the firm may not be able to meet its debts as they fall due.

- Whether there is cause for concern in relation to the firm's history (eg has it ever been the subject of a receiving or administration order or entered into a Deed of Arrangement or failed to satisfy a judgment debt under a Court Order within the last 10 years?).

- Whether the firm has taken reasonable steps to identify and measure any risks of regulatory concern.

- Whether the firm has appropriate systems and controls (including appropriate human resources) to measure risks of regulatory concern.

- Whether the applicant's business plan is soundly researched and based.

5. Suitability 3.24

The FSA will also need to be satisfied that the applicant is 'fit and proper' to undertake the regulated activities in question. This involves a wide-ranging consideration of the applicant's resources, systems and controls (as proposed) and of persons connected with the intended business. Will the firm be equipped and staffed by suitably qualified and appropriate approved persons? The FSA will be looking to see if the firm can demonstrate that it will conducts its business with 'integrity and in compliance with proper standards'. Does the business profile indicate that it will be run by 'a competent and prudent management'? Can the firm demonstrate that it will conduct it affairs with all due skill, care and diligence?

This is a key area where a realistic, satisfactory and workable compliance model is required. The firm will need therefore to show that it has put in place procedures reasonably designed to ensure its employees are aware of and will be compliant with the requirements and standards relevant to the proposed business; the systems and procedures so designed will need to be such as to ensure that the firm's approved persons understand how the regulatory requirements will apply to them and how they will be implemented; a system for measuring ongoing compliance will be a necessary ingredient in the business model.

Critically, the FSA will be concerned to ensure those comprising the governing body of the firm are constituted by individuals with an appropriate range of skills and experience to operate and manage the firm's business in compliance with the regulatory requirements applying to the venture. The FSA's expectations of all such approved persons are considered at 3.25 below.

Further, where a firm has its head office outside the EEA but appears to be seeking to carry on a regulated activity relating to insurance business in the UK, the FSA will need to be satisfied that there is a representative resident in the UK with authority to bind the firm in its relations with third parties and to represent it in dealing with the FSA and the Courts of the UK.

Finally, save in respect of a Swiss general insurance company, the UK representative must be a limited company entitled under the law of the place where its head office is situated to effect and carry out contracts of insurance; it must have in the UK assets of a size agreed between the FSA and the supervisory authorise in the relevant home states.

Approved Persons 3.25

In relation to the conduct of a firm's affairs, persons able to exercise any significant influence over the business (so far as it relates to the performance of any regulated activity) or who undertake any regulated activity in dealing with either customers of the firm or property of customers of the authorised business will be required to obtain approved person status. The need for approval is accordingly activity related. The significant influence or customer related functions are grouped by reference to the following generic and specific descriptions. Each controlled function is designated in accordance with the following table. Approval must be sought in respect of each of the (described) controlled functions the particular office holder will perform.

Type	Controlled function	Description of controlled function
Governing functions:	1	Director
	2	Non-executive director
	3	Chief executive
	4	Partner
	5	Director of unincorporated association
	6	Small friendly society
	7	Sole trader
Required functions:	8	Apportionment and oversight
	9	EEA investment business oversight
	10	Compliance oversight
	11	Money laundering reporting
	12	Appointed actuary function
Systems and controls functions:	13	Finance
	14	Risk assessment
	15	Internal audit
Significant management functions:	16	Significant management (designated investment business)
	17	Significant management (other business operations)
	18	Significant management (insurance underwriting)
	19	Significant management (financial resources)
	20	Significant management (settlement)
Customer functions:	21	Investment adviser
	22	Investment adviser (trainee)
	23	Corporate finance adviser
	24	Pension transfer specialist
	25	Adviser on syndicate participation at Lloyd's
	26	Customer trading
	27	Investment management

3.25 *Applying for Authorisation*

These may be diagrammatically represented in outline as follows:

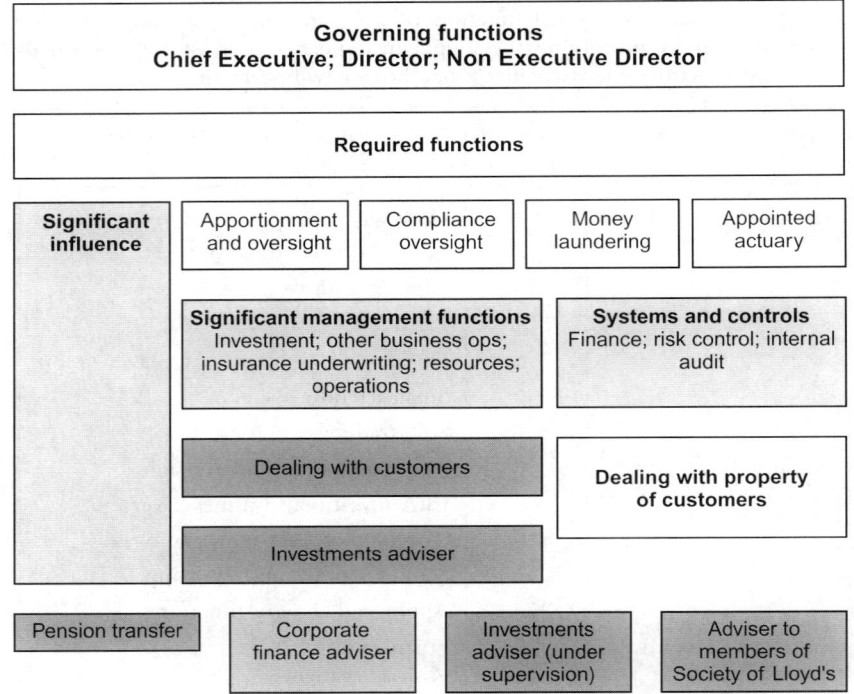

Although not all controlled functions are shown, the intention is to position the high level functions at the top of the hierarchy; the lighter shading is intended to depict the significant influence functions; and the darker shading the different investment advisory functions.

In making the application for a Part IV permission the identity of the proposed approved persons will be included and form part of the FSA's overall assessment. The size and nature of the business will determine which of the controlled functions will be likely to arise. That said, every firm will (obviously) have one or more person responsible for directing its affairs. In the case of limited companies this may include the directors (including non executive directors) and (often) a Chief Executive Officer. Where the firm is a partnership, the business will be run by the partners. In the case of a limited liability partnership, the partner function (CF4) extends to the firm as if it were a partnership and a member of the firm were a partner. In the case of unincorporated associations the director in charge will typically be the person exerting the relevant significant influence.

In all cases, however, the nature of the work carried out determines whether the person responsible is in fact performing a controlled function so as to attract a requirement for individual approval. The job description or label is not in itself determinative.

Required functions 3.26

A firm must appropriately allocate to one or more individuals the functions of dealing with the apportionment of responsibilities among its directors and senior managers. This will include responsibility for overseeing the establishment and maintenance of systems and controls appropriate to the operation of the business in question. A firm which carries on designated investment business with or for customers must also allocate to a director or senior manager the function of responsibility for oversight of the firm's compliance and reporting to its governing body in respect of the discharge of that particular responsibility.

In larger businesses with a complex or group structure, the group Head of Compliance will often be responsible for the performance of the compliance oversight function. If compliance is outsourced the responsibility for the compliance oversight function nonetheless must rest with one or more director or senior manager in the firm.

A firm must also have a Money Laundering Reporting Officer unless it is a sole trader with no employees, carries out certain insurance business as its only regulated activities, or is an incoming firm providing only services in the UK.

Save in respect of certain kinds of friendly society, a long-term insurer must appoint an actuary responsible for the appointed actuary function.

System and control functions 3.27

The finance, risk assessment and internal audit functions will typically be performed by senior managers of the business. The scope of the work undertaken in these areas will obviously reflect the size, nature and complexity of the business itself.

Significant management functions 3.28

Save in respect of very large and complex business structures, it is unlikely a firm will appoint anyone to perform dedicated significant management functions. In practice, those approved to carry out governing functions, required functions and systems and controls functions are likely to be exercising all relevant significant influence at senior management level. Where the firm is of such a size that it is appropriate to appoint individuals to carry out dedicated significant management functions, the firm is subject to an annual reporting obligation to the FSA as to the name of every individual approved to perform such a function and must provide brief details of the job performed by each such individual.

Customer functions

These are activity related and accordingly determined by the job the individual in fact performs, whether advising on investments (other than in respect of pension transfers and opt-outs for private customers) as a fully trained and competent advisor, advising on investments when still a trainee, advising clients solely in connection with corporate finance business, providing pension transfer and opt-out advice to private customers, or acting as an investment manager and dealing in investments with all four private or intermediate customers.

The Statements of Principle for Approved Persons

In determining an application for approval, which will usually be submitted by the sponsoring applicant for the Part IV permission, the FSA will assess the fitness and propriety of the individual in question by considering all matters relating to his:

- honesty, integrity and reputation;
- competence and capability; and
- financial soundness.

In looking at a person's honesty, integrity and reputation the matters to which the FSA will have regard include any extant conviction in respect of any criminal offence (particularly any offence relating to dishonesty, fraud or financial crime); any adverse finding or any settlement in civil proceedings (particularly any relating to investment or financial business); any previous investigation or disciplinary process by previous regulators and other dealings with any regulatory body so far as apparent candour and truthfulness are concerned.

Competence and capability are able to be more objectively assessed by determining whether the person satisfies the relevant requirements in the FSA's Training and Competence sourcebook.

In investigating issues of financial soundness the FSA will take into account any unsatisfied judgment debt or award against the individual concerned and any evidence of past acts of bankruptcy. Normally, however, a candidate will not be required to supply a statement of assets and liabilities. The FSA also indicates that the fact a person is of limited financial means will not necessarily render him unsuitable to perform a controlled function.

The candidate will, however, be expected to demonstrate an ongoing willingness and ability to comply with the Statement of Principle for approved persons. Helpfully, the FSA has published a Code of Practice for Approved

Persons which indicates types of conduct which will be regarded as infringing the requirements of the Statements of Principle.

The first four Statements of Principle address conduct by the approved person himself; the remaining three Statements of Principle deal with the approved person's role in the business of the firm. Because of the importance of the Statements of Principle and the Code it is appropriate to consider each requirement in brief.

Statement of Principle 1 3.31

'An approved person must act with integrity in carrying out his controlled function.'

Examples of conduct likely to be regarded as involving a breach of this Principle are given as conduct which is deliberately misleading to a client, the firm or the FSA. This may arise from any falsification of documents, misleading advice to a client about the likely performance of an investment product, providing false or inaccurate information to the firm, its auditors or appointed actuary. Such misconduct may also be exemplified by omissions eg failing to correct any misunderstanding under which a customer, the authorised firm or the FSA is appreciated to be labouring.

Statement of Principle 2 3.32

'An approved person must act with due skill, care and diligence in carrying out his controlled function.'

Examples of conduct falling below this indicated standard of care include omissions to inform a customer of material information of which (eg) an investment advisor is aware of ought to have been aware. Inadequate or misleading descriptions of risk attaching to particular products where the inaccuracy in the form of promotion ought to have been identified are further examples.

Statement of Principle 3 3.33

'An approved person must observe proper standards of market conduct in carrying out his controlled function.'

Here, it is worth noting that compliance with any relevant rules governing any business in question will tend to show compliance with this Statement of Principle. Other factors which will be taken into account will include whether the person's conduct complies with (where appropriate) the relevant provisions of the Code of Market Conduct.

Statement of Principle 4

'An approved person must deal with the FSA and with other regulators in an open and co-operative way and must disclose appropriately any information of which the FSA would reasonably expect notice.'

Importantly, the guidance offered in respect of this Statement indicates that it does not give rise to a duty on an approved person to report such matters directly to the FSA unless the individual is one of the approved persons responsible within the firm for reporting matters to the FSA. Any attempt, however, to influence a decision not to report a relevant matter to the FSA will involve a breach of the Statement.

Statement of Principle 5

'An approved person performing a significant influence function must take reasonable steps to ensure that the business of the firm for which he is responsible in this controlled function is organised so that it can be controlled effectively.'

Falling within this Statement is (naturally) the duty to take reasonable steps to apportion responsibilities for all areas of business under the approved person's control. An omission so to do will be likely to involve a clear breach of the Statement. Other types of infringing behaviour given by the FSA as examples include implementing confusing or uncertain reporting lines, authorisation levels and/or job descriptions and responsibilities. Likewise, failing to review the competence, knowledge, skills and performance of staff (particularly where there is evidence of unacceptable performance) is likely to be regarded as infringing conduct. The essence of this principle touches on the culture of the firm so that (by way of further example) the giving of undue weight to financial performance when considering the continuing suitability of an individual for a particular role may involve a breach.

Statement of Principle 6

'An approved person performing a significant influence function must exercise due skill, care and diligence in managing the business of the firm for which he is responsible in his controlled function.'

This Principle focuses attention on the appreciation of risks to the firm (and risk management). Conduct of a kind exemplified as falling short includes the permitting of business expansion without reasonably assessing the risks of such growth; inadequate monitoring of highly profitable transactions or unusual transactions; and permitting transactions without a sufficient understanding of the risks involved. The FSA expects a degree of pro-active behaviour so that a failure to review the performance of outside contractors in connection with delegated business or an omission to take personal action where unsatisfactory explanations for apparent business failings exemplify further potentially infringing conduct.

Statement of Principle 7 3.37

'An approved person performing a significant influence function must take reasonable steps to ensure that the business of the firm for which he is responsible in his controlled function complies with the relevant requirements and the standards of the regulatory system.'

This is an area where the monitoring and reporting activity of the compliance department may be important. This ought to identify, through the operation of appropriate systems of control, compliance failings in respect of applicable requirements and the standards of the regulatory system. An approved person performing a significant influence function will be expected to implement and act on information provided by a vigilant and adequately resourced compliance department. This may include acting on recommendations for improvements in systems and procedures the compliance department may advocate.

Breaches of the above Statements of Principle may attract disciplinary proceedings by the FSA. The circumstances in which disciplinary action is likely to be taken against approved persons is discussed in CHAPTER 5.

Application and Determination 3.38

The process of applying for an appropriately worded Part IV permission and for approval in relation to key individuals is a serious and complex business. Professional advice is likely to be necessary from legal, accountancy, compliance (and in some instances actuarial) disciplines. The FSA will encourage a pre-application meeting to discuss the proposals. Thereafter a detailed application pack will need to be submitted. This will include the presentation of a realistic business plan.

An application for a Part IV permission is to be determined within six months from the date of receipt. If the application is incomplete the FSA has 12 months in which to determine it. Although applications for approval should be determined within three months, approval will not be given to any person to carry out a controlled function in respect of a relevant business unless and until the Part IV permission is forthcoming.

If the application is not contentious and is able to be satisfactorily approved, a decision may be taken by internal staff at the FSA. If the FSA staff have decided to recommend a refusal then the final decision will be taken by the Regulatory Decisions Committee. Likewise, if an application is likely to be subject to any limitation or specific requirement the decision will be made by the RDC.

3.39 *Applying for Authorisation*

Decisions to refuse permission for approval are subject to the Warning and Decision Notice procedures and may be referred to the Financial Services and Markets Tribunal.

In assessing an application the FSA may also require a firm (at its own expense) to provide a report (as appropriate) from an auditor, reporting accountant, actuary or other qualified person approved by it in respect of relevant aspects of the firm's proposed business/plans. Applicants seeking to carry on long-term insurance business will also be required to provide a certificate from an actuary confirming the appropriateness of the projections for its business and in particular the adequacy of premium rates and technical provisions and margin of solvency. This will include addressing how the business will be able to overcome capital strains from effecting new business.

Conflicting directorships 3.39

In considering the fitness and propriety of directors to hold office, key issues arise as to:

- the standards to be met by such persons in the conduct of the office of director (including non executive and shadow directors);
- the extent to which directors may delegate responsibility for management decisions; and
- the circumstances in which directors may safely act for different companies (whether connected or not).

Standard of care expected – executive directors 3.40

In broad terms the expectations of company director conduct are stated in the *Insolvency Act 1986, section 214(4)* as being the conduct of:

> 'a reasonably diligent person having both (a) the general knowledge, skill and experience that may reasonably be expected of a person carrying out the same functions as are carried out by that director in relation to the company, and (b) the general knowledge, skill and experience that that director has.'

This includes an obligation that an executive director may not compete with the company of which he is a director.

Non executive directors 3.41

Having a supervisory role is less restrained for a non executive director, but the duties owed by non executive directors are to be reviewed in the proceedings brought by Equitable Life against its former directors and it is possible a more stringent regime will be recognised by the UK courts on fuller consideration. There the Court has indicated:

> 'the extent to which a non executive director may reasonably rely on the executive directors and other professionals to perform their duties is one in which the law can fairly be said to be developing and is plainly "fact sensitive". It is plainly arguable ... that a company may reasonably at least look to non executive directors for independence of judgment and supervision of the executive management.'

Shadow directors 3.42

The definition of 'director' includes a person in accordance with whose directions or instructions the directors are accustomed to act. Such a person is defined in the *Companies Act 1985, section 71* as a shadow director. The directors of a holding company would not, as such, be shadow directors. However, where, for example, a member of a holding company board frequently gives instructions to directors of a firm, either on his own or through a committee which takes frequent executive decisions, the firm should consider carefully whether he (and other members of the committee) should be approved to perform this function. An individual is not a shadow director (or director) because his job description includes the word 'director'. Whether a director is a director within the definition is a question of fact in each case.

Delegation of responsibility 3.43

In litigation arising out of the collapse of Barings (*Re Barings Plc (No 5) [2000] 1 BCLC 523*) it was pointed out that:

> 'whilst directors are entitled (subject to the articles of association of the company) to delegate particular functions to those below them in the management chain, and to trust their competence and integrity to a reasonable extent, the exercise of the power of delegation does not absolve a director from the duty to supervise the discharge of the delegated functions.[...] The extent of the duty, and the question whether it has been discharged, must depend on the facts of each particular case, including the director's role in the management of the company.'

Holding competing offices 3.44

Merely holding office as an executive director of competing companies does not involve a breach of duty to either, but if in acting for each company the director in fact promotes the interests of one employer to the disadvantage of the other then this will involve:

- a breach of the director's duty to act with good faith towards the financially harmed company;
- a breach fiduciary duty of loyalty;
- (possibly) a breach the Articles of the company if they contain a provision prohibiting directors accepting competing directorships; and
- (possibly) a breach of any service contract prohibiting directors accepting competing directorships or requiring dedicated service to one employer company.

An example of problems in practice 3.45

Consider a group structure with Holding Co Plc ('HC') having a:

- 55% shareholding in Mortgage Broker Subsidiary (MBS);
- 100% shareholding in Mortgage Loans Ltd (ML); and
- 100% shareholding in Mortgage Funding Ltd (MFL).

MFL and MBS are identified as whole-of-market brokers for mortgage products; ML is identified as a lender. Common directorships presently exist or are proposed in respect of HC, MBS, ML and MFL. The company ML, as lender, will require a Part IV permission to enter into any Regulated Mortgage Contracts (RMCs). MBS and MFL will require a Part IV permission to arrange/advise on RMCs. Common directorships and control of the group will raise issues of concern to the FSA because of:

- director conflict of duty issues (how can a director of ML act dispassionately in running the MBS and MFL companies which supply a whole-of-market brokerage package without detracting from his duty to promote the interests of the lender company and vice versa?);
- inter-company funding if any (the financial fortunes of the group may linked yet the sales interests of ML conflict with those of MBS and MFL).

Such conflicts at director level are best avoided.

Limitations and Requirements 3.46

In considering whether to grant a permission the FSA may decide it is appropriate to impose some limitation in the description of the regulated activities contemplated. Examples include limiting the types of client with which a firm may deal and/or the number of clients with whom a firm may carry on a particular regulated activity (eg where the FSA is not satisfied that the firm's systems are adequate to process high volume business). A limitation may be imposed on the types of specified investments in which the firm can deal or the type of insurance business the firm may write. It may (for example) limit the types of client with whom the firm may transact particular types of business. The power to impose such limitations will be exercised so as to enable the FSA to comply with its regulatory objectives.

The FSA may also impose requirements in relation to a Part IV permission. For example, it may use a requirement to define the scope of a number of regulated activities proposed to be carried on by the firm. Thus (in an example given in FSA guidance) an applicant wishing to act as a corporate finance advisory firm may be given permission to carry on the activities of advising on investments subject to a requirement that the firm carries on those activities only within the definition of a corporate finance advisory firm. Other examples of requirements include ones to submit financial returns more often than would otherwise be routinely required, to submit audited financial accounts of a parent company or (in the case of an insurer) to carry on only reinsurance business.

The imposition of a limitation or a requirement may be referred to the Financial Services and Markets Tribunal.

EEA and treaty firms 3.47

A business with its head office in an EEA state other than the UK is entitled to 'passport' activities for which it has a home state authorisation covered by a single market directive into the UK by either establishing a branch here or providing cross-border services into the UK. Likewise such a firm wishing to carry on a regulated activity in a like manner in the UK which is not covered by any single market directive (eg reinsurance) will be entitled to exercise the right of establishment and the freedom to provide services afforded by the Treaty of Rome.

In addition, a person who for the time being is an operator, trustee or depository of a scheme which is a recognised collective investment scheme constituted in another EEA state is permitted to carry on as far as is appropriate to the capacity in which it acts in relation to the scheme the activities of establishing, operating or winding up of a collective investment scheme (and any activity in connection with or for the purposes of the scheme).

EEA firms with a UK branch 3.48

Before an EEA firm exercises a passport right it will need to satisfy certain establishment conditions. These are:

3.49 *Applying for Authorisation*

- That the FSA has received a consent notice from the EEA firm's home state regulator that it has given the firm consent to establish a branch in the UK.

- The consent notice must be given in accordance with a relevant single market directive and identify the activities to which the consent relates (including the provision of certain prescribed information).

- The EEA firm must then be informed of any FSA rules intended to be applied to its operations in the UK (and in default only commence activity after two months have elapsed from the date the FSA received the consent notice). If the EEA firm is passporting under an insurance directive any provisions the FSA intends to notify as applicable to its UK operations must in that case also be notified to the home state regulator.

A similar notice and notification regime is operated in relation to the provision of cross-border services into the UK.

The particular applicable provisions which will be likely to be notified include:

- Any obligation (as relevant) to comply with the *Consumer Credit Act 1974*.

- If the business involves motor vehicle third party liability insurance then the firm will be required to become a member of the Motor Insurers' Bureau.

- The firm will be expected to comply with the approved persons' regime.

Top-up permissions   3.49

Where a non UK firm is not able to exercise an EEA right (eg because the activity falls outside the scope of a single market directive) and where the activity is not covered by a treaty right then the FSA may grant a top-up permission. Thus, a top-up permission will normally be required for the marketing of life insurance contracts by intermediaries and designated investment business activities carried on in relation to commodities derivatives. Where such a permission is granted, the FSA is responsible for the prudential supervision of the incoming EEA firm.

Systems and controls   3.50

Following on from the Principles for Businesses in the FSA's Handbook is Senior Management Arrangements, Systems and Controls (SYSC). The SYSC rules apply (with limited exceptions) to all authorised firms. The content of the SYSC requirements reflects and implements the Principles for Businesses. Although written (again) at a high level of generality, the purposes of the SYSC rules are clear enough: to encourage a firm's directors and senior managers to take appropriate practical responsibility for the firm's arrangements on matters likely to be of interest to the FSA and to vest responsibility for effective and responsible organisation of the firm's business in specific directors and senior managers.

Key requirements of SYSC 3.51

Two key requirements are as follows.

- The requirement that a firm take reasonable care to maintain a clear and appropriate apportionment of significant responsibilities among its directors and senior managers so as to identify clearly who has each relevant responsibility and so that the business and affairs of the firm can be adequately monitored and controlled by the responsible directors, senior managers and firm's governing body.

- The obligation on the firm to take reasonable care to establish and maintain effective systems and controls for compliance with applicable requirements and standards under the regulatory system and for counteracting the risk that the firm may be used to further financial crime.

Specific SYSC rules 3.52

The detail of the rules requires that the firm must appropriately allocate to one or more individuals the functions of both dealing with the apportionment of responsibilities and the oversight of the establishment and maintenance of the firm's required systems and controls.

A record of the arrangements it has made to satisfy the SYSC rules as to apportionment and allocation must be made and kept up to date.

The nature and extent of the systems and controls must be such as are appropriate to the firm's business. In broad terms they must cover compliance with applicable requirements and standards under the regulatory system and include measures for countering the risk that the firm might be used to further financial crime. There must be allocate to a director or senior manager the function of:

- having responsibility for oversight of the firm's compliance; and
- reporting to the governing body in respect of that responsibility.

Here 'compliance' means compliance with the rules in, for example, COB (conduct of business), CIS (collective investment schemes), ICOB (insurance mediation services) and MCOB (regulated mortgages). As part of a properly documented control procedure the firm must also take reasonable care to make and retain adequate records of matters and dealings (including accounting records) which are the subject of requirements and standards under the regulatory system.

The decisions as to the apportionment of responsibilities and overseeing the establishment and maintenance of appropriate systems and controls falls to those effectively in charge of the business (the firm's chief executive, directors or senior managers responsible for the overall management as appropriate). The extent of the necessary systems and controls for securing compliance with the FSA's requirements will vary depending on the size of the business (and the risks generated by its activities).

A record must be kept (and retained for six years) of the arrangements made in respect of the apportionment of responsibilities and the (subsequent) allocation of individual responsibilities to particular personnel. The areas of activity the systems and controls are expected to address (appropriate to the nature of the business concerned) include the following:

- the establishment of clear reporting lines appropriate to the nature, scale and complexity of the business being pursued;
- the establishment and maintenance of procedures for securing compliance with the applicable requirements and standards imposed by the FSA;
- the setting up (where appropriate) of risk assessment procedures for determining the risks to which the firm is exposed and for advising the governing body/senior managers upon them;
- arrangements for providing reliable, timely and relevant information to those in charge of the business;
- a system for ensuring the suitability of the firm's employees and agents eg assessing an individual's honesty, competence and ongoing response to training;
- the establishment (in larger firms) of an audit committee to oversee the firm's systems and controls;
- the firm will require a business strategy as part of seeking to control in a responsible manner its business risks;
- the firm will be expected to address remuneration policy issues so as to manage appropriately tensions which may arise between the ability of the firm to meet the requirements and standards of the regulatory system and the personal advantage of those acting for it; and
- the firm will be expected to have in place appropriate arrangements to deal with any unforeseen interruption of business.

Each of the above operations needs to be the subject of properly maintained and compiled records.

Handbook design and terminology 3.53

The rules and guidance applying to all regulated business with which the FSA will expect compliance is set out in the FSA Handbook. This is conveniently divided into key blocks as follows:

Applying for Authorisation **3.53**

- Block 1 – High Level Standards
- Block 2 – Business Standards
- Block 3 – Regulatory Processes
- Block 4 – Redress
- Block 5 – Specialist Sourcebooks
- Block 6 – Special Guides

Within each block the relevant sourcebook or manual is located. A reference code is applied. The scheme of the handbook is best gathered from the following table.

Block	*Sourcebook or manual*	*Reference code*
High Level Standards (The standards applying to all firms and approved persons)	Principles for Businesses (The fundamental obligations of all firms under the regulatory system)	PRIN
	Senior Management Arrangements, Systems and Controls (The responsibilities of directors and senior management)	SYSC
	Threshold Conditions (The minimum standards for becoming and remaining authorised)	COND
	Statements of Principle and Code of Practice for Approved Persons (The fundamental obligations of approved persons)	APER
	The Fit and Proper test for Approved Persons (The minimum standards for becoming and remaining an approved person)	FIT

3.53 *Applying for Authorisation*

Block	Sourcebook or manual	Reference code
	General provisions (Interpreting the Handbook, fees, approval by the FSA, emergencies, status disclosure and the FSA logo)	GEN
Business Standards The detailed requirements relating to firms' day-to-day business	Interim Prudential sourcebook for banks (The prudential and notification requirements for banks)	IPRU (BANK)
	Interim Prudential sourcebook for building societies (The prudential and notification requirements for building societies)	IPRU (BSOC)
	Interim Prudential sourcebook for friendly societies (The prudential and notification requirements for friendly societies)	IPRU (FSOC)
	Interim Prudential sourcebook for insurers (The prudential and notification requirements for insurers)	IPRU (INS)
	Interim Prudential sourcebook for investment businesses (The prudential and notification requirements for investment firms)	IPRU (INV)
	Conduct of Business (The requirements applying to firms with investment business customers)	COB

Applying for Authorisation **3.53**

Block	Sourcebook or manual	Reference code
	Insurance: Conduct of Business (The requirements applying to firms with insurance business customers – in force from 14 January 2005)	ICOB
	Mortgages: Conduct of Business (The requirements applying to firms with mortgage business customers – in force from 31 October 2004)	MCOB
	Client Assets (The requirements relating to holding client assets and client money)	CASS
	Market conduct Code of market conduct Price stabilising rules Inter-professional conduct Endorsement of the Takeover Code Alternative trading systems (What is acceptable market conduct and what is market abuse?)	MAR
	Training and competence (The commitments and requirements concerning staff competence)	TC
	Money Laundering (The requirements for anti-money laundering systems and controls)	ML
Regulatory Processes The manuals describing the FSA's authorisation, supervisory and disciplinary functions	Authorisation (Guidance on whether authorisation is needed, how to apply for it and related issues)	AUTH

3.53 *Applying for Authorisation*

Block	Sourcebook or manual	Reference code
	Supervision (Supervisory provisions including those relating to auditors, waivers, individual guidance, notifications and reporting)	SUP
	Enforcement (Details of the FSA's disciplinary and enforcement arrangements)	ENF
	Decision making (The FSA's decision making processes)	DEC
Redress The processes for handling complaints and compensation	Dispute resolution: Complaints (The detailed requirements for handling complaints and the Financial Ombudsman Service arrangements)	DISP
	Compensation (The rules governing eligibility under, and levies for, the Financial Services Compensation Scheme)	COMP
	Complaints against the FSA (Details of the scheme for handling complaints against the FSA)	COAF
Specialist sourcebooks Requirements applying to individual business sectors	Collective Investment Schemes (Requirements for collective investment schemes)	CIS
	New Collective Investment Schemes (The special requirements for collective investment schemes (to replace CIS))	COLL
	Credit Unions (Requirements applying to credit unions)	CRED

Applying for Authorisation 3.54

Block	Sourcebook or manual	Reference code
	Electronic Commerce Directive (Requirements for firms providing financial services by electronic means)	ECO
	Electronic money (Requirements for firms issuing electronic money)	ELM
	Lloyd's (Requirements applying to Lloyd's and members of Lloyd's)	LLD
	Professional firms (Requirements applying to professional firms (whether exempt or authorised))	PROF
	Recognised Investment Exchanges and Recognised Clearing Houses (Requirements applying to recognised bodies)	REC
	Later: United Kingdom Listing Authority; for current materials see The Listing Rules and Further Information	UKLA
Special Guides	For EMPS, FREN, OMPS, and SERV	

Alphabetic designations 3.54

In the course of the sourcebook and manuals the FSA uses a number of alphabetic designators. These are as follows:

- 'R' indicates a general rule, introducing a regulatory obligation with which compliance will to the extent indicated be compulsory.

- 'E' signifies an evidential provision, ie compliance with the subject matter of the evidential provision will be relied upon as tending to demonstrate compliance with a rule (the converse is also true).

- 'G' indicates guidance. This is used to provide additional explanations of the rules.

3.54 *Applying for Authorisation*

- 'D' indicates directions and requirements given under various provisions of the *Financial Services and Markets Act 2000*; these are binding on the person or groups of persons to whom the directions are addressed.
- 'P' refers to the Statements of Principle for approved persons.
- 'C' is employed in relation to conduct which in the opinion of the FSA falls short of market abuse.

Chapter 4
Risk Based Compliance

Risk Assessment Framework 4.1

The Financial Services Authority (FSA) has a statutory obligation imposed by the *Financial Services and Markets Act 2000 (FSMA 2000)* to secure four key statutory objectives:

- maintenance of confidence in the UK financial system;
- securing an appropriate degree of protection for consumers;
- the promotion of public understanding of the financial system; and
- the reduction of financial crime.

When the FSA accordingly speaks of 'risks' posed by authorised firms, it is using the phrase in a specific sense which refers to the 'risk' a regulated firm presents to the fulfilment of its statutory objectives.

In order to assess such 'risks' the FSA has devised a risk assessment framework which it will be important for Compliance Officers to understand. The extent to which a particular firm is identified as posing a risk to all or any of the four statutory objectives will determine the intensity of the regulatory programme FSA will consider appropriate to the firm.

Whilst responsibility will, of course, remain with the senior management of a firm to address FSA requirements, the Compliance Officer will be concerned to have an awareness of risks viewed from the FSA perspective; likewise, he will be concerned to understand and to a greater or lesser degree monitor the firm's handling of risk areas identified within the risk assessment framework. This chapter describes the scheme for assessing risk and the mechanisms operated by the FSA to contain, reduce or eliminate risks.

The 45 risk elements 4.2

In order to identify potential risks posed by an authorised firm's activities the FSA has mapped out some 45 'risk elements' which to a greater or lesser extent will be common to all financial services undertakings. The first 15 risk

4.2 Risk Based Compliance

elements are generically referred to as 'business risk' components; the remaining 30 risk elements are seen as aspects of 'control risks' presented by a firm to the key statutory objectives. The individual risk elements to the business which fall to be assessed in terms of their impact or potential to affect the FSA's ability to serve and secure its statutory objectives.

The 45 risk elements are as follows:

1. Quality of the firm's strategic planning process
2. Strategic nature of the firm's business
3. Type of credit risks undertaken by the firm
4. Insurance underwriting risk
5. Nature of the market risks under taken by the firm
6. Operational risks posed by the firm's activities
7. Litigation/legal risk evident with the firm
8. Adequacy of capital
9. Liquidity
10. Earnings of the firm
11. Type of customer/user/member
12. Sources of business and distribution methods
13. Types of products and services
14. Market efficiency
15. Proper markets
16. Sales force training and recruitment
17. Basis of remuneration of employees
18. Financial promotions
19. Accepting/advising/reporting to customers/users/members
20. Dealing and managing
21. Security of customer/users/members' assets
22. Disclosure and adequacy of literature
23. Membership arrangements
24. Clarity of legal/ownership structure
25. Jurisdiction/characteristics of controllers/group entities
26. Relationship with rest of group

27. Risk management
28. Policies, procedures and controls
29. Management information
30. IT systems
31. Financial, regulatory and accounting policies
32. Compliance
33. Internal audit
34. Outsourcing/third party providers
35. Professional advisers
36. Business continuity
37. Money laundering controls
38. Market cleanliness
39. Settlement and clearing arrangements
40. Corporate governance
41. Allocation and definition of management responsibilities
42. Quality of management
43. Human resources
44. Relationship with regulators
45. Cultural issues and business ethics

Business risks

Broadly the 'business risk' elements centre on the sorts of issues which would feature in a business development plan, being those risks concerned with:

- The firm's business strategy – in terms of business objectives and the management's ability to achieve any intended establishment, maintenance and development of a market share.

- Market, credit, insurance underwriting and operational risk eg what is the nature of on and off balance sheet counter-party exposures? Do the firm's activities involve any 'insurance underwriting risk'? If so, what is the nature of the insurance risk exposures in terms of size, complexity and cancellation provisions? Is the firm concerned with property and casualty insurance underwriting or life and health policies? How does the firm participate in the market eg through direct sales or third party representatives?

4.3 Risk Based Compliance

- Financial soundness.

- Nature of the firm's customers and its products/services eg is the firm targeting high net worth individuals or seeking to sell products where any demand is located in the lower market?

It is appropriate to consider some of these headline issues in a little more detail. Thus, what 'operational risks' does the business disclose in terms of the appropriateness of required training and supervision of staff relative to the nature of the business and development strategy being pursued? What is the resource profile of the firm in terms of the number of employees? What is the permanent versus temporary staff ratio? Is there a high turnover of staff? Does the nature of the firm's business indicate a potential for 'litigation/legal risk' ie is the firm selling products in a market where the underlying investment contract may not be enforceable? Are the policy terms of a particular product ambiguous so as to give rise to risks of legal proceedings? What steps has the firm taken to mitigate/address such risks eg through insurance cover.

The financial framework of operation is also (understandably) seen as of key importance in risk elements labelled 'adequacy of capital,' 'liquidity' and 'earnings'. The FSA will here be concerned (for example) to consider what processes the firm employs for evaluating capital requirements in the context of current and projected business activities and the level of associated risks. How sensitive is the firm to the need to monitor the adequacy of its capital taking into account trends and projections in, on and off balance sheet growth? What reserves does the firm have in respect of insurance claims, loan loss, liquidity reserves and litigation reserves? How accessible is the capital eg in a group structure? Where is it located? What is the earnings profile of the firm? The FSA will look at the sources, volatility and concentration of revenues and profits. The performance of the firm relative to the peer group will be important as will the firm's ability to demonstrate responsiveness to anticipated changes in the operating environment. How geared up is the firm to deal with competitor behaviour, technology and anticipated legislative or regulatory changes?

Another 'business risk' is the customer profile of a firm. For example, if the firm has a history of dealing with individuals domiciled in higher risk jurisdiction the potential for executing financial crime may increase. If the firm's business centres upon clients of modest or low financial means with poor financial literacy skills the risk of customer misunderstanding or allegations of product mis-selling will increase.

In further assessing business risks the FSA will also look at the sources of business and distribution mechanisms. If direct sales techniques are used, the accuracy and fairness of mail shots, advertising and Internet promotions will need to be scrutinised. If customers are attracted or engaged through the use of decision trees or non-advised filtering questions, how safe and reliable are the processes in avoiding risks of product mis-selling?

The types of products and services is another key risk element. For example, is the firm concerned with a discretionary portfolio management service or an advisory investment service? Does the firm purport to limit activity to 'execution only' transactions?

In the case of major market entities, what view may be taken of the authorised concern's market efficiency? For example, how transparent are its arrangements for price information, procedures to ensure fair and orderly trading and its commitment to the prevention of improper trades? In the case of recognised investment exchanges the operation of proper markets is the identified risk element falling for consideration. Here, attention focuses on the characteristics of the market in terms of the range of investors dealing in a given investment, the means to deliver or settle contracts for dealing in the investment and the nature of information available in the public domain to enable market participants to make a reasonably informed judgement about the volume of the investment to be traded and the associated risks.

Control risks 4.4

'Control risks' relate to the following five elements:

- treatment by the firm of its customers;
- the nature of the firm's organisation;
- the nature of its internal systems and controls;
- the firm's board, management and staff; and
- the firm's business and compliance culture.

As with the above described areas of business risk, the remaining risk elements numbered 16 to 45 will be relevant to a greater or lesser degree to the firm in question depending on the nature of its activities.

Treatment by the firm of its customers 4.5

The firm's ability to control risks will be looked at here by reference to identified risk element areas such as sales force training and recruitment; the basis of remuneration of employees together with its processes for accepting, advising and reporting to customers. The FSA will be concerned to address the policies and procedures operated in respect of financial promotions, product literature and disclosure together with the firm's approach to and mechanisms for dealing with and managing customers and customer assets.

The nature of the firm's organisation 4.6

The organisation of a firm in terms of the clarity of its legal/ownership structure, the jurisdictional base and quality of home country regulatory

4.7 *Risk Based Compliance*

oversight and the relationship of the firm within a wider group represent further control risk elements which the FSA will address.

The nature of its internal systems and controls 4.7

These are 13 discrete risk elements representing possible aspects of a firm's internal systems and controls. The control risks in this instance are those associated with:

- the firm's risk management skills;
- the policies, procedures and controls in place;
- processes for delivering management information;
- the adequacy of the IT system;
- reliability of financial and regulatory reporting and accounting policies;
- the integrity of internal audit procedures;
- the extent of any outsourcing/third party service providers;
- the use and role of professional advisers engaged by the firm;
- the firm's business continuity arrangements;
- money laundering controls and market cleanliness (in the case of recognised bodies); and
- processes for settlement and clearing arrangements (in the case of major market entities).

Included in the internal systems and controls as a key risk element is compliance. The FSA will be concerned to establish the risks posed from the nature and effectiveness of the compliance function within the firm. This will involve consideration of the mandate, structure, staffing, methodology and effectiveness of compliance. Does the compliance department/officer have access to the firm's governing body? What is the quality and experience of the compliance staff? How comprehensive and well documented are the compliance policies and procedures? How adequate are the compliance monitoring processes for ensuring compliance with internal and external rules including desk reviews, trade surveillance and managing conflicts of interest. Does the compliance function enjoy credibility with senior management?

The firm's board, management and staff 4.8

The final group of control risk elements relate to the board, management and staff of the authorised firm. In particular, how effective is the firm with regard to issues of corporate governments, allocation and definition of management responsibilities, ensuring quality of management, proper deployment and use of human resources, maintaining appropriate relations with regulators and ensuring proper approach to handling cultural issues and business ethics?

In relation to each of the above described business risk (see 4.3) and control risk (see 4.4) elements, the FSA, in its risk assessment framework, will 'score' the individual elements according to six levels of risk:

- high risk (indicating action will need to be taken to mitigate risk);
- medium high (where significant risks are identified as indicating mitigating action);
- medium low (where identified risks will be 'flagged' with mitigating action being optional);
- low (a default score requiring no action to be taken in the particular area);
- D/K (indicating insufficient knowledge so that further investigation will be undertaken if considered relevant); and
- M/A (where the FSA finds no relationship between the risk element and delivering its statutory objectives).

Risks to objectives groups

In order to link business and control risks to the statutory objectives in a meaningful way, the FSA accordingly assigns the individual risk elements to one or more of seven regulatory risk groups called RTO (risk to objective) groups (or RTOGs). The seven RTO groups are as follows:

1. Financial failure (ie which threatens market confidence and consumer protection objectives).
2. Misconduct and/or mismanagement (ie further threats to market confidence and consumer protection).
3. Consumer understanding (as it relates therefore to consumer protection and public awareness objectives).
4. Fraud or dishonesty (threatening market confidence and reduction of crime objectives).
5. Market abuse (which poses threats to market confidence, reducing crime and consumer protection).
6. Money laundering.
7. Market quality.

4.9 *Risk Based Compliance*

This may be diagrammatically presented as follows:

	Market confidence			
RTOG	Financial failure	Misconduct	Financial Crime / Market abuse / Money laundering / Fraud/dishonesty	Market malfunction

	Consumer protection				
RTOG	Financial failure	Mis-conduct	Market abuse	Market mal-function	Consumer under-standing

	Financial crime		
RTOG	Fraud or dishonesty	Misconduct	Money laundering

	Public awareness
RTOG	Consumer understanding

Risk failings in any of the 45 risk element areas may pose a threat (to a greater or lesser degree) to anyone or all of the four statutory objectives. The marketing and selling of products against inadequate product literature, for example, could present a risk to market confidence, consumer protection and public awareness objectives.

In assessing risks the FSA will consider the probability of a risk materialising and the impact of the risk if it eventuates. If a firm is assessed as low impact it will not have an individual risk assessment or risk mitigation programme. Such low impact firms will simply be monitored on the basis of standard monitoring returns and notifications. The FSA is keen to explain that the risk assessment framework is not a 'one size fits all' approach but rather its expectations for a firm's controls will be tailored to and reflect the nature and scale of the particular authorised entity's activities.

In using the risk assessment framework there are various stages to be followed. Firstly, an initial impact assessment ie all firms other than those designated as low impact will be subject to an individual risk assessment with risk elements scored as described above.

Secondly, there will be a probability assessment to determine the scale and likelihood of identified risks materialising and impacting on the statutory objectives. Thirdly, after completion of the probability assessment the FSA will develop a risk mitigation programme for the individual firm. This will require the firm to take steps to deal with risks thrown up by the assessment. The tools used as part of this regulatory process are diagnostic (ie for the identification and measuring and risks), monitoring, preventative and remedial. Where high or medium high risks have been uncovered, particularly involving control risk elements, mitigation action will generally be required to be taken. If the risks uncovered are categorised as 'medium low', the FSA may decide to monitor the position eg by requiring desk based reviews of information to assess changes in risk. Low risks will generally not require further action.

Fourthly, the FSA, once it has undertaken the risk assessment process and developed a risk litigation programme, will seek to validate the risk mitigation programme internally before sending it to the firm. The review is intended to ensure amongst other things that any programme is proportionate including to the firm's resources and so as to provide some overall quality and consistency of control across firms.

Fifthly, the results of the assessment are then communicated to the firm.

The final stage comprises ongoing assessment – usually a desktop exercise involving a review at an appropriate interval of risk factors, issues and the regulatory tools employed. If the risk mitigation programme appears on review not to be achieving its objective, the FSA may consider other action including enforcement action.

In carrying out a risk assessment visit, the areas of particular interest so far as compliance is concerned will be the firm's treatment of customers; its internal systems and controls; business and compliance culture; and the nature of the firm's organisation. The Compliance Officer will accordingly be concerned with ensuring an open and responsive dialogue between his department, the firm and the FSA so far as risk mapping and risk reduction measures are concerned.

Chapter 5
Enforcement Action

Introduction 5.1

Compliance failures ultimately invite enforcement action by the FSA. In the detection, investigation and management of any action taken the Compliance Officer is likely to play a significant part. An understanding of the FSA's powers is accordingly important – not only to enable the Compliance Officer to report to the firm's management as to its duties and responsibilities where enforcement action is threatened or taken, but also so as to be able to deal effectively with any enquiries made by the FSA into potential compliance breaches.

This chapter considers accordingly the investigative, supervisory and disciplinary powers of the FSA as they bear upon authorised firms.

Uncovering non-compliance 5.2

Compliance failures usually come to the attention of the FSA in one of three ways. Firstly, the firm has an overriding responsibility to notify the FSA as a result of Principle 11 of the Principles for Businesses of 'anything relating to the firm of which the FSA would reasonably expect notice.' This would naturally extend to material compliance failures. Secondly, regulatory breaches may also come to light as a result of routine monitoring and supervision of the authorised firm. Thirdly, a firm's activities will often come to the attention of the FSA as a result of external (usually consumer) complaints about a particular product or service supplied.

In that which follows attention is confined to the FSA's powers as they are available once a matter has come to its attention.

Obtaining Information 5.3

The first step in any FSA investigation will involve the furnishing of information to the Authority. The FSA will make a written request to the authorised firm for information and documents reasonably required in connection with the exercise of its powers. It may require that the information and

5.3 Enforcement Action

documentation supplied is authenticated in any manner it may reasonably require. In this context the reference to provision of 'documents' extends beyond paper records to include (for example) tape recordings, film and video recordings and email communications. Further, information and documents may be requested from persons connected with the firm. Connected persons include any member of the authorised firm's group, a controller of the firm, any other member of a partnership of which the authorised firm is a member and certain other categories of individual (officers, managers, employees and agents of the firm).

The Compliance Officer may have an important role in the collation of material and information – including advising on its relevance and the scope of disclosure required. For example, certain types of information and documentation called protected items are exempt from any disclosure obligation. These relate in particular to communications between professional legal advisers and the firm made in connection with the giving of legal advice or in relation to contemplated legal proceedings.

In practice, difficult issues can arise in respect of particular documents which require careful thought. Consider as an example a consumer complaint about an alleged act of product mis-selling. Various documents may be generated in response to the complaint as a result of the firm's internal investigation of it: a statement from the relevant financial adviser; a compliance assessment of the transaction by the compliance department; or a senior manager's letter of response setting out the firm's position. At any stage in the firm's consideration of the complaint advice may be sought from in-house or external lawyers. To the extent the documents referred to are generated as part of the firm's response to the complaint and compliance with its obligations under its complaints review machinery they will be properly discloseable to the FSA in the result of any further investigation. To the extent the documents are obtained with the dominant purpose of obtaining legal advice, however, they may well properly attract the description of 'protected items'.

Whilst it is tempting to conclude that materials should in any event be volunteered to the FSA upon request as part of the firm's open co-operation with the Regulator, it is important to bear in mind that once the documents have been so disclosed it will be very difficult if not impossible thereafter to maintain any legal privilege in the documents in question. In other words, once disclosed to the regulator the documents would also become discloseable to the aggrieved consumer. If the content of the documents are sensitive, the firm's position in maintaining any proper legal defence of the claim may thereby become prejudiced.

A further similar issue arises in respect of any simultaneous report or notification made to professional indemnity insurers.

Careful consideration, document by document, is appropriate before collating a package of information and documents designed to comply effectively with any FSA request.

Skilled Person's Report 5.4

In addition to obtaining documents and information relevant to investigations of compliance failures as described above, the FSA may also require a firm to co-operate in the provision of a report on its activities by an appropriately qualified person. The first step, where this power is to be exercised, will involve receipt of written notice to the firm that a report is required. This may typically be solicited from an accountant or external compliance consultant and be designed to address financial issues relating to the firm's conduct of business or compliance systems and procedures.

A common example where the power is exercised arises in relation to a series of product mis-sales where the Authority requires consumer redress payments to be made by the firm. A report on the firm's response to and fulfilment of any consumer redress plan may be required as a step in securing compliance with the FSA's requirements.

There is a duty imposed on any person who has provided services to the firm in relation to a matter on which a report is required to give the appointed skilled person any assistance reasonably required.

General Investigations 5.5

This chapter has so far considered the FSA's powers to obtain information and documents (including by means of a skilled person's report) from authorised firms and connected parties. The Authority, however, has wider powers in the event that it considers there is good reason for undertaking a general investigation. The target of the investigation will in this instance be the nature, conduct or state of the business of an authorised person or of any appointed representative (including any particular aspect of the business or the ownership or control of the authorised person).

Where any such general investigation is to be undertaken, the FSA (or the Secretary of State) must give written notice of the appointment of an investigator to the person who is the subject of the investigation and indicate the reason for the appointment. If the scope of the investigation comes to be extended, the FSA need only give notice if it forms the opinion that the person subject to investigation is likely to be significantly prejudiced by not being made aware of it. An example of such prejudice would arise where a person may inadvertently incriminate himself by not being informed of the change in scope of the investigation.

These general investigation powers arise in respect of both authorised persons and their appointed representatives – including 'connected persons'. In this instance, the range of relevant connected persons is wider than those from whom documents may (for example) be requested by a 'skilled person' for the purposes of a report. Here, 'connected persons' includes not only officers, managers, partners, employees and agents but also appointed representatives, bankers, auditors, actuaries or solicitors of the person under investigation; a parent or subsidiary undertaking of the person under investigation and a subsidiary undertaking of a parent undertaking; or a parent undertaking of a subsidiary undertaking under investigation.

An investigator duly appointed under the above regime is given wide powers including:

- power to require the person under investigation or any person connected with him to attend for questioning;
- power to require any of the above to provide information to the investigator;
- power to require any person (ie whether or not the subject of the investigation or a connected person) to provide documents.

In managing such an enquiry the Compliance Officer may be called upon to advise and assist those being called for interview. Guidance on what documents may be relevant to provide in co-operating with the investigation may be needed; consideration as to whether any documents are 'protected items' as discussed at 5.3 above may be required.

Specific Investigations 5.6

Next, there are two categories of regulatory and/or criminal contraventions where the FSA has modified investigative powers.

The first group comprises:

- Investigations into contraventions of insurance business regulations.
- Investigation of possible offences involving the provision of false information to FSA investigators and/or tampering with documents.
- Failure to notify changes in the controlling interest of an authorised firm.
- Allegations centring upon the provision of false information to an auditor or actuary.
- Allegations relating to the provision of misleading information to the FSA.
- Infringements of Schedule 4 Treaty Rights.
- Conduct of business in the UK otherwise than in accordance with a Part IV permission.
- Money laundering offences.

- Contraventions by an authorised person of any rule made by the FSA.
- Investigations into issues of fitness and propriety of a person to perform functions in relation to a regulated activity carried on by an authorised or exempt person.
- Omissions to prevent prohibited persons from acting.
- Failures by the authorised firm to ensure that no person performs a controlled function without requisite FSA approval.
- Allegations of misconduct by an approved person.

In addition to all of the general powers described above, in the above cases the investigator may also require a person who is neither the subject of the investigation nor someone connected with him to attend at a specified time and place to answer questions or provided information. In this case, the investigator must be satisfied that such attendance is necessary or expedient for the purposes of the investigation.

The second group of cases relates to investigations by the FSA of circumstances suggesting that any of the following has occurred:

- Contraventions of the general prohibition.
- Contraventions of the restrictions on financial promotions.
- Criminal offences of insider dealing.
- Allegations of market abuse.
- False claims to authorisation or exemption.
- Publication of misleading statements or practices.

Here, all of the above investigation powers are (again) available. In this instance the powers may be exercised whenever the investigator considers that a person is or may be able to give information which is or may be relevant to the investigation. In other words, it is not necessary for the investigator also to be satisfied that any interview or request for documents is 'necessary or expedient for the purposes of the investigation.' A test of simple relevance is applied. Further, apart from providing documents and information in the latter group of cases the Investigator may also require any person to give him all assistance in connection with the investigation which could reasonably be afforded.

Search and Seizure 5.7

In certain circumstances the FSA may also obtain a search warrant from a Justice of the Peace. In order to exercise this power the FSA, an appointed investigator or the Secretary of State must be able to swear on oath that there are reasonable grounds for believing any one or more of three specified conditions applies.

The first relates to circumstances where a request for information has not been fully complied with and there are reasonable grounds to believe that there may be documents or information on premises specified in the warrant relevant to an investigation. Here, a magistrate may authorise a constable to enter the premises to search for and seize relevant documents or information.

The second scenario relates to circumstances where there are reasonable grounds to believe that an authorised person or an appointed representative, if presented with a request for documents, would either not comply or would remove, tamper with or destroy such documents.

Finally, an application for a warrant to search premises and seize documents may also be made where there are reasonable grounds for believing that particular offences have been or may be committed – notably offences relating to insider dealing, market abuse, breach of the general prohibition, unlawful financial promotions or misleading statements and practices. In this case the Court must be satisfied that a simple requirement to produce the documents would be ignored or lead to documents or information being destroyed or interfered with.

Supervisory Powers

In the supervision of authorised firms the FSA has a range of 'own initiative powers' of which the Compliance Officer should be aware. In terms of the exercise of such powers the Authority states in guidance on the Enforcement Manual that it will

> 'proceed on the basis that a firm (together with its Directors and Senior Management) is primarily responsible for ensuring that the firm conducts its business in compliance with the [Financial Services and Markets] Act and the Principles and the Rules. In the context of its enforcement activities, the FSA will take formal action affecting the conduct of a firm's commercial business only if that business is being conducted in such a way that the FSA judges it necessary to act in order to secure compliance with those requirements and/or address the consequences of non-compliance.'

In practice, much may be achieved by co-operation with the FSA in addressing identified causes for concern by (for example) agreeing modifications to systems and control procedures and (where appropriate) ensuring any wrongs caused by breaches are appropriately redressed. Where co-operation and conciliation do not meet the regulatory objectives of the FSA the more serious 'own initiative powers' discussed at 5.9 and 5.14 below may be exercised. These are considered (briefly) in turn below.

Varying permissions 5.9

The scope of a firm's Part IV permission is intended to be tailored to its business and trading needs whilst also ensuring that only firms appropriately resourced, controlled and organised conduct business of a kind covered by the relevant permission. To balance these commercial and consumer protection interests the FSA may attach limitations to a permission (eg restricting the number or category of customers with which a firm may deal or limiting the number of specified investments in which a firm may deal). The permission may also be circumscribed by the imposition of formal requirements (eg prohibitions on holding client money or trading in certain categories of specified investment).

Where the FSA considers it desirable in order to protect the interests of consumers or potential consumers such limitations or restrictions may be introduced by a variation to a Part IV permission. Likewise, the FSA may vary a permission by removing a regulated activity from it or modifying the description of the permitted regulated activity.

Such powers are only likely to be exercised where the FSA has serious concerns about a firm or the way its business is being conducted falling short of any regulatory anxiety indicating the firm's permission should be cancelled altogether. Such variations may be directed to take effect immediately – particularly where the FSA is acting on information suggesting any significant risk of losses to consumers may arise or where a firm's ability to continue to meet the threshold conditions is in question.

A proposal to vary or cancel a Part IV permission must be notified to the authorised firm (which then has a right to refer the proposal to the Financial Services and Markets Tribunal).

Withdrawal of approval 5.10

In broad terms, as discussed in CHAPTER 3, a person will only be approved to perform a particular controlled function if the FSA considers the individual is 'a fit and proper person' to perform the function to which the approval relates. When considering an application for approval the FSA will take into account the applicant's qualifications, training and level of competence relevant to the particular function to which the application relates. In addition, the individual's honesty, integrity and reputation will be taken into account along with his solvency. Any criminal record or history of disciplinary proceedings by the FSA or any other Regulator will be important – as will the existence of any unpaid Judgment debts or Bankruptcy Orders.

There is, however, an ongoing duty to demonstrate continuing competence, fitness and propriety. If the FSA accordingly had reasonable grounds to conclude an approved person has ceased to be a fit and proper person to

5.11 Enforcement Action

conduct the controlled function to which approval relates it may withdraw the particular approval given. The onus of proof in demonstrating that the person concerned has ceased to be fit and proper is on the FSA.

An indication is given as to the quality of conduct expected by the FSA in the Statements of Principle for Approved Persons and the Code of Practice for Approved Persons.

It goes without saying a Compliance Officer will have a personal responsibility to demonstrate personal fitness and propriety as well as considering the extent to which others exercising controlled functions in the firm continue to measure up to appropriates standards.

Prohibition Orders 5.11

In addition to the power to withdraw approval, the FSA may, in appropriate cases, go further and prohibit an individual regarded as no longer fit and proper from performing a specified function, any function falling within a specified description or (indeed) any function at all. This power may be exercised not only in relation to approved persons but also to unapproved and exempt persons and members of professional firms and unauthorised individuals. Breach by an individual of a Prohibition Order is a criminal offence. Further, an authorised firm must take reasonable care to ensure that no function in relation to the carrying on of a regulated activity is undertaken by a prohibited person.

The Authority maintains a public record of individuals against whom Prohibition Orders have been made so that firms should have no difficulty in ensuring that any prohibited individual is not inappropriately employed.

In practice, a Prohibition Order is only likely to be made where the FSA determines the individual in question represents a significant risk to consumers or to the market. Such a risk may be more easily apparent where the individual is not someone vulnerable to withdrawal of approval or any alternative FSA disciplinary measure.

Injunctions 5.12

The FSA or the Secretary of State may apply to the High Court for an injunction restraining any person from contravening a requirement arising under the *Financial Services and Markets Act 2000* or from committing any offence for which the FSA or the Secretary of State has a power to prosecute. The Court may also be asked to direct any such person to take remedial steps in relation to any breach and may likewise seek such an Order against any person who has been 'knowingly concerned' in any contravention of the requirements of the Act. Further, the Court may be asked to make an Order preventing the disposal of or dealing with any assets under the control of those against whom the Order is sought.

A similar right to apply for a Restraining or Remedial Order is available to the FSA where it can satisfy the Court there is a reasonable likelihood of conduct being committed, continued to repeated amounting to market abuse.

Restitution 5.13

In similar circumstances to those described at 5.12 above in relation to the obtaining of an injunction the Court may also (on the application of the FSA or the Secretary of State) require a 'contravenor' or any person knowingly concerned in a contravention of the provisions of the Act or rules made thereunder to pay restitution to the FSA. The Court must be satisfied that the person concerned has made a profit as a result of the contravention in question or be satisfied that one or more persons have suffered loss or otherwise been adversely affected by the relevant contravention. The restitutionary payment must then be distributed by the FSA to any qualifying persons as the Court may direct ie any person appearing to the Court to be someone to whom the profits arising from contravention are attributable or who has suffered a loss or other adverse effect. Like powers are available in cases involving market abuse.

Redress 5.14

In respect of authorised firms, the FSA may itself require restitutionary payments to be made in similar circumstances to those which apply in respect of Court Orders described at 5.11 above. It will be necessary in this instance for the FSA to be able to identify quantifiable profits or losses linked to identifiable persons. In practice, the FSA may consider it more appropriate for (for example) consumers to pursue claims personally against a particular firm or through the Financial Ombudsman Service. If the effect of ordering redress would be to expose the firm to a risk of insolvency, the FSA may consider obtaining a compulsory Insolvency Order rather than directing restitution.

Prosecution of criminal offences 5.15

The FSA is also given power to prosecute a variety of offences which may be listed as follows:

- unauthorised trading;
- false claims to authorisation or exemption;
- issuing of unlawful financial promotions;

5.16 *Enforcement Action*

- performing or agreeing to perform functions in breach of the Prohibition Order;
- certain Listing Rule infringements;
- provision of false information to FSA investigators, provision of misleading information to the FSA and issuing misleading statements and practices;
- failing to comply with provisions about control over authorised persons;
- offences of insider dealing;
- money laundering infringements;
- provision of false or misleading information to actuaries and auditors.

Plainly, the above list of offences are ones in relation to which other prosecuting authorities may have an interest, such as the Serious Fraud Office (SFO), the Department of Trade and Industry (DTI) and the Crown Prosecution Service. Generally, the FSA is more likely to be concerned where the defendant is an authorised or approved person in relation to whom particular regulatory contraventions arise which may also involve possible criminal conduct.

In contrast, serious or complex fraud issues are likely to be dealt with by the SFO. Proceedings relating to the disqualification of directors under the *Company Directors Disqualification Act 1986* will normally be appropriately dealt with by the DTI.

Rather than initiate a formal prosecution, the FSA may also choose to administer a formal caution in respect of any criminal conduct. It will do so where there is sufficient evidence of an offender's guilt to give a realistic prospect of conviction and the offender admits the offence and gives his informed consent to being cautioned.

Disciplining Firms and Approved Persons 5.16

In *Meeting our Responsibilities*, published in August 1998, the FSA indicated that:

> 'Disciplinary action against regulated firms and approved persons will be considered where misconduct is sufficiently serious to warrant formal sanctions, in order to correct and deter non-compliance with regulatory or statutory requirements. In the case of individuals, primary responsibility for checking that they comply with their regulatory obligations – and for taking appropriate action if they do not – lies with the management of the firm concerned.'

The first line for disciplinary action will accordingly be the firm and its senior management. Thus any serious breach of the FSA requirements and rules relating to the conduct of the firm's business and (in particular) breaches of the Principles for Businesses will expose the firm to a risk of disciplinary action. The sanctions available where a breach is proved are:

- (in an appropriate case) the issue of an informal private warning;
- the publication of a statement that the firm has contravened the relevant requirement;
- the imposition of a financial penalty.

If the conduct is sufficiently serious to result in a withdrawal of authorisation, the FSA may not, however, also impose any financial penalty.

So far as approved persons are concerned, they will be guilty of disciplinary misconduct if they have either failed to comply with a Statement of Principle or been knowingly concerned in a contravention by the authorised firm of a requirement imposed by or under the *Financial Services and Markets Act 2000*.

Consistent with the approach indicated above, attaching primary responsibility for ensuring compliance with a firm's regulatory obligations to the firm itself, the FSA will only take disciplinary action against an approved person where there is evidence of personal culpability. This means conduct which is deliberate or falling below a standard of behaviour which would be reasonably expected in all the circumstances.

There are three potential sanctions available in respect of approved persons subject to discipline:

- the issue of a private warning;
- the publication of a statement of misconduct;
- the imposition of a financial penalty.

Importantly, the FSA's disciplinary power against approved persons is subject to a limitation period. In brief, no action may be taken against an approved person after the end of the period of two years beginning with the first day on which the FSA knew or ought to have known of the relevant misconduct.

In the case of both authorised firms and approved persons the choice of sanction is likely to reflect the regulatory history of the offender, the nature and seriousness of the misconduct in question, the extent to which any misconduct was deliberate or reckless and the offenders means to satisfy a financial penalty (where appropriate).

Procedural Issues in respect of Enforcement and Disciplinary Action 5.17

The procedural steps relevant to enforcement and disciplinary action are contained in the Decision Making Manual (DEC) of the FSA Handbook. Such action is likely to arise out of investigations of the kind described at the beginning of this chapter.

The FSA will usually provide a preliminary findings letter setting out the results of its investigations and inviting a response. This is a critically important opportunity to co-operate with the Authority in agreeing any compliance failures which have come to light and some remedial strategy with a view to fending off more serious enforcement or disciplinary action.

Once this process has come to an end, the FSA will decide whether to refer the matter to the Regulatory Decisions Committee (the RDC). This is the body responsible for deciding whether disciplinary action should be instituted and carries on its functions outside the FSA's management structure.

Where the RDC determines that enforcement action would be appropriate, it will issue a Warning Notice. Such a Notice is required where the FSA proposes:

- cancellation of an authorised person's Part IV permission;
- the making of a Prohibition Order;
- the exercise of disciplinary powers for misconduct;
- the imposition of penalties for market abuse;
- the publication of a statement of public censure or the imposition of a penalty on an authorised firm;
- a disqualification Order in relation to auditors/actuaries.

The Warning Notice will notify the recipient of a right to inspect the material on which the FSA has relied in taking the decision giving rise to the issue of the notice. The Warning Notice will also identify secondary material ie material which in the opinion of the authority might undermine the decision it is proposing to take. The recipient of the Notice will be given 28 days to make representations which may be given in writing or provided orally to the RDC. This again affords an opportunity to settle matters with the FSA by negotiation with the enforcement staff.

In cases not involving criminal offending or fitness issues relating to honesty and integrity and/or where the FSA is proposing to exercise own initiative powers, a deal may be brokered through a dedicated mediation scheme. Inspection of the materials relied upon by the FSA will obviously be important in deciding how to deal with the threat. This process which may typically take a couple of months, will then lead to the RDC either confirming that no enforcement action will be taken or result in the issue of a Decision Notice specifying what action is proposed.

The Decision Notice must be in writing and provide reasons for the proposed decision and alert the recipient to a right to refer the matter to the Tribunal. If the decision is not accepted by the person or firm concerned then it must be referred to the Tribunal. The process will be concluded by the issue of a Final Notice after acceptance by the firm or person concerned of the action proposed by the Decision Notice or otherwise as directed by the Tribunal following a reference.

In the event of a reference to the Tribunal, the right of access to the material relied upon by the FSA is again afforded to the firm or person concerned. Two types of material which will be referred to in the Warning and Decision Notices have already been highlighted. There are, however, four categories of material which the FSA may withhold:

- Protected items ie legal advice obtained by the FSA.

- Public interest material – ie material which the FSA considers it would not be in the public interest to disclose or which it determines would be unfair to be disclosed given its significance to the recipient of the Notice and the potential prejudice to the commercial interests of other persons.

- Comparative material – ie material relating to a case involving another person which was taken into account by the FSA only for the purposes of comparison.

- Excluded material – ie material which was intercepted in obedience to a warrant issued under enactments relating to the interception of communication or which indicates that such a warrant was issued or that material was intercepted in obedience to such a warrant.

Where disclosure is withheld on public interest or protected item grounds the FSA must, however, inform the recipient of the Notice of the existence of the withheld material.

Insolvency Orders 5.18

Included in the FSA's range of enforcement powers are procedures for it to seek administration, compulsory winding up and bankruptcy orders against authorised firms. The FSA may also participate in such procedures where these are initiated by a firm's creditors. The relevant materials are to be found in *Part XXIV* of the *FSMA 2000* with policy guidance contained in Chapter 10 of the Enforcement Manual.

5.19 *Enforcement Action*

Effective use of the powers and rights conferred by Part XXIV of the Act is to be seen in the context of the fulfilment of the regulatory objectives of maintaining market confidence, protecting consumers and reducing financial crime in particular.

In considering whether to seek an insolvency order the FSA will take into account the following factors:

- Any prior steps taken by the company or partnership to petition for its own administration, place itself in voluntary winding up or enter into a company voluntary arrangements.
- Whether any consumer or other creditor has sought an insolvency order from the Court.
- The effect on creditors if an order is made.
- Whether consumer interest may be better protected by using any other enforcement option available to the FSA such as a restitution order or Court injunction.
- The nature and extent of the relevant bodies assets and liabilities.
- The impact of any order on foreign assets/trading of a business with a significant cross-border or international element.
- The risk of preferential treatment of creditors in the context of an application for an insolvency order.

Administration Orders   5.19

In the case of a company or insolvent partnership which either is or has been either an authorised person or an appointed representative, the FSA may in an appropriate case petition the Court for an administration order. The same relief may be sought against a company or insolvent partnership which is carrying on or has carried on a regulated activity in contravention of the general prohibition. The Court may, however, only make such an order:

- if it is satisfied that the company/partnership is or is likely to become unable to pay its debts; this is deemed to be the case where the company/partnership is in default in respect of an obligation to pay a sum which is due and payable in pursuance of one its regulated activities; and
- it considers that the making of the order would be likely to achieve any one or more of four specified purposes, namely:
  - the survival of the company/partnership and the whole or any part of its undertaking as a going concern;
  - the approval of a company voluntary arrangement;

- the sanctioning of a compromise arrangement under the *Companies Act 1985, section 425* and/or
- a more advantageous realisation of the assets of the company/partnership would be thereby achieved than would arise on a winding up.

Winding up by the Court 5.20

The FSA may also present a winding up petition against any of the above insolvent trading entities. The two grounds specified for such an application are that:

- the body in question is unable to pay its debts; or
- it would be 'just and equitable' that the body should be wound up.

A similar deeming provision in relation to the ability to meet its debts as described at 5.19 above applies.

Voluntary winding up 5.21

In the case of an authorised person (other than an insurance company carrying on long-term insurance business) which is going through a voluntary winding up, the FSA may apply to the Court to determine any question which arises from the procedure or ask the Court to exercise any of the powers which would be available if the company were being wound up by the Court.

Further, the voluntary winding up of an authorised person is no bar to the FSA applying for the concern to be wound up by the Court in any event.

In deciding whether it would be appropriate to apply to the Court to wind up a company/partnership on just and equitable grounds, the FSA will consider whether (in particular) customer claims and client assets may be best preserved by such a course of action or otherwise adequately addressed by the exercise of its alternative enforcement powers (restitution, redress and injunction remedies).

The FSA will also take into account whether such risks may be dealt with by a withdrawal of authorisation, whether the body in question may have been used as a vehicle for financial crime and the extent to which the firm's management has co-operated with it.

Bankruptcy Orders 5.22

Where an individual appears to be unable to pay a regulated activity debt (or to have no reasonable prospect of doing so), the FSA may petition for bankruptcy.

Given the personal and professional ramifications of such an order, the FSA has indicated in the relevant guidance that:

- it will petition for bankruptcy only if it believes that the individual is in fact insolvent;
- even then, it will also consider identified factors eg whether it can deal with the individual using other powers available to it under the Act without the need to seek a bankruptcy order.

This makes sense given that where the individual controls assets belonging to consumers or holds them on trust, such assets will not vest in the insolvency practitioner appointed in the bankruptcy. Again, relevance will be attached to the number of consumers affected, the extent of their claims against the individual, the risk of financial crime, the history of the individual's dealings and co-operation with the FSA and whether there are any special personal or professional implications for the individual if a bankruptcy order were made.

FSA Powers in relation to Voluntary Arrangements 5.23

The FSA is given certain rights to challenge voluntary arrangements entered into at a corporate and individual level. Where a voluntary arrangement has been approved in respect of a company which is an authorised person, the FSA may apply to the Court either where the corporate voluntary arrangement (CVA) approved at the relevant creditors' meeting unfairly prejudices the interests of a creditor, member or contributor of the company or if there has been some material irregularity at or in relation to the meetings.

Likewise, there is a right to apply to the Court if the FSA is dissatisfied with the conduct of the supervisor of a CVA. Similar powers to intervene by an application to the Court apply in respect of individual voluntary arrangements.

The FSA has indicated, however, that it 'will ... not normally challenge an arrangement approved by a majority of creditors.' The exceptional considerations which may prompt such a challenge are identified as follows:

- the ratio of consumer to non consumer creditors;
- where the FSA has reason to be concerned about the regularity of the meeting or the identification of connected or associated creditors and the extent to which creditors with similar concerns could make an application;
- where the company, partnership or individual has control of consumer assets which may be affected by the voluntary arrangements;
- the complexity of the arrangement and all of the regulated activity constituting the relevant business;

- the company's, partnership's or individual's previous dealings with the FSA, in particular the extent of co-operation with the FSA and the compliance history.

Transactions at an Undervalue 5.24

The FSA may also apply to the Court in relation to transactions entered into at an undervalue by a person carrying on a regulated activity (whether or not in contravention of the general prohibition) if the victim of the transaction is/was party to an agreement with the debtor, the making and performance of which was part of the regulated activity carried on by the debtor.

The FSA's application is treated as made on behalf of every victim of the transaction. The objective will be to secure an order from the Court restoring so far as is possible the position which would have obtained had the transaction not been put into effect. The factors relevant to the FSA's exercise of this power are:

- the extent to which the impugned transaction involved dealings in customers funds;
- the number of consumers or other creditors likely to be affected by the application;
- whether it would be appropriate for matters of concern to be addressed through alternative insolvency orders;
- the size of the transaction to be impugned.

The Financial Services and Markets Tribunal 5.25

The Financial Services and Markets Tribunal is available to receive references where the FSA proposes:

- disciplinary action against a firm;
- disciplinary action against an approved person;
- exercise of certain own initiative powers (eg variations of permissions, cancelling of a firm's permission or withdrawal of approved person status).

The Tribunal is presided over by a President appointed from a panel of chairmen, appointed by the Lord Chancellor. Proceedings will take place before the Chairman (who must be legally qualified), together with two members appointed from a lay panel. The latter can be expected to be individuals with relevant consumer and industry experience.

5.25 Enforcement Action

The procedure involved in referring a matter to the Tribunal involves the service of a Reference Notice on the Tribunal and the FSA within 28 days, beginning with the date on which the relevant FSA Notice was itself first given. The Reference Notice must give the name and address of the Applicant (along with any Representatives), state that it is a Reference Notice and set out the issues concerning the FSA Notice which the Applicant wishes the Tribunal to consider.

The FSA will then respond within a further period of 28 days by service of a Statement of Case specifying the basis for its proposed action. This will be accompanied by a list of documents on which the FSA proposes to rely and any further material which in the opinion of the FSA might undermine the decision it proposes to take.

Thereafter, the Applicant is given a further 28 days in which to file a reply setting out the grounds on which he relies in the reference and indicating those matters in dispute arising from the FSA's Statement of Case. The Applicant must also supply a list of documents relied on in support of his case.

A pre-hearing review will then be conducted before the Chairman who will give appropriate directions to manage the reference. These will relate (for example) to exchange of witness evidence and any need for preliminary hearings in respect of any questions of fact or law which may enable the reference to be disposed of more expeditiously.

Although substantive hearings may take place in private, it is to be anticipated that in practice proceedings will be in public. Private hearings are only likely to be directed where they are necessary, having regard to any unfairness to the Applicant or prejudice to the interests of consumers that might result from a hearing in public *and* a private hearing would not prejudice the interests of justice. More often than not these conditions will not be satisfied.

Whatever the result of the reference, the losing party will not be directed to pay the costs of the reference as a matter of routine. Orders for costs against a losing party will only be made where the Tribunal considers that party has acted vexatiously, frivolously or unreasonably or whether the FSA's decision, the subject matter of the reference, was itself unreasonable.

The Tribunal may, within 14 days of reaching its decision, review matters and set aside a relevant decision if satisfied it was wrongly made or if new evidence has become available justifying a different conclusion. Once the Tribunal has determined the reference, it must remit it to the FSA with any appropriate directions designed to give effect to its decision.

A right of appeal then lies to the Court of Appeal with permission of the Tribunal or the Court of Appeal. Permission may only be granted, however, where a 'point of law' arises.

Chapter 6
Compliance Models

Introduction 6.1

It has been noted thus far the regulatory emphasis now placed on the board or senior management of a firm accepting responsibility for the proper organisation and running of its affairs. In taking responsibility for the firm's compliance function there are two approaches which have been traditionally taken. These may be loosely called 'compliance output supervision' and 'compliance input supervision.'

Compliance Output Supervision 6.2

According to the first model, the function of compliance is seen as monitoring the quality of sales output from a regulatory perspective. This involves adopting procedures for reviewing and appraising sales transactions (whether individually or by representative sampling). Here, the compliance function will focus on a paper audit. For example does the file relating to a transaction contain evidence of appropriate terms of business being given to a client, an adequate fact find and reason why letter with ancillary material to enable suitability of any recommendation to be demonstrated?

This approach, in practice, often proves to be inadequate. The following difficulties often emerge:

- A client's file may appear to be compliant in containing evidence of the materials which may be expected to be found (referred to above); this is not, however, a reliable indicator/guide that non-compliant investment advice has been provided: experience shows that where mis-selling complaints arise investors frequently allege that other reasons were given for a transaction which turns out to be unsuitable than is apparent from the content of contemporaneous documents.

- Even statistically relevant sampling of files will not establish that compliant, appropriate and suitable advice was given in all cases.

- Relying upon the compliance function to detect inappropriate sales is accordingly a precarious business model to adopt and one whose presence in a firm does nothing usually to encourage compliant selling practices; on the contrary, it often fosters a view among the sales force that 'we will sell as best we may and wait for any problems to be identified by compliance'; responsibility for the firm's compliance is seen accordingly as resting with the Compliance Officer/compliance department rather than with the individuals in the firm transacting day-to-day business.

Compliance Input Supervision 6.3

The alternative model, compliance input supervision, addresses the issue of compliance from the other end of the telescope. According to this model, the compliance function is intimately concerned with engendering a good compliance culture on the part of each member of the firm, supported in this endeavour by the responsible board or senior management. Responsibility for compliance is seen as part of each member of the firm's day-to-day activity. In practice inputting compliance rather than monitoring output results in a firm far less vulnerable to compliance failures.

At the most basic level, the compliance function of a firm largely reflects the firm's culture or business ethics. The FSA is concerned to promote good, ethical business practices in the financial services markets rather than to impose a prescriptive regime of regulation. Its intention is to encourage firms to embrace good business standards rather than look for regulatory loopholes which may be exploited to a firm's commercial advantage at the expense of respect for overarching ethical principles. An attempt to capture and define the expected ethical standards is inherent in:

- the FSA's statutory objectives (maintenance of confidence in the UK financial system; securing an appropriate degree of protection for consumers; the promotion of public understanding of the financial system; and the reduction of financial crime);
- the Principals for Businesses; and
- the Statements of Principal for approved persons.

Assessing a firm's culture by reference to the above high aspirational standards is difficult. Objective self-assessment is hard, particularly where any ground for criticism identified may lead to unwelcome changes in business practices. In truth, however, a realistic self appraisal is likely in the long run to be more beneficial than waiting for external signs/symptoms of a poor culture to manifest. When the compliance culture of a firm is allowed to deteriorate, sooner or later three particular problems will develop:

- increasingly poor consistency in maintaining sales; self evidently, in the long run this is economically disruptive.

- an increase in investor complaints; again, this can prove economically disadvantageous and impose increasing strains on the firm's relationship with professional indemnity insurers; and
- ultimately, disciplinary action will be provoked.

Rather than wait to be confronted with the results of a poor compliance culture, the firm would be best advised to get to grips with its existing culture, measured against the high aspirational standards referred to above. Attempting to define a firm's individual ethos, however, is, as noted, difficult. The concepts are, to a degree, illusive; the tendency to a subjectively satisfactory assessment is often compelling; who is to be responsible for the assessment? Consistent with making the board or senior management of a firm primarily responsible for regulatory compliance, it is suggested the assessment is one which ultimately needs to be instituted by those responsible for the firm. The (non-exhaustive) areas to consider include the following:

- What conduct does the board/senior management reward? Is there, for example, any emphasis on rewarding the achieving of sales targets alone?
- What is the firm's practice and policy towards dealing with regulatory breaches committed by individuals in it? Are these ignored or do they attract internal discipline?
- What takes priority in employment appraisals? Again, is there an emphasis on achieving sales figures or does the appraisal consider and applaud evidence of good compliance in selling practices?
- How is the Compliance Officer/department/function viewed by the board or senior management and the wider business staff? Is compliance seen as a business facilitator or business inhibitor?
- How is the board's or senior management's attitude towards the compliance function viewed by the wider firm personnel? Is the board or senior management viewed as supportive of compliance or merely tolerant of the function as a required evil?
- What resources and authority are allocated to the compliance department? Is this department seen as having the final say? Is it afforded time and resources to train and instruct? What role does it play at board or senior management meetings?

The profile of a firm with a good cultural attitude towards compliance is likely to reflect the following.

- The senior management or board will be publicly visible as accepting responsibility for delivering good compliance; it will be positive about the compliance function.
- Compliance Officers will be identified as key value players at board and management meetings, seen as having an important role to play in business development decisions.

6.3 Compliance Models

- There will be clearly defined recruitment, training and business processing systems in which the Compliance Officer/department will be intimately involved.

Where compliance is afforded an appropriate place of honour in the conduct of the firm's affairs the function is likely to be able to be developed and will be seen as affording a valuable asset of the business. Correctly positioned, the Compliance Officer/department will demonstrate what may be called the six As of good compliance:

- *Authority* to direct adherence; it is important that business authority is given to the compliance department for requiring and enforcing the meeting of regulatory standards. This may take the form of delegated authority from the board or senior management or be clear from well documented and publicised reporting lines. A good culture will take infringements seriously.

- *Availability* for consultation; it is important that the Compliance Officer/department is seen as user friendly, approachable and available to give advice and guidance when requested.

- *Ability* to train and instruct; the Compliance Officer/department will have a key role to play in providing ongoing training and instruction, including giving necessary advice and guidance to the board or senior management. This may include advising on business changes which may be necessary.

- *Awareness* involving detailed knowledge of the regulatory requirements specific to the regulated business concerned.

- *Arbitration* on compliance conflicts; if the sales force, board or senior management takes a view as to a particular product line or sales practice which conflicts with a regulatory requirement, the Compliance Officer/department should be at liberty to arbitrate and facilitate the adoption of a compliant business practice.

- *Auditing* of the firm's implementation of compliance will also form a key part of the Compliance Officer's/department's job description.

The activities lying behind each of the above (authority, availability, ability to train/instruct, auditing, arbitration and awareness) will be best delivered and flourish given the necessary support by the board or senior management. This will include allocating sufficient resources to the compliance function to enable it properly to operate. At a practical level this involves:

- Ensuring the recruitment of an adequate number of compliance staff (appropriate to the size and complexity of the business).

- Ensuring the recruitment of staff with requisite rule expertise, knowledge and experience.

- Ensuring the recruitment of individuals able to relate well with the business departments of the firm so as to be able effectively to communicate and deliver compliance knowledge, skills and training.
- Provision of IT systems to assist in the promotion and monitoring of good compliance practices.

Having established the correct cultural framework and ethos, adequately resourced and equipped the compliance function and appropriately positioned compliance as a vital part of the firm's business operations, the test of the effectiveness of the arrangements will lie in its ability to monitor the maintenance of business practices complying with the regulatory regime.

The systems the compliance function employs to identify risks and detect regulatory breaches will in practice be likely to reflect the risk based approach taken by the FSA and described elsewhere in this work.

In classifying risk the matters of concern will be those giving rise to a potential for regulatory infringements. The presence of a rule of course carries with it the risk of non-compliance. If the culture and ethos of the firm is right the risk of non-compliance is naturally reduced. In quantifying risk, however, it is important to consider both the likelihood of a particular risk manifesting and the impact the realisation of a particular risk may have on the business in question. A low probability risk resulting in a low impact on the firm's affairs will call for less rigorous systems for monitoring and detecting such occurrences compared with low probability but high impact or high probability but low impact events.

Designing an appropriate modelling system will therefore start with an analysis of the existing regulatory risk profile of the firm in question. Once the areas of particular regulatory risk are identified, the types of monitoring regimes and the frequency of monitoring will be able to be determined. Take as an example a traditional firm offering independent advice in arranging life and pension products but which also advises and arranges on wider short- and long-term investments.

The Compliance Officer/department is likely to need to be alive to any of the following:

- Any sudden increase in transactions in a particular product area eg a significant increase in new business written in respect of some newly marketed offshore fund.
- Changes in the profile of the concentration of business being written by the firm.
- A sudden increase in the number of policies/plans/investments in a particular sector lapsing.
- A sudden increase in the number of complaints being made in relation to eg a particular product, a particular branch or a particular individual.

6.3 Compliance Models

- Evidence of any increase in rule breaches (whether in a particular sector of the firm or in respect of particular individuals in it or in respect of particular investment products) uncovered by periodic file reviews.

It goes without saying that these diagnostic indicators will only be meaningful if part of an overall system requiring regular reporting of transactional data, regular appraisal and review of such material and the maintenance of accurate historical data against which to judge the significance of any emerging trend(s).

Such procedures as are established should be written down and clear in content and objective. Having been alerted to changes in the profile of business operations the next step in the compliance function is to assess the significance of the changes and report appropriately to the board or senior management. It will be important to gain an understanding as to what may be going wrong and to agree a programme of timely remedial action. In a well run firm, where the culture is right, there will be built into the timetable of those responsible for the firm's affairs routine meetings with the Head of Compliance, where regular briefings as to the firm's activities can be delivered. Ad hoc access to management personnel will also be available to deal appropriately with any urgent situation which develops.

Where causes for concern are identified, a well run firm will appreciate the need for inter-departmental/inter-disciplinary discussion and meetings. Thus, to take an example, assume a sudden increase in recommended investments into a newly advertised offshore fund promoted by a particular product provider. Assume within three months of a surprisingly large volume of business being written complaints begin to come in from investors alleging losses from the transactions and complaining about inadequate warnings as to risks.

From this simple scenario a range of department/disciplines may be identified as relevant contributors to any investigatory and remedial action. In particular:

- The HR department responsible for recruiting the adviser/salesman concerned: how rigorously were the individuals appraised in terms of their fitness and propriety to act on behalf of the firm?

- Those on the board or forming part of senior management responsible for approving or including the product as one appropriate for marketing and arranging through the firm: what steps were taken to (a) verify the true nature of the investment and (b) ensure any advisers/salesmen were properly instructed in how to sell such an investment?

- The in-house legal department (if any): what legal liability issues may arise as a result of the complaints being made?

- The firm's insurers: ought a report to be made to insurers alerting them to potential claims?

- How ought the matters being uncovered to be reported to the FSA – a likely responsibility of the Compliance Officer?

Prompt detection of problems and a responsible dialogue with the Regulator is likely to be critical in fending off disciplinary action or the exercise of own initiative powers by the FSA.

Dealing with Professional Indemnity Insurers 6.4

The prudent need for professional indemnity (PI) insurance cover in the operation of all businesses concerned with offering professional advice and services is self evident and reflected in the regulatory requirement for authorised firms to have appropriate cover in place. A compliance officer will often have responsibilities associated with the arrangement of cover including taking some part in the renewal process; he may also be concerned to ensure that the policy terms are operated properly so that the benefit of cover is available when required in response to a client complaint. This may involve working with in-house or independent lawyers in dealing with complaints whether they lead to proceedings in a Court or before the Financial Ombudsman Service. The following paragraphs look at some of the key issues to be considered in obtaining and preserving PI insurance cover.

Arranging cover and renewal 6.5

As contracts of utmost good faith, the PI insurers will require candid disclosure of any matter material to the underwriting risk. Information required to be disclosed in obtaining cover is that which passes 'the awareness test of materiality'.

This is information which would have affected the insurer's judgment in the sense of reinforcing a decision to contract or in the sense that together with other information it might have been sufficient to lead to different contract terms but considered in isolation it would have made no difference to the contract or its terms. If 'material' in this sense then the information (or the withholding of it) will be taken to have induced the particular policy and entitle insurers later to avoid the policy if it emerges the initial underwriting risk was inaccurately presented.

It will therefore be important for any Compliance Officer dealing with arranging or renewing cover to make sure that the following types of information are accurately provided to the insurers (this list is not exhaustive):

- gross turn-over figures (often allocated to specific areas of business);
- details of product lines/business activities;
- information as to complaints or claims made during the year;
- information as any known circumstances that may give rise to claims;

- details of any adverse comments or action by the FSA on aspects of the regulated business;
- details of concern over or discipline of any of the sales force or management in respect of regulatory breaches.

Inaccurate or incomplete information may well lead to a later avoiding of coverage.

Giving notification 6.6

Most PI policies, particularly those applying to the financial services industry, cover claims made by an insured firm's clients during the year of cover. A 'claims made' policy imposes a stipulation in almost all cases that the insured must report or notify the insurer about a claim immediately and, furthermore, report at once any circumstance coming to the attention of the insured which could give rise to a claim being made later. Provided notification is given, the policy will respond even if a claim is pursued outside the year of cover in which a notification is provided to the insurers.

Conversely, a failure to notify as required will generally be tantamount to a breach of policy condition and allow the insurer the right to avoid cover either in respect of the particular non-notified claim or to avoid the whole policy.

The purpose of prompt notification is of course to allow the insurers the best and earliest opportunity to investigate matters which a delay in reporting may otherwise prejudice. Many independent financial adviser businesses were forced into insolvency as a result of failures to ensure the availability of PI insurance cover in relation to complaints/claims arising out of the Pensions Review. A sudden discovery of under-insured areas of the business may therefore also result in a breach of the firm's capital adequacy requirements and threaten the ability to continue trading. The issues discussed here are of immense practical importance and great sensitivity.

What is a notifiable claim? 6.7

The Compliance Officer with any responsibility in this area of business will therefore need to be clear as to what amounts to a claim or a notifiable circumstance. The words 'claim made' require not only the assertion of a claim or of some remedy as due but also the bringing of that assertion to the notice of the assured. Thus, a letter from a client of the firm complaining about an investment recommendation and demanding compensation for alleged losses would obviously amount to a notifiable claim.

What is a notifiable circumstance? 6.8

What may amount to a circumstance requiring notification is not always so straightforward. In general terms a complaint by a customer of the firm is often an event which may ripen into a claim and as such may be seen as a notifiable circumstance. The discovery of some systemic weakness in (for example) marketing literature or repeated compliance failures at point of advice may also be identified as circumstances which may lead to claims.

Guidance is to be found in a key legal decision in this area – *J Rothschild Assurance Plc v Collyear et al, 29.09.1998* – where the Court gave some general guidance on a number of issues relating to the liability of professional indemnity insurers to respond to calls on a standard-worded PI policy made in the context of the review of past sales of personal pension plans. Issues the Court was asked to adjudicate upon included:

- When could or ought notification of a possible claim to be made so as to preserve entitlement to cover under a claims made policy?
- What may amount to non-disclosure by an assured sufficient to justify a repudiation of cover?
- What amounted to a 'claim' on the policy?

The policies in the *Rothschild* case all offered cover on a 'claims made' basis in respect of the period from 1 February 1993 to 31 January 1994. The insuring clause offered an indemnity to the assured 'against any claim or claims first made against them during the period of insurance … in respect of any civil liability whatsoever.'

J Rothschild Assurance Plc (JRA) was required as a condition of cover to 'give notice to the underwriters as soon as possible during the period of this policy … of any circumstance of which the assured shall become aware which may give rise to a claim or loss against them.'

It was further provided that 'any claim or loss to which that circumstance has given rise which is subsequently made after the expiration of the period [of cover] shall be deemed for the purpose of this policy to have been made during the subsistence hereof.' How did these terms apply to notifying insurers of risks of claims arising from the Pensions Review?

History relates that the problem of mis-selling of personal pension plans was first clearly highlighted by a report to the Securities and Investments Board made by KPMG in December 1993. Shortly thereafter LAUTRO wrote to its members in a letter of 22 December 1993 stating 'there is a problem which needs to be tackled.'

Rothschild's response was to forward a letter dated 27 January 1994 to its PI insurers, indicating that in the light of the KPMG report and LAUTRO letter, and the fact of its own reviewable pension transfer business there were circumstances which 'may in respect of each policy identified [in a list attached to the letter] and to be identified give rise to a claim by each client against the assured.' A schedule of some 2500 pension transfers was then attached. This blanket notification was held both to be justified and sufficient to obtain cover under the policy.

The Court pointed out that the test for materiality for notice was a weak one ie any circumstance which may give rise to a claim. It did not have to be a circumstance which was likely to give rise to a claim.

Faced with this the insurers then sought to argue that an earlier LAUTRO enforcement bulletin 16, published in July 1992, warning of the likely non-compliant nature of sales of personal pension plans to members of occupational pension schemes ought to have led to notification in similar terms to those of the letter of 27 January 1994. The absence of such earlier notification was argued to entitle the insurers to avoid cover.

This contention was given short shrift by the Court. The bulletin referred to potential for concern which merited investigation. By the time of the KPMG report, the compliant nature of pension transfer transactions had been examined and evidence revealed to justify a conclusion that the majority of occupational scheme transfers would most likely be such as to justify investor claims.

The insurers argued that even if there was a liability to respond under the policy, it was a liability to respond to claims. Since the investors had been sought out by the assured as part of the carrying out of the review directed by the Regulators, a claim could not be said to have been made on the policy in the sense in which that matter was usually understood.

This argument also failed. The investors were held to have made a claim on JRA by participating in the review process and/or in accepting the redress offered in the light of its terms.

Getting the reporting balance right 6.9

When potential for complaints and investor claims against a firm become 'a circumstance which may give rise to a claim' so as to require notification is therefore a delicate issue. Whilst insurers are in practice reluctant to accept blanket notifications of circumstances which may give rise to claims, preferring claim-by-claim or case-by-case notifications, as the arguments in *Rothschild* and experience show firms may find that reporting individual claims where there is prior knowledge of a wider problem may lead the insurers to rely on an earlier omission to report the circumstance as justifying repudiation of cover in relation to individual claims.

A practical approach is to discuss any circumstance with a potential for multiple claims with insurers and brokers and agree if necessary a protocol for accepting notifications on a case-by-case basis when individual claims arise. The downside is that if the firm has been involved in selling a particular product on a large scale, such that many claims could arise, these may not be identified and notified within any particular policy year: the insurers may decline renewal for the next year appreciative of the risk of further claims coming in or may load the premium or excess in a way which is financially unattractive to the insured.

Conversely, a blanket notification of circumstances apt to give rise to future claims, whilst capturing if effectively worded and properly made, all the possible claims that may arise out a particular piece of business activity to one year, the insured may find that the scale of the potential value of the claims exceeds the total level of cover for any one year and or makes the firm uninsurable (save at a prohibitive premium) in future years. A case-by-case approach may thus serve the interests of insurers and insured alike.

The same thorny issues arise in respect of the annual renewal of the policy; circumstances which may give rise to claims and which ought to have been reported as such in the preceding year will be excluded from cover in respect of the new year's cover by a standard policy condition to that effect; there would be a duty to disclose the risk of claims arising from such circumstances as part of the obligation of utmost good faith in any event.

If the identity of the PI insurers is to change at renewal the issue is of acute significance in that any liability must be appropriately captured to the outgoing insurers or at least the new insurers must be able to be satisfied that the insured did not have knowledge of circumstances which may give rise to claims in fact prior to inception of the new policy.

Timing of giving of notice 6.10

Where the duty to notify has arisen, the majority of policies require 'immediate notice in writing to be given' often to a particular department/address set out in the policy: a failure to do so, however innocent, will generally give the insurers a right to refuse cover. In this context, 'immediate' is usually taken to mean as soon as is reasonably practical.

Standard duties 6.11

The scope of a broker's responsibility in each case may of course depend on the precise terms of engagement but in the absence of any attempt to define the scope of responsibility in any terms of business agreement, the core minimum duties will generally include the provision and competent operation of a strategy for:

- arranging suitable cover; and
- making appropriate notifications under the terms of cover arranged.

Brokers' duties

Where there is a gap in cover it may be that a claim will lie against the firm's brokers. This paragraph sets out briefly the standard duties owed by brokers in this situation. The ordinary function of the insurance broker or other intermediary is in short to receive instructions from his principal as to the nature of the risk or risks, the rate or rates of premium at which he wishes to insure, to communicate the material facts to the potential insurers and to obtain insurance for his principals in accordance with the principal's instructions and on the best terms available. In many cases these duties will include advising the client on the type of insurance best suited to his requirements and subject to client's instructions, exercising reasonable care to obtain insurance which will best meet those requirements. The duties thus described are easy enough to follow.

A recent example

A recent example of a failure by brokers to live up to the above standards is provided by *Alexander Forbes v SBJ Ltd [2003] Lloyd's Rep IR 432*. In that case, for years 1994/95 Alexander Forbes effected errors and omissions (E&O) insurance cover through SBJ Ltd. For regulatory reasons the cover effected was separate from an umbrella policy for the benefit of the group maintained by the parent holding. The policy was a claims made one with standard requirements to notify claims and circumstances as a condition of cover.

In late 1994 Alexander Forbes received a complaint of pensions mis-selling which it reported to the brokers. In doing so it drew attention to a potential for other claims arising as a result of the Pensions Review obligations that were to be engaged. The brokers inadvertently reported the single claim to the group insurers and not to the relevant PI underwriters responsible for dealing with this insured subsidiary. In addition, the notification was not one which extended to reporting the risk of further claims of a similar kind which the implementation of the Review may bring out.

When the mistake as to the identity of the underwriter to notify was appreciated, a late out-of-time notification was made to the correct insurers. The latter agreed to cover the actual complaint of mis-selling but refused retrospectively to provide blanket cover for all claims arising from the Pensions Review. There was no mechanism for requiring the insurers to accept a block notification out of time.

The Court held that the brokers had been negligent not only in omitting to forward notification to the correct insurers but that SBJ Ltd ought also to have considered and advised in respect of the need for a blanket notification of circumstances. It was indicated the damages which could be claimed for these defaults would be such sum as would have been obtained if a blanket notification had been given, which the Court concluded the insurers would have been obliged to accept.

In principle these would cover not only the lost indemnity (minus excess) but any defence (legal) costs that the original policy if operated would have given.

Recovering costs 6.14

Most policies also provide for insurers to 'indemnify the assured in respect of all costs and expenses incurred with their written consent in the defence or settlement of any claim which falls to be dealt with under the policy.' This is an area for vigilance on the part of any Compliance Officer involved in overseeing the process of complaints handling and reporting to insurers.

Frequently, although a claim may be notified appropriately, the insured will often with the insurer's consent become involved in investigating the complaint as part of its regulatory duty and incur expense in so doing. Careful consideration should be given as to whether any part of this expense is incurred in defence or settlement of the claim. If it is, then insurer's consent to the incurring of the expense should be obtained so as to ensure that the cost can be said to be covered by the policy.

In the *Rothschild* case (see 6.13) an argument arose as to whether part of the costs of complying with the Review, where these were also incurred in defending or settling claims were covered by the policy. As to the scope for recovering the costs of the review exercise under the policy, the Court gave some limited comfort in suggesting that the costs of settlement may have started to have been incurred when the claim was potential rather than actual. Provided that in any case a claim has been made, then the costs of settling it, whether before or after it was made, are costs incurred in the settlement of a claim which fall to be dealt with under the policy.

Insurers and the Regulator 6.15

There is no doubt that all of these issues are of great practical consequence to the industry. Accommodating regulatory expectations and dealing with insurers' requirements can also create opportunities for conflict: in announcing the Pensions Review the SIB for example required authorised firms responsible for advising on and arranging the sales of personal pension plans to seek out investors and assess the quality of the advice given, offering redress where it was found to have been non compliant.

This obligation at first blush ran directly counter to the expectations of insurers who are responsive to claims and not pro-active in eliciting them. The balance between satisfying the firm's regulatory duty to comply with the Review obligation and not taking any step which would invalidate cover was a fine one. PI policies routinely contain an express condition that no claim will be admitted or settled without insurer's consent. Contacting clients and offering

6.15 Compliance Models

compensation without careful handling of the process created the ever-present risk of breaching policy terms and conditions.

Likewise, it is not unknown for insurers to take a more optimistic view of the ability of a firm to demonstrate that its advice was complaint than the FSA or the Financial Ombudsman Service (FOS). Insurers may insist that particular lines of defence are run in an attempt to defeat a claim in circumstances where the FSA or the FOS may not regard the point as meritorious. Firms can find themselves between a rock and a hard place.

The practical advice is to keep an open dialogue with insurers and Regulator alike in this situation. It is relevant also to bear in mind that whilst insurers can decide on the tactics to be pursued in handling a claim, they must do so in what they bona fide consider to be the common interest of themselves and the insured.

Equally, the insurer's right to object to settlement must always be exercised in good faith, having regard to the interests of the insured as well as to its own interests. Further, in the exercise of its power to withhold consent the insurer must not have regard to considerations extraneous to the policy of indemnity.

Chapter 7
Training and Competence

Core Standards 7.1

Fundamental to the compliance delivery of financial services in all aspects of the market is the operation of an adequate 'training and competence' regime. This is a key area in which Compliance Officers will have a responsibility – often in assessing, appraising or commenting upon defined levels of competence required from those carrying out the firm's regulated activities and in designing or ensuring the delivery of adequate training. The training and competence regimes operated by a firm will be important to HR, having regard to their relevance to employment issues in relation to both recruitment and retention of employees; they will be relevant to senior management both in relation to the need to satisfy the requirements of Principle 3 of the Statements of Principle for businesses and the regulatory obligation 'to take reasonable care to organise and control their affairs responsibly and effectively'. The subject of training and competence is equally critical to a firm's ability to continue to satisfy threshold condition 5 ie the need to satisfy the FSA that the firm's approved persons are fit and proper to carry out the regulated activity for which each is engaged. Competence is a key aspect of an approved person's fitness and propriety.

High Level Standards 7.2

The approach taken by the FSA to the provision by a firm of an adequate training and competence regime is to specify five high level commitments which must apply to the regime designed and operated. The commitments which a firm must satisfy are that:

- its employees are competent;
- its employees remain competent for the work they do;
- its employees are appropriately supervised;
- its employees' competence is regularly reviewed; and
- the level of competence is appropriate to the nature of the business.

Recruitment 7.3

The issue of an employee's competence and need for training is first met at the stage of recruitment. Where the firm intends to recruit an individual with a view to him either engaging in or overseeing certain activities with or for private customers the firm's recruitment procedures must 'take into account the knowledge and skills of the individual in relation to the knowledge and skills required for the' job in question. At a practical level this involves:

- ensuring an accurate and detailed job description is formulated;
- determining correctly the level of knowledge and degree of skills likely to be required to carry out the job described;
- investigating fully the knowledge, experience and past training of the candidate in question;
- identifying in the light of the above any further training or educational needs which may be required on the part of a particular candidate; and
- devising an appropriate method of recording the above processes and conclusions.

Competence Levels

Pre-competence status 7.4

Broadly there are two levels of competence which may be referred to as the 'pre-competence' and the 'competent adviser' level. Where an individual is recruited at the pre-competence level the firm must ensure that before such an employee engages in a relevant activity with or for a private customer:

- he has first to pass the relevant regulatory module of an appropriate examination;
- he has an adequate level of knowledge and skills to act with or for a private customer while under supervision; and
- he does not so act otherwise than under the supervision of a competent person.

At this pre-competence level the prospective employee adviser must have an adequate knowledge of:

- the firm's relevant systems and procedures as they apply/relate to the activity in question;
- the kinds of designated investment business carried on by the firm and any other members of its marketing group;

- how to deploy the appropriate skills necessary in analysing a private customer's needs and circumstances; and
- the necessary ability to apply his knowledge of the firm's (and its group's) procedures and products.

Competent adviser status 7.5

Natural career progression will lead to attaining competent adviser status. Before a firm can assess an employee as competent it must be satisfied that he:

- is competent to apply the knowledge and skills necessary to engage in or oversee the relevant activity without supervision; and
- has passed each module of an appropriate examination.

This will involve (in particular) consideration of the following:

- Has the employee passed an accredited examination to the required level in respect of the activity to be undertaken? A comprehensive guide to the approved examination requirements is provided by the Financial Services Skills Council. This is activity specific, so that it is relatively straightforward to enquire of the Council (through its dedicated website at www.fssc.org.uk) as to (for example) the examination requirements for acting as a broker fund adviser or 'acting as a pension transfer specialist.
- Assessing whether the employee has developed the requisite skills to apply the technical knowledge acquired, eg is he able to assess accurately the client's needs so as to be able to identify and recommend suitable financial products?
- Assessing whether the employee has developed the skills necessary to solicit relevant information from a client, eg how accurate and thorough is his fact-finding analysis?
- Determining his level of knowledge of the firm's products (and those offered by any marketing group).
- Appraising his knowledge and awareness of the market in general, including other products, applicable legislation and relevant regulatory provisions.

The firm's training and competence regime must also make provision for the recording (and retention of records) of the criteria applied in assessing competence and how and when the decision was arrived at to confer competent adviser status on a particular employee.

'Employee' and 'Activities' 7.6

The paragraphs above refer generically to a firm's employees and their individual engagement in respect of relevant activities. These are defined terms

7.6 Training and Competence

for the purposes of the training and competence regime. Firstly, so far as the application of the training and competence requirements to a firm is concerned, the high level commitments referred to above apply to all authorised firms except that:

- an incoming EEA firm or treaty firm is not obliged to embrace the high level commitments insofar as responsibility for any matter covered is reserved by a European Community instrument to the firm's home state regulator;

- the commitments apply to a UCITS (undertakings for collective investment in transferable securities) qualifier only insofar as may be relevant to the manner in which the firm communicates or approves a financial promotion.

The term 'employee' means an individual 'who is employed or appointed by a person in connection with that person's business, whether under a contract of service or for services or otherwise or whose services, under an arrangement between that person and a third party are placed at the disposal and under the control of' the firm; the term also embraces an appointed representative of the firm or an individual employed or appointed by an appointed representative of the firm.

The relevant activities include:

- advising on and/or dealing with investments with or for clients (being securities other than stakeholder pension schemes or broker funds and/or derivatives;

- managing investments;

- advising on packaged products (other than broker funds), investments comprising Friendly Society tax exempt policies and investments in the course of corporate finance business;

- the activity of broker fund adviser;

- advising on syndicate participation at Lloyd's; and

- the activity of a pension transfer specialist.

Secondly, the training and competence requirements described above apply to employees overseeing on a day-to-day basis the following activities:

- operating or acting as a trustee or depository of a collective investment scheme;

- safeguarding and administering investments or holding of client money;

- certain administrative function in relation to managing investments and effecting or carrying out life policies;

- taking private customers through decision making processes in connection with stakeholder pension schemes; and
- certain administrative functions in relation to the operation of stakeholder pension schemes.

Further Controls on Training and Competence 7.7

There are three particular controls which apply in respect of the training and competence requirements described above:

- Firstly, the requirement to pass each module of an appropriate examination to attain competent adviser status does not apply if a firm is satisfied that an employee has at least three years' up-to-date relevant experience in the activity in question obtained while employed outside the UK, has not previously been required to comply fully with the relevant examination requirements as otherwise stipulated and has nonetheless passed the relevant regulatory module of an appropriate examination. This relaxation, however, does not apply in respect of an employee engaging in the activities of a broker fund adviser or pension transfer specialist nor the activities of advising on investments which are packaged products (where the advice is given to private customers) or on syndicate participation at Lloyd's. Further, the ability to be designated as competent adviser without having previously complied fully with currently stipulated examination requirements is not relaxed in relation to an employee intending to perform the functions of investment adviser, corporate finance adviser and/or investment management.

- Secondly, a firm must ensure that an employee does not recommence engaging in the activities of advising on or dealing in investments for clients comprising securities (other than stakeholder pension schemes or broker funds) and/or derivatives if he has not engaged in that activity for twelve months and two years have passed since he passed an appropriate examination in respect of the relevant activity. This embargo is disapplied, however, if the firm can demonstrate that the employee nonetheless has sufficient experience and has kept his technical and regulatory knowledge up to date. Otherwise, the firm must require the employee to pass an appropriate examination (afresh).

- Thirdly, a firm must ensure that an employee under supervision passes an appropriate examination within specified time limits running from the date (which must be recorded) on which he began engaging in the relevant activity – and in default of an examination success, the firm must ensure the employee ceases to engage in or oversee the relevant activity and does not resume it without first passing an appropriate examination. In broad terms, the relevant time limits are as follows:

- The relevant examination(s) must be passed before employees engage in the activities described above of advising on/dealing in certain investments without supervision.
- Relevant examination(s) must be passed within thirty months of commencing the activities of managing investments.
- In respect of all other activities referred to above the relevant examination(s) must be passed within two years of starting the activity in question.

Maintaining Competence

Having devised and operated an appropriate system for recruitment and initial training and instruction of the employee adviser so as to bring him to the status of competent adviser, the firm must then also have appropriate arrangements in place to ensure that any employee who has been assessed as competent to engage in or oversee an activity maintains competence. There are two aspects to this process: firstly, the firm must maintain a system for monitoring an employee's competence; secondly, the firm must at intervals appropriate to its circumstances determine the training needs of its employees and organise appropriate training to address those needs. The training must be timely, planned, appropriately structured and evaluated.

The task of monitoring competence of an ongoing basis is an important part of the task of risk based supervision entrusted to the firm. In ensuring ongoing training is appropriately targeted to those individuals/activities likely to pose the greatest regulatory risks, it is (naturally) important to decide objectively where the risks lie. It is suggested the following 'weak links' may be the appropriate focus of attention:

- recently qualified and (accordingly) relatively inexperienced field advisers;
- employees whose sales profile relates to high risk products;
- employees with a poor record in respect of the completion of fact finds and/or maintenance of regulatory compliant files;
- employees who have attracted a high level of complaints and/or who evince poor persistency; and
- employees with a poor record of attending training/instruction.

The programme of training and instruction which is devised should take into account, in terms of frequency, duration and intensity, the above risk areas. As to how it is delivered, the firm may rely on a range of services provided by:

- in-house compliance;
- attendance at external training events, courses and seminars;

- attendance at CPD accredited conferences;
- face-to-face reviews;
- a requirement to sit further examination(s).

Supervising Employees 7.9

Where the firm allows an employee to engage in an activity with or for private customers at pre-competence level the firm must ensure he does so under supervision and that the level of supervision is 'appropriate in relation to the employee's ability to apply the necessary knowledge and skills.' Part of the instruction and supervision process will include ensuring the employee undergoes a review and assessment of his work and is provided with individual coaching (which may include role play and accompanied private customer visits).

Where the employee at pre-competence level engages in the activity of advising on packaged products for private customers the firm must also ensure that the supervisor has himself passed an appropriate examination and has the technical knowledge, assessment skills and coaching skills to act as supervisor. The firm must also ensure these supervisory skills are themselves maintained to a competent standard.

Record Keeping 7.10

The firm must also make appropriate records so as to be able to demonstrate compliance with the training and competence requirements summarised here. These must be retained by the firm for at least three years after an employee ceases to engage in or oversee an activity; in the case of records in respect of pension transfer specialists, these, however, must be retained indefinitely.

Chapter 8
Money Laundering

The FSA's Objectives 8.1

One of the four key FSA objectives is the reduction of financial crime. In July 2001 it published *The Money Laundering Theme: Tackling our new responsibilities*. This document identified, following research, six 'risk clusters' where money laundering activity was perceived as most likely to occur. These were:

- international banking and high risk jurisdictions;
- independent financial advisers and offshore fund investments;
- domestic banking;
- online broking;
- credit unions; and
- spread betting.

A gap analysis following an industry study identified particular weaknesses perceived as likely to facilitate money laundering activity. These were:

- failures to carry out adequate customer verification exercises;
- a lack of awareness and training on the part of staff in respect of money laundering risks;
- inadequate procedures for internal and external reporting;
- a failure to keep adequate records;
- omissions to acquire source of wealth information;
- failures to carry out sufficient enquiry into the background of those with whom firms had established correspondent relationships;
- systemic defects in the role of money laundering Reporting Officers;
- a failure by firms to consider the geographical location of customers and conduct additional due diligence for non-Financial Action Task Force jurisdictions.

8.2 Money Laundering

In pursuing the regulatory objective of 'reducing the extent to which it is possible for a business carried on by a regulated person to be used for a purpose connected with financial crime', the FSA is further required to 'have regard to the desirability of regulated persons taking adequate measures to prevent money laundering, facilitate its detection and monitor its incidence.'

These objectives find expression so far as the industry is concerned in the FSA's *Money Laundering Sourcebook*. In addition to the requirements of this *Sourcebook* firms will also be obliged to comply with the *Money Laundering Regulations 2003 (SI 2003 No 3075)* and certain criminal legislation containing anti-money laundering provisions, particularly the *Proceeds of Crime Act 2002*. The contents of the *Money Laundering Sourcebook* largely reflect the basic provisions of the (now) *Money Laundering Regulations 2003*.

The role of the authorised firm in helping the FSA to achieve its statutory objectives is given a high profile in so far as Rule 3.2.6 of *Senior Management Arrangements, Systems and Controls* provides in terms that firms 'must take reasonable care to establish and maintain effective systems and controls for compliance with applicable requirements and standards under the regulatory system and for countering the risk that the firm might be used to further financial crime.'

This section will accordingly consider the broad requirements of the *Money Laundering Sourcebook*, the duties imposed by the *Money Laundering Regulations 2003* and take a brief look at the impact of the *Proceeds of Crime Act 2002* on the financial services sector.

The Sourcebook and its application 8.2

The requirements of the *Money Laundering Sourcebook* are expressed to apply to every 'relevant firm' with respect to its 'relevant regulated activities.' The term 'relevant firm' includes every firm except:

- a firm whose *only* regulated activities comprise general and certain other insurance business (including certain Lloyd's insurance activity);
- a UCITS qualifier;
- an incoming EEA firm to the extent that it is *not* conducting activities from an establishment in the UK.

The term 'relevant regulated activity' means any regulated activity apart from the categories of general and certain other insurance business (including certain Lloyd's activities) referred to above.

Specific duties 8.3

A relevant firm must appoint an individual as its Money Laundering Reporting Officer (MLRO). It will generally be convenient for this individual also to be the 'nominated officer' for the purposes of the *Money Laundering Regulations 2003* discussed below. The MLRO must be a person with a sufficient level of seniority within the firm and have sufficient resources (including time and, if necessary, support staff).

Resourcing is an important consideration given the extensive range of duties and other responsibilities imposed by the *Money Laundering Sourcebook* on the MLRO. These require the firm to ensure the MLRO is able (amongst other things):

- to monitor the day-to-day operation of its anti-money laundering policies; and
- to respond promptly to any reasonable request for information made by the FSA.

In addition, the MLRO is responsible for:

- Receiving internal reports from others in the firm in respect of suspected money laundering activity.
- Taking reasonable steps to access relevant 'know your business information' (ie in particular data collected by the firm on customers which will enable him to assess an internal report and decide whether to make a further external report to the National Criminal Intelligence Service).
- Making external reports to the National Criminal Intelligence Service.
- Obtaining and using national and international findings in carrying out his role, which takes the form of data and information available inter alia from the Financial Action Task Force and the Joint Money Laundering Steering Group.
- Taking reasonable steps to establish and maintain adequate arrangements for awareness and training (both of himself and others).
- Providing an annual report to the firm's senior management in respect of the firm's handling of money laundering responsibilities. The report should:
    - assess the relevant firm's compliance with the *Money Laundering Sourcebook*;
    - indicate how (for example) national and international findings have been used during the year in handling money laundering responsibilities; and
    - provide information about the number of reports made internally by staff of the relevant firm.

These detailed responsibilities of the MLRO reflect the day-to-day implementation of the broad requirements of the rules for the relevant firm to 'set up and operate arrangements including the appointment of a Money Laundering

8.4 *Money Laundering*

Reporting Officer' which are designed to ensure that it and any appointed representative acting on its behalf are both able to and do comply with the *Money Laundering Sourcebook*.

Identification of clients 8.4

As noted above, one of the key failings in the FSA's gap analysis comprised inadequate client verification procedures. In the rules the word 'client' is defined more widely than for the purposes of other sections of the FSA Handbook. In relation to money laundering, 'client' means 'any person engaged in or who has had contact with the relevant firm with a view to engaging in any transaction with that relevant firm (a) on his own behalf or (b) as agent for or on behalf of another.'

In relation to a 'client' the relevant firm must take reasonable steps to obtain sufficient evidence of the client's identity so as to be able to show that the client 'is who he claims to be.' If the 'client' appears to be acting on behalf of another, the same verification duty arises in respect of the other person. The firm must carry out this verification exercise as soon as reasonably practicable after it has contact with a client with a view either to agreeing to carry out an initial transaction for him or to reaching an understanding with the client that it may carry out future transactions. If the client does not supply appropriate evidence of identity, the firm must discontinue any regulated activity it is conducting for him and bring to an end any understanding it may have reached with the client (unless in either case the firm has already thought it appropriate to make a report to the National Criminal Intelligence Service, which will have caused it to cease to act in any event).

What amounts to 'sufficient evidence' is not specified. The relevant guidance indicates, however, that it would include passports, driving licences or utility bills. If a client is unable to produce any of the foregoing and the firm concludes it would not be reasonable to expect him to do so (for example a hospital inmate whose affairs are being handled by the Court of Protection) then the firm may accept a letter from a person in a position of responsibility verifying the individual's identity (ie name and address).

Exceptions 8.5

The above verification duty does not apply in the following situations:

- Where the client is a credit institution or a financial institution covered by the *Money Laundering Directive* (91/308/EEC as amended by 2001/97/EEC).

- A one-off transaction or series of related transactions where the total value is less than 15,000 euros.

- A client who is introduced by an authorised firm which has provided a written assurance that it obtained sufficient identification evidence of the individual concerned.

- Where the proceeds of a one-off transaction are invested on the client's behalf and are to be recorded as such, where the same can only be reinvested on his behalf or paid directly to him.

- Long term insurance contracts with a one-off premium not exceeding 2,500 euros or where annual premium payments do not exceed 1,000 euros.

These exceptions of course do not apply if the relevant firm otherwise knows or suspects or has reasonable grounds to know or suspect that the client (or the person on whose behalf he appears to be acting) is engaged in money laundering.

Reporting 8.6

The *Sourcebook* imposes (initially) internal reporting obligations on staff handling transactions which may involve money laundering to report these promptly to the MLRO if the person 'knows or suspects or has reasonable grounds to know or suspect' that the client is engaged in money laundering. Implicit in this duty is a requirement on the part of the firm to ensure its staff are appropriately trained and instructed in *both* the identification of potential money laundering activity *and* the firm's procedures for internal reporting.

External reporting 8.7

Once the MLRO has received a report, he needs to decide whether to make a report to the National Criminal Intelligence Service (NCIS). To assess whether a report would be appropriate, he will need to know more about the particular transaction and client. The relevant firm is accordingly obliged to take reasonable steps to provide to its MLRO any 'know your business information.' This means information about the financial circumstances of a client (or any person on whose behalf he appears to be acting) and the features of the transaction which the firm has entered into with or for the client. The guidance provided in respect of this obligation makes it clear, however, that the firm is not expected to obtain additional information above and beyond that which would normally be gathered from a client in the course of conducting its business; the expectation is that the firm should use its existing client information effectively by making this available to the MLRO.

If the MLRO, having considered the internal report and any relevant 'know your business information' concludes that money laundering is suspected or apparent, a further report to NCIS must then be made.

Record keeping requirements 8.8

There are onerous record keeping obligations in respect of steps taken to comply with the *Money Laundering Sourcebook*.

A firm must make records of the following:

- the evidence used to verify client identity;
- details of every transaction carried out by the relevant firm with or for a client in the course of regulated activity;
- all internal and external reports; and
- decisions not to make an external report.

The above records must be retained:

- as to a client's identity, for five years from the end of the relevant firm's relationship with the client (or last transaction conducted for him);
- in any other case for five years from the date information was obtained or the record was created.

Here, however, 'transaction' does not include advice given to a client where it is not followed by a transaction with a monetary value.

The Money Laundering Regulations 2003 8.9

The *Money Laundering Regulations 2003* (SI 2003 No 3075) are of broader application than the *Money Laundering Sourcebook* requirements in that they apply to the conduct of all 'relevant business', which is defined to include regulated investment business activity but also includes other business activities such as that carried on by insolvency practitioners, accountants and providers of legal services. That said, the Regulations must also be complied with by 'relevant firms'. Insofar as (in practice) the relevant obligations in the Regulations overlap with those in the *Sourcebook* this should not present any additional burden to firms.

Systems and training 8.10

Regulation 3, for example, requires every person carrying on a relevant business to establish such procedures by way of internal control and communication 'as may be appropriate for the purposes of forestalling and preventing money laundering'; these will include taking appropriate measures so that relevant employees are made aware of the provisions of the Regulations and related legislation including the *Proceeds of Crime Act 2002* and given training in how to recognise and deal with transactions which may be related to money laundering. Each relevant business carried on in the UK must ensure it complies with further requirements set out in the Regulations relating to identification of clients, internal reporting and record keeping procedures.

The identification procedure requirements in essence mirror those described at 8.4 above as applied by the *Sourcebook*; similar exceptions apply in respect of certain low value transactions, insurance related transactions and where introductions are effected by a third party who has provided a written assurance that evidence of the identity of the relevant person was obtained and recorded under their own procedures.

The requirements for record keeping are again broadly similar, being five years commencing with the date on which the relevant business relationship ends.

Suspected money laundering detected by those carrying on the relevant business must be internally reported to a nominated officer, who will then have the responsibility to decide whether a further report to NCIS is required.

The Proceeds of Crime Act 2002

The *Proceeds of Crime Act 2002* ('the 2002 Act'), so far as is relevant for present purposes, creates four relevant offences:

- Concealing criminal property.
- Arranging in relation to the acquisition, retention, use or control of criminal property.
- Acquiring, using or possessing criminal property.
- Failing to report suspected money laundering of any proceeds of crime by those working in the regulated sector, which includes those carrying on regulated activities.

'Criminal property' in relation to the above first three offences includes both the proceeds of an offender's crime as well as those of another. It extends, however, to property which the alleged defender knows or suspects constitutes or represents the benefit of criminal conduct ie any conduct which amounts to an offence in any part of the UK (or which would constitute an offence if it occurred in the UK).

The 2002 Act provides a defence in respect of the first three offences if the alleged offender:

- made an authorised disclosure before carrying out the prohibited act eg transferring the property from the UK ('concealing' criminal property includes disguising, converting or transferring it or removing it from the UK);

- made an authorised disclosure after the event with an excuse for the delay; or
- intended to make a disclosure but had a reasonable excuse not so to do.

In practice, delay in disclosure or non-disclosure will be very hard to justify.

Regulated sector offences 8.12

As noted above, the 2002 Act creates a new offence where those in the regulated sector fail to report suspicions of money laundering. The initial reporting obligation is to the nominated officer ie usually the firm's MLRO; the MLRO will also commit an offence if an external report is not then made where the internal report discloses evidence of a suspicion of money laundering. It is important to note the threshold triggering the reporting obligation is set very low. It is sufficient that a reasonable person would, on the information available, have reasonable grounds for either knowing or suspecting that another person was engaged in money laundering. Incompetently failing to appreciate what was taking place is accordingly no defence.

It is also made an offence to disclose suspected money laundering to a person where this is likely to prejudice the money laundering investigation ie giving a 'tip off'. Here, however, it is a defence to show that the person making the disclosure did not know or suspect that it would prejudice an investigation.

Penalties 8.13

There are potentially serious penalties for those convicted of offences under the 2002 Act: for those convicted of the offences of concealing, arranging and/or acquiring there is (potentially) a maximum term of imprisonment of fourteen years, an unlimited fine or both. A person convicted of a 'tipping off' offence or failure to make an appropriate disclosure is liable on conviction to a maximum term of imprisonment of five years, an unlimited fine or both.

Chapter 9

Complaints Handling, the Financial Ombudsman Service and the Financial Services Compensation Scheme

Complaints Handling

Regulatory requirement 9.1

In general, every authorised firm carrying on regulated investment business from an establishment maintained in the UK is obliged to maintain a complaints handling system. The requirement does not apply to:

- firms which do not conduct business with eligible complaints ie a person eligible to refer a complaint to the Financial Ombudsman Service (described at 9.2 below);
- UCITS qualifiers;
- authorised professional firms insofar as their non-mainstream regulated activities are concerned;
- credit unions; and
- the Society of Lloyd's, Members of the Society and Managing Agents (subject to a separate complaints handling regime).

The particular requirement is for the firm to 'have in place and operate appropriate and effective internal complaint handling procedures.' These must be written down and cater for 'handling any expression of dissatisfaction, whether oral or written and whether justified or not' made by or on behalf of an eligible complainant. The procedures must provide for:

- receiving complaints;

9.2 Complaints Handling

- responding to complaints;
- investigating complaints; and
- notifying complainants of their right to refer a complaint not resolved to their satisfaction to the Financial Ombudsman Service.

The procedures put in place must be notified to clients of the firm 'at or immediately after the point of sale' of a financial product. Details of the internal complaint handling procedures must also be supplied if requested by an eligible complainant and furnished automatically when a relevant complaint is received. A firm must also display in each of its branches or sales offices to which eligible complainants have access a notice indicating that it is covered by the Financial Ombudsman Service.

Who is an eligible complainant? 9.2

As indicated above, an eligible complainant is any person entitled to refer a complaint to the Financial Ombudsman Service. This comprises in essence any:

- private individual;
- business with a group annual turnover of less than £1m;
- charity with an annual income of less than £1m; or
- trustee of a trust which has a net asset value of less than £1m.

In addition, the relevant complainant must be 'a customer or potential customer of the firm.' A potential customer is somebody whose complaint arises out a firm's actions or its failure to act. An eligible complainant also includes a person who may be regarded as an 'indirect customer' of the firm. Examples include a beneficiary under a trust or estate where the direct client is the trustee or personal representative; a person for whose benefit a contract of insurance was taken out (or intended to be taken out); and a person to whom the benefit of a claim under an insurance contract has passed (amongst other methods by assignment or subrogation).

Time scales 9.3

Time scales are laid down for dealing with complaints as follows:

- A complaint must be acknowledged within five business days of receipt (save in respect of minor complaints able to be dealt with on the day or otherwise able to identify as falling outside the complaints regime).

- A final response must be provided within four weeks of receipt of the complaint or the complainant notified that the matter is still under investigation.
- Within eight weeks of receipt of the original complaint a final response letter must be issued or the complainant notified that the matter is still under investigation; reasons for the delay must be given and the complainant notified of his right to refer any dissatisfaction to the Financial Ombudsman Service.

In acknowledging the complaint the firm must identify the person responsible for dealing with it.

What is a complaint? 9.4

A complaint is defined as 'any expression of dissatisfaction, whether oral or written and whether justified or not.' Firms must accordingly be astute to recognise communications from clients amounting to 'expressions of dissatisfaction.' Given that it is a requirement that complaints are handled 'fairly, consistently and promptly', the setting up of appropriate management controls to meet this standard will include ensuring all personnel having or likely to have any contact with members of the public are properly trained in the identification of complaints and aware of the firm's internal complaints handling procedures.

Five key issues in complaints handling 9.5

There are in essence five key aspects to handling communications identified as complaints by eligible complainants. These are:

- A firm must ensure it is dealing with the complainant or his nominated representative and likewise permitted by the complainant to solicit relevant information required as part of the investigation process from third parties. If a complaint is made 'on behalf of an eligible complainant', eg by a professional adviser or member of the complainant's family, it is necessary to ensure authority has been given by the complainant himself for the firm to deal with his appointed agent; where it will be necessary to solicit information from third parties, eg product providers or (perhaps) the complainant's accountant, authority must be obtained to discuss the complaint with such concerns (in particular to avoid potential infringements of the provisions of the *Data Protection Act 1998*).
- The terms of the complaint must be clearly understood. Does it relate to inadequate commission disclosure? Is the complaint more radically related to an allegation of product unsuitability? If the original package of advice included arranging a variety of linked investment products, does the complaint extend to all or only part of the original advice? It may be appropriate to seek clarification in writing or (occasionally) by telephone.

9.6 Complaints Handling

- The person appointed to investigate the complaint must be someone with 'appropriate competence' to address the issues raised, should be independent of the individual(s) involved in the original advice and must have authority (or access to someone with authority) to settle the complaint.

- In investigating the complaint, it will be appropriate to consider whether the allegations (if accepted/established) evidence a breach of conduct of business rules, a breach of any expressed or implied terms in the terms of business letter of engagement or involve negligence; if the investigation shows a likely breach of duty then the next question will be as to whether the relevant breach of duty identified has caused the loss and damage to which the complaint relates. If these issues appear to be likely to be established in the complainant's favour then it will be appropriate to consider whether any (legal) defence exists. In particular, may it be that the complaint relates to advice given so long ago that a time bar defence applies. The issue of time bars is considered at 9.15 below in respect of the Financial Ombudsman Services jurisdiction.

- Having addressed the above issues as part of the investigation process, the final step will be the issue of a final response letter. This should:

    – summarise the facts as found by the firm;
    – state the conclusion(s) reached by the firm as a result of the investigation and provide reasons for the views reached;
    – offer redress if appropriate. The calculation of redress is often a complex exercise and firms should bear in mind any relevant guidance given by the FSA and/or the Financial Ombudsman Service. For example, in cases involving allegations of mis-sold personal pension plans, detailed specifications as to the form and calculation of compensation have been provided by the FSA; similar guidance has been provided in relation to dealing with complaints about the mis-selling of endowment plans;
    – if redress is to be offered then the letter should invite the complainant to return an acceptance expressed to be given in discharge of any liability which may arise out of the issues involved in the complaint;
    – the complainant's right to refer the matter (in any event) to the Financial Ombudsman Service within six months of receipt of the final response letter must be identified; a leaflet published by the Financial Ombudsman Service describing its procedures should be included.

Ancillary issues 9.6

In operating the complaint procedures it should be at once apparent that the receipt of a complaint may trigger an obligation to notify the firm's professional indemnity insurers. The internal procedures should therefore accommodate this step. The insurers may well then be involved in agreeing the wording and content of any further communication(s) to the complainant and in agreeing the level of any offer of compensation to be made.

Further, the final response letter is intended to be final. Experience is that complainants often seek to engage in further correspondence, disputing the findings and conclusions of a final response letter. Unless the further communications involve the correction of some accepted error on the part of the firm and/or the firm sees some good reason to change the view arrived at it is usually best to notify the complainant politely that the conclusions reached in the final response letter are ones by which the firm stands; it will not (accordingly) enter into further correspondence and if the complainant remains dissatisfied he should take advantage of the Financial Ombudsman Service.

Two-stage complaints procedures

A firm may operate a two-stage complaints procedure. In this event, the firm must ensure that any response it issues informs the complainant how to progress his complaint further within the firm if dissatisfied with the outcome and must also refer the complainant to the ultimate right to complain to the Financial Ombudsman Service. Where a two-stage procedure is adopted, the firm must indicate in its first response that it will regard the complaint as closed in the absence of a reply from the complainant with eight weeks. Provided these milestones are adhered to the firm will be relieved of any need to issue either a holding letter or a final response letter at the four- or eight-week stages mentioned above (save where the complainant indicates he remains dissatisfied, in which event the firm must still issue a final response letter within eight weeks of the receipt of the initial complaint).

Firms should consider carefully whether the two-stage complaints procedure is appropriate. In practice, it is sometimes apt to lead to hurried and inadequate investigation coupled with an instinctive response to reject a complaint. It is well to remember that there are two key benefits to a well organised complaints machinery:

- Its proper operation in fact generally inspires consumer confidence in the firm in question (and leads to client retention rather than loss of business).
- The results of data emerging from the complaints handling procedures are helpful in identifying any remediable weaknesses in the firm. For example, does the process disclose evidence of a pattern of complaints in relation to a particular:
    - product line?
    - salesman?
    - branch?

If so, does this identify a need for additional training/instruction or possible discipline of any of the sales force? It is equally important to assess whether the reason for complaints reflects some systemic problem with the business or whether rather it is linked more specifically to particular fault on the part of the financial adviser responsible for the original transaction.

Records and reports

A firm must make and retain records of complaints for a minimum period of three years from the date of initial receipt. This does not apply where:

- the complaint is not made by or on behalf of an eligible complainant;
- the complaint does not relate to an activity of the firm coming within the jurisdiction of the Financial Ombudsman Service; and
- the complaint does not involve an obligation of actual or prospective financial loss or material distress or inconvenience.

In addition, the firm must report twice yearly to the FSA with information about:

- The total number of complaints received by the firm categorised as to whether the complaint (in substance) relates to the following:
    - overcharging/incorrect charges;
    - delays;
    - other administrative errors;
    - unsuitable or misleading advice;
    - a failure to carry out the client's instructions;
    - provision of a poor customer service;
    - misleading advertising/product information;
    - disputes over sums/amounts payable;
    - switching/churning;
    - a breach of the customer agreement; or
    - some other matter.
- The total number of complaints closed by the firm with four weeks or less of receipt, closed between four and eight weeks of receipt and more than eight weeks after receipt (also identifying the total number of complaints outstanding at the end of the reporting period).
- The total amount of redress paid to consumers in the period.
- The number of complaints referred to the Financial Ombudsman Service in the period.

The above information forms an important part of the FSA's approach to risk and desk based monitoring.

When is a complaint closed? 9.9

There are three circumstances in which a complaint is regarded as closed. These are where:

- the firm has sent a final response;
- the complainant had indicated in writing acceptance of the firm's earlier response;
- the firm operates a two-stage complaints process and the complainant has not indicated dissatisfaction with the initial response containing the warning that if the firm does not receive a further reply within eight weeks it will regard the complaint as closed.

The Financial Ombudsman Service 9.10

The jurisdiction of the Financial Ombudsman Service over firms is subject to a number of gateways. This section considers the extent of the Service's remit. The detailed provisions are to be found in the section of the FSA Handbook dealing with disputes (DISP).

Territorial scope 9.11

The territorial scope of the Ombudsman Service embraces complaints about an authorised person's or a voluntary jurisdiction participant's activities conducted in or from the UK. It therefore includes incoming EEA firms and incoming treaty firms.

Compulsory jurisdiction 9.12

The Ombudsman has compulsory jurisdiction in relation to acts or omissions by a firm in carrying on one or more of the following activities:

- regulated activities;
- lending money secured by a charge on land;
- lending money (other than restricted credit);
- paying money by a plastic card (other than a store card);
- the provision of ancillary banking services;
- (and activities ancillary to the above).

Voluntary jurisdiction 9.13

The Ombudsman may also consider a complaint under the voluntary jurisdiction if it falls outside the above areas of compulsory jurisdiction and it relates to an act or omission in the carrying on of one or more of the following activities by a 'VJ participant':

- general insurance business;
- accepting deposits;
- lending money secured by a charge over land;
- lending money (other than restricted credit);
- paying money by plastic card (other than a store card);
- the provision of ancillary banking services;
- acting as an intermediary for a loan secured by a charge on land;
- acting as an intermediary for general insurance business or long-term insurance business;
- any financial services activity carried on after commencement of the Financial Ombudsman Service and which had been covered by a former scheme insofar as the VJ participant was a member of that former scheme in respect of the activity immediately before commencement day;
- any activity carried on or after 29 April 1988 which was a regulated activity when the VJ participant joined the voluntary jurisdiction (or became an authorised person if later) but which was not a regulated activity at the time of the act or omission in question;
- (and in respect of any activities ancillary to the above).

Eligible complainants 9.14

The definition of 'eligible complainant' is discussed at 9.2 above in the context of complaints handling where such a person is defined by reference to a default entitlement to pursue a complaint through the Financial Ombudsman Service. The description given above is not repeated here, save to add that excluded from the categories of eligible complainants are:

- any individual, business, charity or trustee who was an intermediate customer or market counter-party in relation to the firm in question at the time of the act or omission giving rise to the complaint; and
- any firm or VJ participant whose complaint relates in any way to an activity which the firm itself has permission to carry on or which the VJ participant itself conducts and which is subject to the compulsory or voluntary jurisdiction of the Service.

Time limits for referral 9.15

There are a number of time bars which apply in relation to the referral of a complaint to the Financial Ombudsman Service. In summary:

- The Ombudsman cannot consider a complaint if it is referred to the Service less than eight weeks after the receipt of the complaint by the firm or VJ participant (unless a final response letter has been issued); this obviously makes sense in allowing the firm an adequate time to investigate the complaint in accordance with the required complaints procedures.

- The Ombudsman cannot consider a complaint if it is referred 'more than six months after the date on which the firm or VJ participant sends the complainant its final response advising him that he may refer the matter to the' Service unless the failure to comply with the time limit is a result of exceptional circumstances.

- The Ombudsman also is disabled from considering a complaint referred 'more than six years after the event complained of or (if later) more than three years from the day on which he became aware (or ought reasonably to have become aware) that he had a cause for complaint'; this time bar is subject to two particular dispensations. Firstly, it may be dis-applied where the time limit is missed 'as a result of exceptional circumstances'; secondly, it is dis-applied if the complainant referred the complaint to the firm or V J participant or to the Ombudsman within the six- or three-year period and has a written acknowledgement or some other record of the complaint having been received.

Further exceptions 9.16

There are two further (discrete) exceptions to the six-year/three-year time limit which relate to the following:

- complaints concerning a contract or policy the subject of the Pensions Review (including specific categories of FSAVC business); and

- complaints relating to the sale of endowment policies for the purpose of achieving repayment of a mortgage, which are subject to a separate time limit where time starts to run from the date the complainant receives a letter from a firm or VJ participant warning that there is a high risk the policy will not produce at maturity a sum large enough to repay the target amount and ends six months from the date the complainant receives a second letter containing the same warning or other reminder of the need to act.

In the latter case, the Ombudsman is empowered in any event to apply (in effect) the six/three-year time limit where it is appropriate to do so. This would be the case where a firm can show that in respect of a particular complaint the three-year period had started to run before the complainant received the high risk warning letter.

Summary dismissal 9.17

Whilst it is the responsibility of the Ombudsman to consider initial issues/questions going to jurisdiction, it is possible for certain types of complaint to be summarily dismissed without consideration of the merits. In this instance, any jurisdiction over adjudication on the complaint is short-lived. The categories of complaint vulnerable to summary dismissal are as follows:

- A complaint which discloses no evidence of actual or prospective financial loss or material distress or inconvenience.
- A frivolous or vexatious complaint.
- A complaint enjoying no reasonable prospect of success.
- A complaint which has already been the subject of an offer of compensation by the firm which is fair and reasonable and which is still open for acceptance.
- A complaint which has been reviewed in accordance with the regulatory standards such as those under review of past business.
- A complaint which has been considered and excluded previously by the Ombudsman Service (or a predecessor scheme).
- A complaint which has already been dealt with by a comparable independent complaints scheme or dispute resolution process.
- A complaint which has been the subject of Court proceedings where there has been a decision on the merits.
- A complaint which is the subject matter of current Court proceedings.
- A complaint which is more suitable for a Court, arbitration or other complaints scheme.
- A complaint relating to a legitimate exercise of a firm's commercial judgement.
- A complaint relating to employment matters in respect of an authorised person's employee(s).
- A complaint about investment performance.
- A complaint relating to a firm's decision whilst exercising a discretion under a will or private trust.
- A complaint which relates to a firm's failure to consult beneficiaries before exercising a discretion under a will or private trust (where there is no legal obligation to consult).

- A complaint which involves or might involve more than one eligible complainant which has been referred without the consent of the other complainant(s) and it is considered it would be inappropriate to deal with the complaint without that consent.
- There is some other compelling reason why it would not be appropriate for the complaint to be dealt with under the scheme.

Dealing with the Financial Services Ombudsman 9.18

Following acceptance of a complaint by the Ombudsman, the process of the Service's investigation will commence. This will (usually) involve a request for production of the file(s) relating to the transaction, the subject of the complaint (including documents generated in relation to the firm's investigation into and closure of the matter). At this stage, the firm has a good, practical opportunity to present the materials in an orderly, coherent manner with a view to demonstrating that the conclusion(s) reached was/were appropriate. The case papers will then be reviewed by an adjudicator, who may well solicit further information and responses from the complainant and the firm.

The DISP rules provide for either party to request a hearing. This may be appropriate where disputed issues of fact emerge as a result of the exchanges taking place or from the firm's investigation itself.

Where the adjudicator's initial assessment (preliminary decision) is not accepted by the parties, either may assist on a final decision from the Ombudsman. An aggrieved party to such a decision has a limited right to challenge the result by instituting (as soon as possible and in any event) within three months of the decision an application for permission to bring judicial review through the Administrative Court. This would involve demonstrating that the Ombudsman, in reaching the decision:

- failed to take into account some material information;
- took into account materially irrelevant information; or
- reached a decision which no reasonable Ombudsman could have reached on the basis of the materials available.

It is unlikely in anything other than an exceptional set of circumstances any of the above grounds would be able to be demonstrated.

Size of the award 9.19

The maximum sum the Ombudsman may award is £100,000 (save that a further sum may be added in respect of costs reasonably incurred by a complainant in respect of a complaint. If the Ombudsman is of the view that proper redress requires payment of a sum in excess of this limit a recommendation to that effect may be made. The recommendation is not binding, however, on the firm.

If the award is accepted by the complainant, the matter is concluded. If the award is rejected then a complainant may consider whether to pursue the complaint through the Court.

An unpaid award which has been accepted may be enforced by any of the enforcement procedures available in the County Court (or in Scotland by the Sheriff and in Northern Ireland as a money judgment under the *Judgments Enforcements (Northern Ireland) Order 1981 (SI 1981 No 226)*).

One scheme for all 9.20

The procedures described above now apply by way of replacement and consolidation into the single Ombudsman Service of some eight pre-existing schemes, namely the:

- Personal Investment Authority (PIA) Ombudsman Bureau;
- Securities and Futures Authority Complaints Bureau and Arbitration Service;
- FSA (formerly SIB) Complaints Unit and Independent Investigator;
- Personal Insurance Arbitration Service;
- Insurance Ombudsman Bureau;
- Office of the Investment Ombudsman;
- Office of the Building Societies Ombudsman; and
- Office of the Banking Ombudsman.

The Financial Services Compensation Scheme 9.21

The Financial Services Compensation Scheme now provides the safety net for certain categories of eligible claimants who have protected claims against firms which they are unable or likely to be unable to satisfy. The scheme replaces similar sector based compensation safety nets previously provided by:

- the Policyholder's Protection Scheme (which applied in respect of most general insurance and life company policyholders);
- the Friendly Society's Protection Scheme (which applied in respect of insurance policyholders with such societies);

- the Investor's Compensation Scheme (providing compensation for investment business regulated by the FSA (formerly SIB) and the self regulatory organisations (IMRO, PIA and SFA);
- schemes for customers carrying on investment business with professional firms supervised by recognised professional bodies;
- the Deposit Protection Scheme for bank depositors; and
- the Building Societies Investor Protection Scheme (available for depositors with building societies).

Although a single compensation scheme now exists, it continues to reflect separate financial market sectors:

- deposit taking;
- insurance; and
- investment.

This affects eligible claimants and the industry alike. So far as eligible claimants are concerned, the compensation limits vary depending upon the sector provider in default. So far as the industry is concerned, the Scheme's power to impose levies in respect of (in particular) compensation costs is also sector determined.

Table of Compensation Limits		
Type of claim	Level of cover	Maximum payment
Protected deposits	100% × first £2,000 90% × next £33,000	£31,700
Protected general Insurance contract in respect of liability subject to compulsory insurance	Unlimited	Unlimited
Protected general Insurance contract in respect of specified claims under the *Third Parties (Rights Against Insurers Act) 1930*	Unlimited	Unlimited
All other protected general insurance contract claims	100% × first £2,000 90% of the remainder of the claim	Unlimited

Protected long term insurance contract	100% × first £2,000	Unlimited
	At least 90% of remaining value of the policy	
Protected investment business	100 × first £30,000	£48,000
	90% × next £20,000	

Pre-conditions to compensation 9.22

There are (in essence) four conditions to be satisfied, as follows:

- The claimant must be an eligible claimant.
- The claimant must have a protected claim.
- The claim must be against a relevant person.
- The relevant person must be in default.

Eligible claimant 9.23

The definition of 'eligible claimant' is complicated. It includes 'any person who at any material time did not come within' the following list except in specific circumstances indicated. The list of prima facie excluded claimants comprises the following:

(1) Firms (other than a sole trader, credit union or a small business whose claim arises out of a regulated activity for which they do not have permission).

(2) Overseas Financial Services Institution.

(3) Collective investment schemes (including anyone who is the operator or trustee of such a scheme).

(4) Pension and retirement funds (including anyone who is a trustee of such a fund except a trustee of a small self-administered scheme or an occupational pension scheme of an employer which is not a large company, large partnership or large mutual association).

(5) Supranational institutions, government and central administrative authorities.

(6) Provincial, regional, local and municipal authorities.

(7) Directors and managers of the relevant person in default (subject to particular exceptions such as directors and managers of eg a small mutual association who do not receive a salary or other remuneration for their services and credit unions).

(8) Close relatives of persons excluded at (7) above.

(9) Corporate bodies in the same group as the relevant person in default.

(10) Persons holding 5% or more of the capital of the relevant person in default (or any corporate body in the same group).

(11) The auditors of the relevant person in default (or of a body corporate in the same group as the relevant person in default), or the appointed actuary of a Friendly Society or insurance undertaking in default.

(12) Persons who in the opinion of the Financial Services Compensation Scheme are responsible for or have contributed to the relevant person's default.

(13) Large companies or larger mutual associations.

(14) Large partnerships.

(15) Persons whose claim arises from transactions in connection with which they have been convicted of an offence of money laundering.

(16) Persons whose claim arises under the *Third Parties (Rights Against Insurers) Act 1930*.

Dis-application of exclusions 9.24

The list of excluded eligible claimants is then subject to the following dis-applications, which are again sector based. In particular:

- A person is eligible to claim compensation in respect of a protected deposit if, at the date on which the relevant person is determined to be in default, he came within excluded category (14) above or he came within any of the categories at (1) to (3) and was not a large company, large mutual association or a credit institution.

- A person other than one which comes within any of the categories listed at (7) to (12) and (15) is eligible to claim compensation in respect of a long-term insurance contract.

- A person falling within categories listed at (1) to (4) is eligible to claim compensation in respect of a relevant general insurance contract if, at the date the contract commenced, he was a small business.

- A person coming within category (14) is eligible to claim compensation in respect of the relevant general insurance contract entered into before commencement of the scheme.

- A person within category (16) is eligible to claim compensation if:
    - the person insured would have been an eligible claimant at the time his rights against the insurer were transferred to and vested in the category (16) person; or

- the liability of the person insured in respect of the category (16) person was a liability under a contract of employer's liability insurance which would have been subject to a liability subject to compulsory insurance if the contract had been entered into after 1 January 1972 or (for contracts in Northern Ireland) 29 December 1975; or
- the extent of the liability of the person insured in respect of the category (16) person had been agreed in writing by the insurer or determined by a Court or arbitrator before the date on which the insurer is determined to be in default.

- A person within the list of excluded claimants is eligible to claim compensation in respect of a liability subject to compulsory insurance.

Protected investment business 9.25

The excluded categories are not, however, dis-applied in respect of claims made in connection with protected investment business.

Protected claims 9.26

Detailed definitions are given in respect of protected deposit claims, protected contract of insurance claims and protected investment business claims. Broadly, deposits made with a relevant person in the UK (including EEA branches) are protected provided the deposit is not a bond issued by credit institution, a secured deposit, a deferred share issued by a building society or a deposit made where the depositor's identity is not disclosed. General and long-term insurance contracts are protected contracts of insurance save for reinsurance contracts. Designated investment business is generally protected investment business for the purposes of the regime.

Relevant persons 9.27

For the purposes of the scheme a 'relevant person' includes any person who at the time the act or omission giving rise to the claim took place was a participant firm in the scheme or an appointed representative of a participant firm.

In default 9.28

The relevant firm will be treated as in default if 'in the opinion of the Financial Services Compensation Scheme or the FSA it is unable to satisfy protected claims against it or likely to be unable' to satisfy such claims.

Rejection of claims 9.29

Significantly, claims may be rejected amongst other circumstances where:

- the application for compensation contains any material inaccuracy or omission; or
- the Financial Services Compensation Scheme considers that a civil claim in respect of the relevant liability would have been defeated by a defence of limitation at the earlier of:
  - the date on which the relevant person is determined to be in default; and
  - the date on which the claimant first indicated in writing that he may have a claim against the relevant person (except in the case of protected investment business where the Financial Services Compensation Scheme may disregard the defence of limitation if it considers it to be reasonable to do so).

Reporting obligation 9.30

There is a reporting obligation upon participant firms to provide the Financial Services Compensation Scheme by the end of February each year with a statement of the contribution group(s) to which it belongs and the total amount of business (measured in accordance with a tariff base or bases) which it conducted as at 31 December of the previous year in relation to each of those contribution groups. A participant firm which does not conduct business that could give rise to a protected claim by an eligible claimant and has no reasonable likelihood of doing so may secure an exemption from specific costs and compensation costs levies. Such an exempt firm is also relieved of the obligation to report.

Quantification of claims 9.31

Subject (where applicable) to the compensation limits set out in the above table, the amount of compensation payable to a claimant in respect of any type of protected claim is the amount of his overall net claim against the relevant person at the quantification date. Rules are provided for the approach to be taken to assessment of compensation in individual instances. For example, given a long-term insurance failure, the scheme may deal with claims by making arrangements to secure continuity of insurance cover; in default, the Financial Services Compensation Scheme:

> 'must calculate the liability of a relevant person to the Claimant under a long term insurance contract in accordance with the terms of the contract as valued in a liquidation of the relevant person or (in the

absence of such relevant terms) in accordance with such reasonable valuation techniques as the Financial Services Compensation Scheme considers appropriate.'

A particularly difficult valuation issue arises in such cases in respect of treatment of bonuses provided for under a long-term insurance contract. These may only be treated as forming part of the claimant's claim if a value to the expectation of a bonus would be attributed to it by a Court in accordance with the *Insurer's (Winding up) Rules 2001 (SI 2001 No 3635)*. The latter provide for a Court to place a value on a policyholder's reasonable expectation of receiving additional benefits to those otherwise guaranteed (including discretionary, reversionary, terminal and other types of bonus allocation). The valuation exercise is complex and will take into account any established practice of the person in default in respect of past bonus allocation.

Chapter 10
Lessons from Past Failures

Introduction 10.1

This chapter will look at lessons which may emerge from past failures. In particular it will consider firstly issues arising out of the downfall of Equitable Life and secondly a series of examples of conduct which has recently attracted FSA disciplinary action.

Lessons from Equitable Life 10.2

Much has been written about the spectacular demise of Equitable Life. The observations which follow are personal reflections of the authors offered with a view to further elucidation of the risk assessment concepts discussed above in CHAPTER 4. It is in this regard pertinent to note that in August 1999 the Insurance and Friendly Society division of the FSA carried out an Initial Risk Assessment of Equitable Life as part of piloting the FSA's risk assessment framework described above in CHAPTER 4.

It is possible to see now where the Society posed threats to a number of the business and control risk elements making up the assessment framework. As discussed above in CHAPTER 4, history reveals the FSA was right to be concerned by the following risk factors posed by Equitable Life business to its statutory objectives: quality of strategy; litigation/legal risk; adequacy of capital; product type; disclosure/adequacy of product literature; risk management; financial and regulatory reporting and accounting policies; and cultural issues and business ethics.

The Initial Risk Assessment set out an overall summary to the effect the Society was perceived as a:

> 'high financial risk because of the level of benefits guaranteed to policyholders, the relatively low free asset position and the difficulty it would face in raising external finance. Equitable would be particularly vulnerable to a sustained and significant fall in Equity prices.'

In relation to its 'cultural attitude' the following comment was made:

10.3 Lessons from Past Failures

'A tendency to arrogant superiority regarding the efficiency of their operations and the high priority given to the interests of policyholders. This can blind them to the financial risks that can arise as a result of guaranteeing high benefit levels.'

To see these comments in perspective and learn from the collapse of the world's oldest mutual life assurance society it is necessary to look back into the history of the fall of Equitable Life.

Background to Equitable Life 10.3

As is well known, Equitable Life is the oldest mutual life assurance society in the world, having been established in 1762. The origin of its problems related to the sale of with profits pension policies effected mainly between 1957 and June 1998 and containing offers of guaranteed annuity rates. These conferred on the policyholder an option to take an annuity at a fixed guaranteed rate or to purchase an annuity at whatever the current rate was when the benefits were taken.

Although guaranteed annuity rate business was a common feature of the life insurance market at the time, it was a critical feature of Equitable's business for two reasons:

- Equitable Life had written 116,000 guaranteed annuity option policies which represent a much bigger proportion of its business and was the case with other companies; and

- it had a long established practice of maximising the distribution of profits to its policyholders with the result that it preserved little excess capital in addition to funds necessary to meet liabilities and satisfy solvency requirements; being a mutual, it had no shareholder funds on which to draw.

For many years, current annuity rates exceeded the guaranteed annuity rates written into the policies. During the 1990s, however, annuity rates fell significantly. Two factors (market and demographic) were mainly responsible.

Firstly, the yield on government gilts with a 15-year term to maturity fell from approximately 7% at the end of 1990 to just over 4.5% at the end of 1998. Since these securities represented the principal investments relied on by life insurance companies to provide for annuity payments, the drop in interest rate mean that the level of annuity income the insurance companies could provide reduced accordingly.

Secondly, recent decades have seen a decrease in mortality rates. The life expectancy (for example) for a retiring male purchasing an annuity has risen from 14.9 years in 1975 to 17.6 years in 2000. The impact on current annuity rates was naturally felt by a reduction in the amount of annuity able to be purchased for the same fund.

In May 1990 (for example) the annuity rate for a male aged 65 was approximately 15%; by June 1999 this had reduced to approximately 9%. A 65-year-old male retiring in mid-1999 was therefore only able to buy approximately 60% of the income for life which could have been secured by a similar man retiring in the spring of 1990.

Equitable Life's awareness of its problems 10.4

The problem became apparent to Equitable Life in (at least) the early 1990s. In late 1993 current annuity rates slumped; despite a brief recovery in 1994, from mid-1995 onwards the guaranteed annuity rate options written into the policies it had sold were consistently higher than the current annuity rates otherwise available. The problem was exacerbated by the increasing margin which became evident between guaranteed and current rates. By September 1998, guaranteed annuity rates in policies issued by the Society between 1957 and 1988 were approximately 30% higher than current annuity rates.

The response of the Board was to introduce and adopt a 'differential terminal bonus practice.' The decision was taken in December 1993 that Equitable Life would allocate to a guaranteed annuity option policyholder a different terminal bonus according to whether the policyholder elected to take an annuity at the guaranteed annuity rate or an alternative benefit (such as an annuity at the current rate from Equitable Life or from another provider).

The financial consequence to the guaranteed annuity rate policyholder can be illustrated by the following example which assumes a current annuity rate of 8% and a guaranteed annuity rate of 10%, with a guaranteed fund of £75,000 and a non-guaranteed final/terminal bonus of £25,000. The differential terminal bonus policy operated in the following manner:

Current annuity: £100,000 × ($8/100$) = £8,000 per annum.

Guaranteed minimum annuity: £75,000 × ($10/100$) = £7,500 per annum.

So actual annuity paid equals £8,000 per annum.

The contrary position for which the guaranteed annuity rate option holders contended was that the guaranteed rate should be applied to the guaranteed fund and their final bonus which should be of an equivalent value irrespective of whether the guaranteed annuity rate option was taken or not. Accordingly, the annuity should be:

£100,000 × ($10/100$) = £10,000 per annum.

10.5 Lessons from Past Failures

If the annuity paid is in fact £8,000 per annum, it follows that the final bonus has been reduced from £25,000 to £8,000 (since (£75,000 + £5,000) × ($^{10}/_{100}$) = £8,000 per annum).

Growing complaints and public statements 10.5

By mid-December 1998 at least 15 complaints had been made to the Personal Investment Authority Ombudsman by individual policyholders about Equitable Life's approach to differential terminal bonuses. In its regulatory returns for years ending 1993, 1994 and 1995 the Appointed Actuary to the Society stated as follows:

> 'Pensions business with profits contracts described as retirement annuity, transfer plan, individual or group business are deferred annuities, the premiums being of the recurrent premium (or variable premium) type. The premiums provide a cash fund at the pension date to which (for policies issued prior to 1 July 1988) a guaranteed annuity rate is applicable.'

In the regulatory returns for 1996, 1997, 1998 and 1999 the wording was changed to the following:

> 'Some older contracts contain minimum guaranteed rates for annuity purchase at retirement.'

At a separate paragraph in the regulatory returns for 1993, 1994, 1995, 1996 and 1997 dealing with the basis of reserves for guarantees and options Equitable Life stated:

> 'It was considered unnecessary in current conditions to make explicit provision for the other guarantees and options described [above].'

The product literature 10.6

So far as investors into the with profits fund between 1993 and 1998 were concerned, the Society's product literature, in the form of its with profits guides, contained no explanation of the differential final bonus policy that had been applied to guaranteed annuity rate policies since 1993; further, the guide did not contain information about market value adjusters that had been imposed or the circumstances in which they had been imposed. The wording of the factors influencing bonus rates section of the Society's August 1999 with profits guide was revised so as to set out some explanation of the differential final bonus policy. There remains, however, no indication of the possibility that the asset shares of all with profit policyholders might be reduced, market value adjusters impose and/or final bonuses reduced so as to meet the cost of funding obligations to guaranteed annuity rate option holders in the event that the differential terminal bonus policy was successfully challenged.

The Hyman proceedings 10.7

In January 1999 the now infamous test case was launched nominally by a policyholder, Mr Hyman (*Equitable Life Assurance Society v Hyman [2000] 3 WLR 529*). It appears the Society had taken legal advice towards the end of 1998, no doubt in the light of the then growing number of complaints about the differential terminal bonus policy. In a note of part of the legal advice given to the Society in late 1998 referred to in the Baird Report, it emerged that leading Counsel had advised that it:

> 'would be feasible but not tactically desirable (at this stage at least) to obtain a test case ruling on the matter. Better to sort matters out quietly and to attempt to undo any damage done to date by getting a clear message across by correspondence, than to risk the publicity, cost and serious potentially adverse result of a Court Hearing.'

Proceedings nonetheless were commenced and further perusal of the Baird Report reveals in that in June 1999, some six months later, the General Council Division of the FSA advised the Insurance and Friendly Society Division and the Government Actuary Department as follows:

'If the Court takes a Chancery approach to this matter, it will favour the Equitable's position but make no mistake, this is a very high risk for the Equitable. You can never predict judicial outcomes. At the High Court level, they are more likely to get a Judge who will take a Chancery approach but we cannot be certain about that. Courts are more and more inclined now to take a wider policy approach to these matters ... if Equitable get the wrong panel or the wrong Judge, they could find themselves on the receiving end of a change in judicial approach. The Court might ... not like what the Equitable has done and might be influenced for that reason. Don't jump to conclusions about this.'

The re-insurance that never was 10.8

The Society took some steps to effect reinsurance against the possibility of an increased uptake of guaranteed annuity options. The difficulty, however, with the initial cover obtained in December 1998 was that the reinsurance was able to be cancelled if Equitable Life changed its practice on guaranteed annuity options (GAOs) – which would necessarily be the case if it lost the Court case. In due course the Society did lose the Court case in the House of Lords, resulting in its closure to new business on 8 December 2000.

Closure to new business and the aftermath 10.9

Since closure Equitable Life has attempted to consolidate its position *inter alia* by obtaining a Court sanction to a scheme of compromise which in exchange for modest policy value enhancements has achieved a bar on members suing the Society in respect of allegations of product mis-selling. The scheme of compromise, however, has not bound investors who surrendered their investments in the with profits fund prior to the compromise scheme taking effect. This has left the Society vulnerable to Court action by aggrieved former investors – principally investors who made investments into the with profits fund after 1993 without any appreciation of the risk that their funds may end up being looked to as a source from which to meet the Society's funding obligations to its guaranteed annuity rate option holders.

The Penrose Report 10.10

Since the closure of the Society to new business the very detailed report of Lord Penrose has revealed that the problems with the Society were far more deep seated than the those arising from a funding obligation to its historic population of GAR (guaranteed annuity rate) policy holders.

At paragraph 113 of chapter 2 of the report, Lord Penrose concludes his section entitled 'Origins of Annuity Guarantee Issue' with the observation:

'The House of Lords' decision in *Hyman* heralded the final phase in the Society's life as an office carrying on an active long term business. Why that should have been the case requires a close examination of the Society's financial position over a long period of time. Superficially claims of £1.5 billion should not have brought down a Society with funds of £32 billion. A movement in liabilities of about 5%, though a significant injury, perhaps, should not have rendered the Society moribund.'

In reality, the GAR issue emerged as the final breaking straw which exposed an underlying significant financial weakness and inappropriate management and marketing structure which dated back to (arguably) 1988 and certainly from 1990. (1988 being the year in which the decision was taken by the Society to market personal pension plans without GAOs without differentiating between such policies and former S226 retirement annuity contracts (RACs) containing GAOs; 1990 being a later year by which there was an entrenched and (largely) ever worsening disparity between aggregate policy values (ie with profit liabilities including terminal bonus) and with profits available assets.)

Prior to 1972, the Society had it appears maintained an 'estate'. In that year it had introduced a 'three call' system (designed to preserve reserves and allow for prudent allocations of policy value growth to members). This system could have been prudently operated to preserve sufficient assets to meet policy values but for action taken in 1973 when Equity markets fell when the estate was then raided in order to maintain competitive and high bonus rates.

As Penrose concludes (chapter 19, para 40):

'Over the 1980s the Society maintained competitive levels of bonus allocation by cutting back on its general reserve until, by 1987 it had over allocated bonus so that its aggregate policy values on a realistic basis exceeded available assets.'

At para 48 of chapter 19 is a fundamental finding that:

> 'in 1990 the aggregate policy values estimated to policyholders were significantly higher than the assets available as a result of the allocations of that year. Thereafter the with profits assets of the Society were never in excess of or equal to aggregate with profits value including accrued terminal bonus.'

Any assertion during this era that the Society was financially sound would, it seems, have accordingly been open to challenge and investments were at risk of not providing the safe return in accordance with the Society's declared policy. It seems likely the lack of accurate accounting information made available to advisers seeking to achieve sales of the Society's products will have (necessarily) resulted in widespread mis-selling into the with profits fund.

From 1989 onwards the Society in its key features literature offered investors a 'uniform smooth investment return allocated to accumulated policy values.' The Penrose Report demonstrates clearly that no such policy was in fact discernibly operated by the Society. At para 22 of chapter 6, in dealing with the 'smoothing technique' Lord Penrose states:

> 'A smoothing policy ... would specify a projected target return, incorporating an assumed rate of growth; maximum deviation above and below the projection; and the duration of the cycle to achieve equilibrium between the projected and actual returns. In reality, such a policy would be unlikely to be realised over time and adjustments would be required to reflect experience. But it would be difficult to envisage any rational smoothing process that did not allow for the holding of surplus assets from time to time, during that phase of the cycle when actual returns exceeded projected returns, to balance periods when over allocation was necessary as against actual returns to support bonus allocation. ... I have sought to demonstrate ... the Society's free assets were eroded over the 1980s by the policies adopted until there was a net excess of policy values over available assets.'

In the circumstances, there was no evidence of any such a 'smooth return' policy being applied. At para 61 of chapter 6 Lord Penrose points out:

10.10 *Lessons from Past Failures*

> 'The most fundamental deficiency in the Society's attempt to smooth was in its approach to claims. Claims on average continued throughout the period of review [1989–2000] to be paid out in excess of their asset share leaving the enforced business to restore balance. Smoothing consequently was not applied at a claims level ... consequently the Society became heavily dependent on unallocated investment earnings on new and enforced business in its attempts to restore fund balance.'

It is also (now) arguably clear that an inaccurate financial picture was presented to the public as a result of the accounting techniques summarised at chapter 19 of the Report (paras 50–55). In short, the Society:

- 'overvalued' its net premium valuation and 'undervalued' its annuity liabilities with the result of inflating the perceived surplus;

- improperly applied a quasi-zillmer adjustment which had the effect of generating (in truth) a non-existent further surplus sum of approximately £1billion;

- relied on mortality factors which had not been updated, serving also to depress the real value of long-term liabilities;

- supported its 'technical solvency' for regulatory purposes by issuing £350m of subordinated debt, making extensive use of implicit profits adjustments and entering into a financial reinsurance agreement which did not materially transfer risk to the Underwriters.

These features of financial weakness were deeply embedded and merely exacerbated by the explicit obligation to meet GAR's liability following the House's decision in *Hyman*.

Further, prior to 1995 the Society through it product literature very arguably misrepresented/mis-stated to investors its bonus policy. GAR and non-GAR policyholders were not differentiated. This was arguably misleading in that:

- from as early as 1983 the Society had decided through its Executive Management to introduce in any period of sustained low interest rates a differential terminal bonus policy which would erode the value of guarantees to GAR policyholders; and

- after the differential terminal bonus policy was formally assented to by the Board in December 1993 its impact was not revealed in any clear statement to investors (historic or prospective).

The reasonable expectations of the GAR policyholders was therefore that the guaranteed rates would be applied to their individual fund values and terminal bonus in full; this was contrary to the Society's intentions formulated in 1983 and approved by the Board ten years later; new investors, however, conversely were not warned that if the differential terminal bonus policy was successfully challenged the value of their investment would be diminished by calls to satisfy the Society's obligation to meet its guarantees to the historic population of GAR policyholders.

In truth, the cost of meeting the latter obligation (£1.5b) was later met from a seven-month non-allocation of growth and was a factor of reduced significance compared with the disadvantage of investing in a financially insecure Society which had been over declaring bonuses relative to net assets for a sustained period.

The misleading nature of the Society's product literature (1990 to 2000) is critically addressed by Lord Penrose in chapter 14 (paras 85–159).

All the above has served to expose the Society to a mass of investor claims from a variety of action groups alleging product mis-selling on a grand scale. Typical allegations include breaches of the *Financial Services Act 1986, section 62* and the LAUTRO code of conduct in respect of disclosure and advisory duties by financial advisers to investors, such as:

- L6 of the Code – failure to give the investor all information relevant to the investment transaction and to use best endeavours to enable the investors to understand the nature of the risks involved in the recommended transaction;

- L12 of the Code – failure to ascertain the investors' attitude to the true scale of the risks associated with the proposed investment;

- L8(1)(a) of the Code – wrongful recommendation of unsuitable investments;

- L6A(1A)(a) of the Code – failing to give the investor key features documents containing any adequate description of the main factors which may have an adverse effect on performance of the investments proposed or otherwise materials of the decision to invest; and

- L5.15(2) – failure to provide (when requested) a with profits guide containing prescribed information including the basis on which any amount available for distribution to policyholders was to be determined along with information as to the Society's policy for ensuring fairness of treatment at maturity or earlier surrender between investors holding policies issued at different times, including the policy with regard to terminal bonuses.

In many instances the direct sales force may have been kept in the dark as to the true position. This will have created the very circumstance conducive to mis-selling. It will be appreciated that the Society during the period after 1994 would have been obliged to comply with the PIA Rules in respect of the management of its business. These included duties to ensure its investment staff were able to make compliant sales of its products (PIA Rule 7.2.1.(1)(a)). In dealing with (in particular) the Society's main accountant's (Mr Ranson's) maxwellisation representations, Lord Penrose concludes:

- 'Ranson did not advise the Board of the risk that persistent practice associated with published statements of practice would develop policyholders reasonable expectations that existing patterns of payment would continue to characterise the Society's bonus practices in the future. In particular the advice that future terminal bonus payments were not guaranteed ... diverted attention from the risks associated with the generation of non-contractual expectations of future terminal bonus payments' (chapter 19, para 121);

- 'Ranson did not advise the Board on the requirements of a systematic policy for smoothing of returns to policyholders that provided criteria for the smoothing cycle and permissible deviations from a specified norm against which to measure total bonus allocation.' (chapter 19, para 125);

- 'Ranson did not provide a regular and adequate information to the Board about the business risks inherent in the general actuarial management of the Society and in particular the business risks associated with the terms and conditions written by the Society from time to time. In particular he did not inform the Board (i) of management decisions in the period 1983–93 related to the recovery of the costs of annuity guarantees from terminal bonus; (ii) that the validity of the 1988 equation of annuity benefits for equal contributions to retirement annuity pensions and personal pensions respectively depended on the decision of 1982/83 that the costs of annuity guarantees would be recovered from final bonuses otherwise payable on retirement annuity pensions; (iii) of the relevance of the prospective differential terminal bonus policy to the gradual withdrawal of guarantees from new with profits business during the 1990s or (iv) of the risks to which policyholders not entitled to annuity guarantees were exposed by the policies and practices adopted' (chapter 19, para 126).

These failures, on the part of an employee of the Society contributed to the ignorance on the part of the sales force as to the risks associated with the policies they were being invited to sell/market.

The reserves question 10.11

It is difficult, even without the benefit of hindsight, to understand why Equitable Life proceeded in this respect as it did. It has always been a fundamental principal in the management of life offices that the value of long-term assets should be at least equal to the value placed on long-term liabilities. The value determined in respect of long-term liabilities has always been required to be calculated so as to take account of the life office's contractual liabilities, including options contractually available to policyholders.

This position was reflected in the *Insurance Companies Regulations 1981 (SI 1981 No 1654), reg 54* which provided that:

'The determination of the amount of long term liabilities shall be made on actuarial principles and shall make proper provision for all liabilities on prudent assumptions in regard to the relevant factors ...'

Specifically the Regulations stated that:

'Provision *shall* be made to cover any increase in liabilities caused by policyholder exercising options under their contracts' [emphasis added]. These 1981 regulations were replaced by The Insurance Companies Regulations 1994. Regulation 64 of the 1994 regulations was even clearer in stating that:

'(1) The determination of the amount of long term liabilities ... shall be made on actuarial principles which have due regard to the reasonable expectations of policyholders and shall make proper provision for all liabilities on prudent assumptions that shall include appropriate margins for adverse deviation of the relevant factors.

'The determination shall take account of all prospective liabilities as determined by the policy conditions for each existing contract ...

'Without prejudice to the generality of paragraph (1) above, the amount of the long term liabilities ... shall take into account, inter alia, the following factors:
— All guaranteed benefits ...
— Vested, declared or allotted bonuses ...
— All options available to the policyholder under the terms of the contract
— Expenses, including commissions.'

Whilst interest rates remained high during the 1970s and for much of the 1980s (and higher than the rates implicit in the guaranteed annuity options) the Society may have been able to conclude that the guaranteed annuity options were of no real value and that even if interest rates dropped, it was unlikely they would fall below guaranteed annuity option rates in the policies. From the late 1980s, however, interest rates began to fall and the possibility of guaranteed annuity rates becoming more valuable than current annuity rates ceased to be a remote likelihood. An appreciation of this no doubt explains why the Society (along with a number of other life offices in the mid-1980s) ceased to issue policies with guaranteed annuity options.

10.12 *Lessons from Past Failures*

By the early 1990s, however, when interest rates had continued to reduce, Equitable Life ought to have concluded that specific provision had become appropriate and necessary in the form of actual reserves being made in respect of its obligations to guarantee annuity option holders. If reserves had been set aside as the regulations referred to above, it is suggested, required then Equitable Life would (plainly) not have needed to introduce the differential terminal bonus policy nor would it have faced complaints from guaranteed annuity option holders such as gave rise to the *Hyman* action.

Equally, having decided not, it appears, to make specific reserves but to introduce the differential terminal bonus policy the risks posed by that strategy ought, it is suggested, to have been made plain to prospective investors into the with profits fund in and after December 1993. Likewise, it is suggested, the Society's direct sales force ought to have been apprised of the reasoning and risks posed by the Board's approach so that its advisers were in a position to provide new investors with an adequate explanation of risk and to facilitate the provision of suitable advice at the point of sale. A review of product literature and sales training/instruction was called for.

Much of the analysis set out here appears to have been evident from the Initial Risk Assessment of the FSA in August 1999. A more developed sensitivity to the risk framework at that time (as would not doubt now occur) may have resulted in a risk mitigation programme being put in place which, it is suggested, would have included:

- improved insurance cover – as indicated above, the initial cover ceased to be available in the event of the differential bonus policy being altered. To that extent, reinsurance cover disappeared at the very point where it was most needed;
- an increase in financial reserves to deal with funding commitments to guarantee annuity option holders who opted for the guaranteed annuity rates;
- a programme of training and instruction to the direct sales force so as to enable proper risk disclosure to be made to new investors;
- amendments to product literature and (in particular) the Society's with profits guides so as to deal clearly and explicitly with the Society's policy with regard to the imposition of a market value adjuster and the factors influencing the value of terminal bonuses.

Summary lessons and conclusions 10.12

On one view, the whole history of the above difficulties can be seen as reflecting a failure to identify and appreciate key risk elements. In introducing and operating the differential terminal bonus policy in and after December 1993 without obtaining (apparently) any independent legal advice, the Society took the risk that the policy would sooner or later be successfully challenged. In choosing to rely on the differential bonus policy as an alternative to making specific financial reserves the Society took the risk that it would find itself financially exposed. In operating a distribution policy that was not properly explained to investors or the direct sales force, it created an opportunity for substantial investor losses and opened the doors to mis-selling claims – all of which resulted in its further destabilisation and ultimate closure.

Particular Case Study Examples 10.13

As described in CHAPTER 5, the FSA has a wide selection of disciplinary and enforcement powers which include:

- variation and cancellation of permissions and withdrawal of authorisation;
- prohibition orders preventing individuals from carrying out regulated activities;
- withdrawal of approved person status;
- the issue of public statements of misconduct and the imposition of financial penalties against approved persons;
- the imposition of financial and other penalties for market abuse;
- powers to disqualify auditors and actuaries;
- powers to seek injunctions restraining unlawful activity carried on in contravention of regulatory requirements;
- powers to order restitution;
- powers to prosecute in respect of certain regulatory offences.

The exercise of these powers is to be seen in the context of the FSA's key statutory objectives. In general, where enforcement or disciplinary action is taken against a firm or individual the result of the FSA's action will be publicised. The FSA's policy is to consider each case on a case by case basis. Publicity may not result if it is considered that public awareness of the enforcement action taken would prejudice consumers' interests. Likewise, the FSA will avoid making public confidential information about an individual or firm. That said, the maintenance of an accurate public record of the status of firms and individuals is an important element in securing the statutory objective of consumer protection.

The publicity afforded to the FSA's enforcement and disciplinary measures taken against firms and individuals provides a useful insight not only into the workings of the FSA but also highlights compliance deficiencies about which firms need to be aware. The following paragraphs consider some of the

10.14 *Lessons from Past Failures*

common issues and themes which emerge from the disciplinary, supervisory and enforcement action taken against firms and individuals since December 2001.

Adequate funding 10.14

Fundamental to the effective implementation of the compliance function is the need to ensure that it is adequately funded and resourced. This requirement reflects the authorised firm's responsibility to organise and control its internal affairs in a responsible manner and to have adequate systems in place to secure compliance with the FSA's rules.

On 15 April 2003, ABM AMRO Equities (UK) Limited (AAE) received a financial penalty of £900,000 by the FSA inter alia for a breach of the principle dealing with the firm's duty to organise and control its affairs. The background to the imposition of the penalty is instructive. AAE was principally concerned with the activities of market making, customer facilitation and research in European equities on behalf of (primarily) institutional clients. The registered Compliance Officer of AAE was also the registered Compliance Officer for two other companies in the group (Hoare Govett Limited, the corporate broking arm) and ABM Amro Corporate Finance Limited (the corporate finance arm). He reported directly to the Senior Executive Officer and the Global Head of UK Equities Compliance.

At the beginning of 1998 the compliance function in respect of these three distinct lines of business consisted of the Compliance Officer, an assistant and an administrator plus a secretary. In April of that year the Compliance Officer warned AAE that the department was seriously under-resourced and requested an increase in Compliance Department staff to seven. Although the request was authorised, recruitment difficulties meant that throughout 1998 the Compliance Department remained unchanged with four members (including only frontline compliance staff). Further, in spite of a requirement in the ABM Amro Bank NV Investment and Banking Global Compliance Manual that local Compliance Officers prepare compliance manuals for each business line or local unit defining compliance procedures consistent with the bank's general policies and procedures, prior to March 1999 no local compliance manual was prepared for AAE.

The procedures manual in place in 1998 was an earlier manual prepared in 1993 and which was seriously out of date. Although compliance monitoring did take place in 1998, there was no record of this activity.

During 1998 AAE was concerned to increase business from US customers and accordingly sought to promote its customer services to clients of ABM AMRO Inc (AAI), a member of the ABM AMRO Group based in New York. In furtherance of this objective the joint Head of the UK Equity Trading Desk participated in April 1998 in implementing trading instructions from the UK sales trader on behalf of the customer, in circumstances where he had good reason to suspect the instructions were being given to pursue an improper strategy to move the closing price of shares to close higher.

In September of the same year the senior cross-border trader accepted and acted on improper instructions on behalf of a customer of AAE to move the price of Volkswagen AG and Metro AG to close higher; a similar improper instruction was also accepted and acted upon by one of the directors of UK Equities later the same year designed to move the price of British Biotec Plc to close higher.

In imposing the above penalty the FSA considered that the misconduct of the traders reflected serious weaknesses in the management systems and internal controls relating to those relevant aspects of AAE's business. These included failures to allocate adequate resources to compliance policies and procedures. The failures were particularly serious given inter alia the fact AAE had been alerted to difficulties by the Compliance Officer.

Adequate training 10.15

In addition to ensuring adequate resourcing of the compliance function in terms of appropriate numbers of appropriately qualified staff with recorded, defined, adequate policies and procedures, an equally critical aspect of 'good compliance' relates to the cultural ethos of the firm and the compliance unit. On 27 January 2004 Deloitte & Touche Wealth Management Limited (DTWM) received a financial penalty of £750,000 from the FSA in respect of a series of compliance failures. These related particularly to deficiencies in the structure and implementation of compliance arrangements governing the conduct of the Pensions Review.

At the heart of the FSA's disciplinary sanctions was the conclusion that DTWM's approach to implementing former PIA rules relating to the documentation of information from clients and recording advice in connection with pensions business was that up to October 2000 these requirements could be disregarded as adding no value to DTWM's business.

It emerged, symptomatic of this cultural attitude, that in 97% of cases reviewed by DTWM as part of its past business review, it was unable to ascertain from its own records whether advice given to individual clients had been suitable or not. DTWM was found to have taken the view that since its client base consisted of sophisticated customers, who had an understanding of the investment market, there was a reduced risk of mis-selling taking place. DTWM also believed it could simply rely on its advisers to give appropriate advice, particularly in light of the fact that it did not charge its clients on a commission basis.

There was material to indicate that one former Senior Compliant Manager and member of the board had circularised a note to DTWM's advisers which,

10.16 *Lessons from Past Failures*

whilst urging compliance with the rules relating to documentation of information from clients and recording of advice, he believed compliance to be a nuisance which did not add to the protection of DTWM's clients. Indeed, between 1997 and April 1999 the Compliance Officer was the sole resource operating DTWM's compliance function. Apart from this role, he also acted as DTWM's Finance Officer.

Although ad hoc assistance was lent from time to time, this did not include the Compliance Officer's main responsibility of ensuring that advisers acted within the PIA rules. A further organisational difficulty was that although DTWM operated through a series of branches its compliance function was centralised at its Cambridge branch, where, until February 2001, the Compliance Officer was based. Such remote monitoring required a robust compliance system which was lacking. When a new Compliance Officer was appointed and carried out a review of files in the London branch as part of the Pensions Review he found compliance shortfalls including inadequate 'know your customer' information, deficient 'reason why letters' and poor file composition. He considered that 58% of the files reviewed demonstrated inadequate 'know your client' information.

Although steps were taken to improve matters, these were initially found to be insufficient by the FSA. The above illustrates that a good compliance culture is of as much importance to avoiding regulatory disciplinary sanctions as it is to minimising risks of mis-selling and any consequential need to pay redress to disadvantaged customers.

Adequate systems 10.16

A central and recurrent theme of disciplinary intervention by the FSA relates to breaches of SYSC Rule 3.2.6R providing that:

> 'A firm must take reasonable care to establish and maintain effective systems and controls for compliance with applicable requirements and standards under the regulatory system and for countering the risk that the firm might be used to further financial crime.'

This is of course similar to the former SIB Principal 9 dealing with internal organisation and control of a company. On 2 December 2002 Abbey Life Assurance Company Limited received a financial penalty of £1m for (in particular) a breach of PIA rules dealing with the need for such procedures to be in place and properly operated.

This case concerned Abbey Life's processes in respect of the sale of mortgage endowments. Deficiencies in this product providers compliance procedures and controls from 1995 to 1999 included inadequate records, inadequate communication of recommendations to customers and weaknesses in its monitoring and supervision of advisers.

A key issue centred on Abbey Life's classification of attitudes to risk which comprised three types of possible investor: cautious, balanced or adventurous. Whilst these descriptions could be appropriate to an assessment of attitude to risk in relation to investment products, they did not (necessarily) deal with the four distinct risks associated with an endowment mortgage ie that the endowment may not realise a sufficient sum to repay the mortgage; that premiums may have to increase to cover potential shortfalls; that any shortfall at maturity may have to be repaid from other resources; and that if other resources were not available, the property may need to be sold to make up the difference.

In criticising Abbey Life's procedures the FSA was particularly concerned that the fact finding processes made no provision for a separate assessment of attitude to mortgage risk as distinct from the degree of investment risk a client may be prepared to take in respect of an investment product. These difficulties naturally meant that records of information in respect of mortgage endowment customers were at risk of containing inadequate relevant information.

Abbey Life established in early 1994 a Sales Verification Department (SVD) responsible for checking that sales recommendations and the application of best advice by advisers complied with corporate guidelines contained in its 'Best Advice Guide.' The SVD, however, was also found not to be providing the necessary and rigorous cross-checking of files and transactions. In the result, Abbey Life instituted a programme of remedial work which was reflected in the mitigated penalty.

At the date of the Final Notice it was indicated that the overall compensation paid out by Abbey Life as a result of the remedial programme (both in respect of mortgage endowments and other products) was realistically expected to be in the region of £90m to £165m. The costs Abbey Life anticipated incurring were put in the range of £6m to £10m. It goes without saying that such expenditure is best deployed in resourcing the compliance function and ensuring compliance with regulatory requirements.

Compliant promotions 10.17

Another risk area which has attracted significant financial penalties concerns non-compliant financial promotions. On 24 March 2003 DBS Financial Management Plc was fined £100,000 by the FSA in respect of a misleading direct offer advertisement in the form of a 24 page brochure distributed with copies of the Daily Telegraph, the Sunday Telegraph and the Sunday Mirror. The case concerned a product called a protected ISA. The advertisement attracted a total of 455 investors.

It was misleading in numerous respects, including wrongly giving the impression that it offered 100% capital security over a five-year investment span; the advertisement did not make sufficiently clear that the capital protection offered

10.17 *Lessons from Past Failures*

applied only at the five-year anniversary; the front cover contained a prominent statement: 'all at no initial charge'. Elsewhere in the advertisement, however (page 21 in a small font), there was information about an initial charge of 6% together with management charges and other expenses.

The advertisement included an example of possible future growth over the five-year investment period of 100% and 200%, equivalent to 14.4% and 22.9% growth per annum respectively; these projections were substantially in excess of the growth rate permissible for ISA type investments. The ability for such an advertisement to be released into the market place reflected inadequate procedures with regard to approval of advertisements.

DBS at that time relied on an Advertising Approval Officer who would check material and either approve or reject it. He had a discretion in the case of advertisements of a very technical nature to refer them to the Research and Technical Department; likewise, he could refer contentious advertisements to the Policy and Audit Manager. The terms 'very technical nature' and 'contentious' were not, however, defined. Further, at that time DBS classified the Advertising Approval Officer as a technical role, sitting within the compliance function.

The Advertising Approval Officer received a two-week period of training on DBS's advertising approval procedures. No ongoing training was provided. He was, accordingly, not able to maintain appropriate levels of current expertise especially as regards developments in relation to new products. It emerged the Advertising Approval Officer had been unfamiliar with protected ISAs. Apart from the financial penalty, DBS was accordingly also obliged to carry out a remedial programme.

Compliance failures facilitating inter alia the issue of financial promotions which were misleading also resulted in Berkeley Jacobs Financial Services Limited receiving a financial penalty of £175,000 in February 2004. In that instance, what was described by the FSA as 'misleading and unbalanced advertising' was said to have been 'aggravated by a production line approach to selling.'

The case largely concerned the promotion and implementation of early vesting of pensions. The emphasis was on early releasing of cash without balancing this against the inherent risks of early vesting. Included in the reasons for the sanction was a failure of compliance oversight. The compliance sign-off procedure of the sales process was evidenced by the completion of a certification of verification of pension transfer and opt-out form.

The FSA's review of 250 customer files identified 19% of cases, however, where there was no defined objective recorded on the client profile form. Only limited advice appeared to have been offered to customers with limited disclosure of the advantages and disadvantages of early vesting of pensions or the consequences of using alternative methods of raising cash rather that accessing preserved retirement benefits.

The monitoring of new business had also failed to prevent the failure by Berkeley Jacobs advisers complying with a number of regulatory requirements in respect of gathering information from customers as to their personal and financial circumstances and making suitable recommendations.

Adequate IT systems 10.18

Failures in the organisation and control of the internal affairs of a business will of course extend to IT issues. This is well illustrated by the £750,000 penalty imposed on the governor and company of the Bank of Scotland in February 2003. Prior to April 1999 the Bank of Scotland (BoS) implemented within its PEP/ISA Department a new computer system known as LISA to manage ISAs other than mini cash ISAs. BoS thereafter migrated approximately 38,000 PEPs to LISA that had until then been managed on QUASR, the predecessor computer system.

Shortly after the implementation of LISA, BoS experienced difficulties in reconciling the cash positions recorded on LISA with the cash position recorded in BoS's bank accounts, a major control over BoS's PEP/ISA business. At implementation in April 1999, LISA had missing funtionality in key areas: dividends, statements, withdrawals, income distribution and fees. To compensate for this missing information BoS relied on a manual process. This proved, however, inadequate for the task.

Of particular concern to the FSA was that BoS migrated the PEPs to LISA even though it knew that extensive manual adjustments would be required to deal with LISA's functionality failings and that it should have appreciated that the PEP/ISA Department would be incapable of dealing with the additional burdens that the manual adjustments/reconciliations required. The functionality problems ought to have been appreciated and addressed so as to be eradicated in advance. The system was eventually made to work but between November 1999 and August 2001 BoS's PEP/ISA Department was unable to reconcile properly the cash that it was holding on it customers' behalf.

It goes without saying that proper prior planning and an orderly introduction of the new system would have avoided or reduced the risk of business and regulatory failings.

Adequate money laundering controls 10.19

We have noted above the emphasis on disciplinary action in respect of 'systems and controls' failures, a particular aspect of difficulties in these areas which has attracted disciplinary action relates to the systems and controls for compliance with money laundering requirements.

The anti-money laundering requirements on financial sector firms were imposed by the 1993 regulations, which took effect on 1 April 1994. These of

10.20 *Lessons from Past Failures*

course required firms to have procedures for inter alia the identification of Clients and the maintenance of records.

Abbey National Plc 10.20

On 9 December 2003 Abbey National Plc received a headline fine of £2m from the FSA for systems and control failures in respect of money laundering requirements. Before November 2000 Abbey National operated a system of centralised monitoring of compliance with its anti- money laundering policies and procedures. From November 2000, however, following a reallocation of resources, reliance was placed on a branch self-certification process. The management information generated by this new process was insufficient for the central MLRO function adequately to assess Abbey National's compliance with money laundering requirements.

In March 2003 its group internal audit function (GIA) reported following an internal review that there were substantial failures in the adherence to the requirements including non-compliance rates of 32% in respect of the identification of new customers. Apart from this significant failure rate, the GIA investigators also reported serious failures in relation to Suspicious Activity Reports (SARs). For example, in respect of transactions occurring during 2002 in excess of half were submitted more than 30 days after they had been reported internally to the central MLRO function. In the result, apart from the above financial penalty, Abbey National was obliged to implement a remedial programme.

Northern Bank Limited 10.21

On 4 August 2003 Northern Bank Limited also received a financial penalty of £1,250,000 in respect of breaches of money laundering requirements. Between March and July 2001 the bank conducted a review of compliance with its account opening procedures which identified significant non-compliance with its own client identification requirements. In January and February 2002 a further review was undertaken (ie after the Money Laundering Sourcebook came into effect) which showed continuing high rates of non-compliance. Nonetheless, it concluded its procedures were 'satisfactory' whilst noting that 'weaknesses existed which required attention.' In September 2002 it carried out a further internal review. In October of that year the January and September review materials were provided to the FSA for analysis.

The FSA concluded that in 35% of the accounts included in the January 2002 review and 18% of the accounts included in the September 2002 review Northern Bank had failed adequately to verify that the client was who he had claimed to be. In the result, the bank was obliged to devote considerable additional resources to correcting the problem and implementing a comprehensive remedial action plan.

Royal Bank of Scotland 10.22

By way of emphasising the importance which the FSA attaches to money laundering systems and controls the financial penalty imposed on the Royal Bank of Scotland in December 2002 of £750,000 for money laundering compliance failures should also be noted. The bank used a process called the 'new account sanctioner' (NAS), intended to ensure that the 'know your customer' information necessary for verifying identity was in place prior to an account being opened. The effectiveness of NAS was monitored by the bank's compliance function.

The procedure employed had also been independently audited by the bank's GIA. A GIA review of 241 accounts opened in November 2001 showed a failure rate of 11.2%, ie either the customer's name or address (or both) had not been verified to the standards laid down in the NAS process. A subsequent FSA investigation also confirmed serious failure rates which lead to a revised remedial programme.

New product lines 10.23

New product lines also pose a variety of threats and challenges to compliance. The dangers are well illustrated by the £1.9m fine imposed in September 2003 on Lloyds TSB Bank Plc (LTSB). The case concerned the sale of some 51,000 policies known as 'extra income and growth plans' (EIGP) which had been effected in four tranches between October 2000 and July 2001.

EIGP was a new product with a medium/high risk rating designed by Scottish Widows Group and distributed by the LTSB branch network shortly after Scottish Widows was acquired by LTSB. The high level controls for the launch into the network of a new product required formal approval by the Network and LTSB Group Risk Management.

There was no formal process in place at group level within LTSB for considering the relative suitability of different distribution channels for different products or for approving products on a channel by channel basis. On 31 July 2000, the LTSB branch network committee approved the sale of the EIGP through the network in principle provided a number of issues could be satisfactorily addressed including training and risk mitigation associated with the product itself.

On the same day Scottish Widows submitted the initial product approval request to Group Risk Management. This indicated in all probability it would not be offered through the network as a distribution channel. Group Risk Management approved the product on that basis on 21 August 2000. The following day the LTSB branch network committee's decision to approve the sale of EIGP through the network was communicated to the head of LTSB group operational risks.

10.24 *Lessons from Past Failures*

Risks of product mis-selling through the network had been identified within LTSB on a number of occasions. Financial consultants within the network were under pressure to perform and meet sales targets for all products. EIGP was a possible way of getting high volumes of business since it was regarded as a potentially successful and popular product due to a high headline rate of income or growth. LTSB recognised that due to the inherent risk of capital loss implied in any equity-linked product and the high headline rate of over 10% income offered by the EIGP, there was a risk customers would not understand the implied risks including misunderstanding the maturity return and that a full return of capital was not guaranteed.

The importance of a balanced range of investments was not emphasised to network consultants. Training in safe selling was not adequate. In order to address the risk of mis-selling in respect of the EIGP, a risk based verification model was used. Files were selected for checking through a central verification unit. In fact, 100% of EIGP's sales were initially verified as compliant by this process.

The central verification unit, however, applied suitability rules developed for the financial consultants in relation to EIGP which did not provide sufficient guidance in respect of 'concentration levels'. In other words, it did not enable proper checking of the extent to which EIGP had been used as part only of an overall investment strategy rather than exposing investors to the risk of putting all their eggs in one higher risk basket.

In the result, the FSA determined that some 22,500 EIGP sales (44% of the total number of policies sold) were made through the network to investors for whom the product was not suitable. LTSB agreed to pay compensation in respect of these sales at a total cost of approximately £98m.

Complaints handling 10.24

When the systems and procedures operated by a firm go wrong or only inadequate procedures are in place, the risk of customer complaint is enhanced. The FSA, however, is equally committed to ensuring that where complaints are made the firm has a fair, rigorous and adequate complaints handling system in place. This is brought home by the £675,000 penalty imposed on Friends Provident Life and Pensions Limited (Friends Provident) in December 2003 in respect of its failure to establish and maintain appropriate and effective procedures for the proper handling of mortgage endowment complaints.

Friends Provident had sold 216,629 mortgage endowment policies between 29 April 1998 and 21 December 2001. Between March 2000, when a dedicated complaints handling unit was established, and February 2003 some 21,788 mortgage endowment complaints were received.

After February 2003 a revised and improved complaints handling machinery was in place; prior thereto, however, the system operated was deficient. The system was considered in the light of a letter sent by John Tiner to the Chief Executives of product providers and large ISAs known to have sold mortgage endowment policies in April 2002. The Tiner letter identified three main issues for firms' attention: the need for firms to assess customers' complaints fairly, particularly in respect of the assessment of consumers' understanding and acceptance of risk at the time of sale; the danger of firms' complaints handlers placing too much reliance on the decision tree process for complaints published by the Financial Ombudsman Service in June 2000 and the need to consider each complaint separately and avoid the application of precedent (especially FOS decisions) without due regard to the facts of the specific case under review.

The approach taken by the FSA in this instance is illustrative also of the need for firms, and Compliance Officers in particular, to be sensitive to the FSA's expectations articulated through its official statements and public announcements.

Monitoring appointed representatives 10.25

The preceding paragraphs looked at recent examples of penalties imposed for breaches by firms in relation to the management of direct sales and organisation of its direct labour. The FSA's concern over the adequacy of business systems and controls, however, of course extends to those required to be in place to ensure adequate monitoring of activities of appointed representatives.

St James Place Unit Trust Group 10.26

This is illustrated by the £250,000 penalty imposed on St James Place Unit Trust Group Limited in November 2003. The conduct there at issue concerned record keeping inadequacies in connection with recommendations made to customers by St James appointed representatives – particularly in relation to the surrender and replacement of existing investment contracts.

St James appointed representatives were commonly recruited from other product providers, sometimes as a result of reduction in or closure of a direct sales force. These new recruits commonly approached previous clients to recommend investment contracts provided by St James which resulted in a lapsing or surrender of an existing policy.

Investigations revealed a widespread lack of adequate recorded file evidence to justify recommendations. Examples of inadequacies in the documentation included the presence of conflicting information with regard to customers' attitude to risk; a lack of any clear reason or explanation for switches from with profits to higher risk unit-linked investments; a lack of evidence that the replacement contract was more advantageous to the investor than the existing product and an absence of evidence to show that the client was made aware of all relevant advantages and disadvantages of the proposed transaction.

The identified defects have not been picked up by St James's compliance systems. A failure to detect inadequately documented or unsuitable sales by City Financial Partners Limited, an appointed representative to Lincoln Assurance Limited, also attracted a penalty of £485,000 in April 2003. The particular issue there concerned the systemic nature of weaknesses in the documentation and sales process (and Lincoln's monitoring thereof) with respect to sales of ten-year savings plans.

A review indicated a lack of adequate evidence in many instances justifying the particular sales. The result of this was that Lincoln was left with an estimated compensation liability to customers put at £8.8m after taking into account the current value of their policies. The position was not helped by the fact that a couple of years earlier the PIA had issued a formal warning to Lincoln that there appeared to be a lack of evidence to satisfy 'know your client' requirements, and poor documentation, requiring the issue of amended 'reason why' letters, along with files which did not clearly demonstrate compliance at the point of sale. These indicated a monitoring failure on the part of Lincoln. In spite of this warning, however, problems were not effectively addressed within a timescale satisfactory to the FSA.

Apart from the above systems and controls examples the public register of Final Notices contains numerous examples of prohibition orders and cancellations of Part IV permissions. Commonly prohibition orders are made in relation to individuals who have carried on significant regulated investment business without a Part IV permission or where the individual has been found guilty of serious criminal (fraudulent) misconduct. Cancellation of permissions are issued commonly where a firm fails to demonstrate an ongoing ability to satisfy one or more of the threshold conditions. Of particular concern is any breach of capital adequacy requirements.

Interdependence Limited 10.27

A further recent example of failures to monitor appointed representatives is afforded by the disciplinary proceedings against Interdependence Limited, culminating in a financial penalty of £125,000 imposed on 24 May 2004. The proceedings concerned sales of income drawdown policies by appointed representatives of Interdependence, particularly during the period 1999–March 2002. The risks associated with pension fund withdrawal contracts were highlighted in detailed regulatory guidance issued by the PIA in Regulatory Update 67. In an attempt to comply with relevant guidance, Interdependence had introduced a system in 1996 requiring appointed representatives advising in respect of pension fund withdrawals to provide details of the intended business to a pensions specialist so that any transaction could be overseen by an individual with relevant specialist, technical knowledge ('the pre-approval system'). The system did not, however, operate fully or effectively. Initially, this reflected a failure by the appointed representative to provide anything other than basic details of proposed transactions; between July 2000 and March 2002 there was insufficient supervision of such business by Interdependence.

The particular failings identified included the absence of any means of ensuring that appointed representatives did actually submit their cases for pre-approval; the absence of any evidence to demonstrate that action had been taken by Interdependence during the relevant period to review the efficiency of the pre-approval system; the complete absence of evidence in 90% of all pension fund withdrawal cases being submitted for pre approval; instances of cases which were submitted for pre-approval being rejected as unsuitable whereafter the appointed representatives had ignored the specialist advice and proceeded to write the business in any event.

Interdependence had two monitoring mechanisms in particular: the activities of the Business Assessment Team (BAT) and the operation of a Professional Standards Visits Team (PSV). Neither had contributed properly to the monitoring of the appointed representatives; the BAT team had made incorrect assessments of the risk posted by individual appointed representatives; and some PSV visits did not identify key regulatory issues, such as failure to comply with the pre-approval system. The absence of record keeping was also a contributory area of concern to the Regulator.

Monitoring conduct of business   10.28

An extreme example of systems failures in respect of compliant selling practices arises from the disciplinary action taken against Carr Sheppards Crosthwaite Limited. These culminated in a financial penalty of £500,000 being imposed in May 2004. The firm carried on the business of private client stockbroking, providing discretionary, non discretionary and advisory services. It had approximately 20,000 discretionary and advisory clients on its books, of which about 15,000 were managed on an active basis. Its customer base fell into three main categories: private clients with more than £200,000 to invest; private clients with under £200,00 to invest; and smaller charities. The company was a wholly owned subsidiary of Investec. In late 2003 the internal audit department of Investec undertook a review of Carr Sheppards Crosthwaite's compliance department and arrangements, producing a detailed written report for the FSA.

The firm's compliance department consisted of a head of compliance (Compliance Officer) with three compliance staff and one secretarial support person. The Compliance Officer reported orally to the Chief Executive Officer on a regular basis and monthly to the firm's management committee (on which occasion his oral reports were minuted).

The firm was found to be operating with reference to a compliance manual which was incomplete and out of date. Further, there was no procedure or register in place to confirm whether staff had read or understood the content of the manual. Following the coming into force of the *FSMA 2000*, Carr Sheppards Crossthwaite had not established and implemented a detailed monitoring programme covering all aspects of FSA rules and regulations. In particular, the firm had failed to ensure that it could demonstrate that it had all relevant facts about its customers so as to be able to show it had taken reasonable steps to ensure its customers' portfolios or accounts remained suitable. Further, there was inadequate documentation in respect of ongoing, personal and financial know your customer information. The Investec internal audit department considered a sample of 70 client files from its London head office and 50 files from the firm's branch offices. These revealed that ongoing know your customer information was not being formally documented: there were inconsistencies in the standard of documentation handled. The majority of the reviewed files had little or no additional information on the client's background and current circumstances, and 635 discretionary customers had no risk level attributed to them.

The level of penalty was no doubt mitigated in the light of prompt and effective remedial action taken to address the issues identified by the Investec internal audit review and the FSA. These took the form of:

- strengthening the resources in the compliance department;
- establishing a detailed procedures manual for the compliance department;
- developing, with the assistance of a major accountancy firm, a detailed compliance monitoring programme; and
- instigating a know your customer project by way of contacting all customers with a view amongst other things to establishing correct risk profiles.

Personal lessons 10.29

The FSA jurisdiction to prohibit approved persons from continuing to carry on regulated activities has been exercised in a number of recent cases. The lesson from each is: play fair with the Regulator and customers. On 1 June 2004 Mr Headdon, the former appointed actuary and a director and chief executive of Equitable Life, was prohibited from carrying out a number of governing and required functions as a result of conduct disapproved by the FSA in relation to a particular aspect of his relationship with the FSA and the Government Actuaries' Department. We have discussed above some of the general lessons arising from the failure of this particular life assurer.

The background to the prohibition order made in this instance (which was expressed to be subject to revocation upon application after 26 May 2010) was as follows. In late 1998/early 1999 Equitable Life agreed with the Regulator to offset a proportion of statutory reserves by a reassurance arrangement valued at approximately £800m. This was ultimately provided through a treaty between

Equitable Life and the Irish European Reinsurance Company Limited (IRECO). In January 1999 Equitable alerted IRECO to the fact that a provision in an earlier draft of the proposed treaty whereby it could be cancelled if withheld claims reached £100m would not provide the necessary cover in respect of its reserves. After some negotiation IRECO and Equitable agreed that the treaty would provide for a renegotiation of terms in the event that withheld claims reached £100m. Further, Equitable agreed to a proposal that if such renegotiations failed, the treaty might be cancelled. This agreement in respect of cancellation was recorded in a side 'letter of understanding'.

Having reached the above understanding, a meeting then took place with the Regulator. It was indicated to the FSA and the Government Actuary's Department that there was no intention that the reassurance treaty should be cancelled in the event that the £100m claims limit was reached. This was contrary to the letter of understanding which was not then disclosed to the FSA and/or the Government Actuary's Department. Subsequently, the annual regulatory returns were signed off in which a value of £793m was attributed to the treaty. The position thus shown in the return for year end 31 December 1998 was repeated in the return in respect of the following year end, 31 December 1999 (notwithstanding that the side letter remained in effect). The failure to refer to the letter of understanding and its real impact on the returns and reserves position was described as 'not a matter of inadvertence but followed from a decision on' the part Mr Headdon.

A further recent example of a failure to deal openly with the Regulator is afforded by the prohibition orders made in respect of Messrs Rayner and Townsend, former directors and shareholders of Townsend Rayner Associates Limited. The latter company had been responsible for the sale of (for present purposes) personal pension plans falling within the Pensions Review Regime. By January 1999 the company had not adequately reviewed its priority (phase 1) cases between 1995 and 1998. After discussion with the FSA, Messrs Townsend and Rayner were informed in August 2000 that the failures in the Pensions Review would be referred to the FSA's Enforcement Division. Within approximately two months, and a week after an FSA visit, Messrs Rayner and Townsend entered into an asset purchase agreement, disposing of their assets in the business for £400,000.

Although some work thereafter continued on the Pension Review, the company ceased trading in October 2000. In May the following year Mr Rayner confirmed to the Pensions Review Unit of the PIA that the company lacked resources to continue to meet its Review obligations. Despite both individuals being in regular contact with the FSA at the time, neither revealed the sale of assets, about which the FSA did not learn until November 2000. It then invited the directors to return the purchase monies to the company, so as to provide a fund to apply to any investor redress obligations arising out of the Review. The directors declined to do so. In the result, prohibition orders were made against each individual. In a statement by the head of department in the FSA Enforcement Division it was indicated 'This is a warning to other individuals who asset strip regulated firms without standing obligations to consumers – they will face enforcement action and are not welcome in this industry.'

High(er) risk products 10.30

In the nature of things the promotion of and dealing in high(er) risk products carries the potential for increased regulatory attention and action. Two recent examples may be considered: the cancellation of the Part IV Permission to David M Aaron (Personal Financial Planners) Limited in August 2004 and a financial penalty of £300,000 imposed in May 2004 on Hargreaves Lansdown Asset Management Limited. Both firms had decided to promote and deal in high(er) risk investments.

The firm of David M Aaron (Personal Financial Planners) Limited had been responsible between January 1998 and June 2003 for the sale of a substantial number of Structured Capital At Risk Products (SCARPs). The total number of sales was estimated at not less than 7,900. Although business was transacted with customers on both an advisory and direct offer basis, the substantial majority of business was conducted (as to 85%) on the basis of direct offers. In such cases, where advice was not provided, it was particularly important that any advertising and financial promotions were accurate and fair. As part of its process for marketing SCARPs the firm used a marketing committee, comprising its directors and senior advisors. These decided upon the risk ratings to apply to various versions of SCARPs marketed. The methods used to assess the risk profile of SCARPs was described by the FSA, however, as 'fundamentally flawed in that it placed undue reliance upon the marketing committee's own subjective views on the past, current and future market conditions and failed to take adequate account of the downside gearing as well as the fixed term nature of SCARPs'.

As indicated, the members of the marketing committee were also directors of the firm with key controlled functions exercised within it. This resulted in the risk assessment process failing to provide customers with a transparent view about the potential impact of an adverse event. Further, much of the literature emanating from the firm was attributed to the views of 'independent' panellists. From September 2003 the firm received a substantial number of complaints in respect of its marketing and sales of SCARPs. After a decision against the firm in respect of one such complaint by the Financial Services Ombudsman in respect of a complaint relating to a direct offer SCARP sale, the firm was placed into voluntary administration and subsequently placed in insolvent liquidation.

In the case of Hargreaves Lansdown Asset Management Limited, this firm had offered between 1992 and 2002 investment opportunities in its Secure Growth Portfolio (SGP). This had been offered as a discretionary management service in zero class shares of split capital trusts. Until 2000 these were confined to shares issued by traditional trusts and properly sold as carrying a lower risk than equities. In the late 1990s, however, splits were introduced that were structured very differently from their predecessors and having the potential of exposing their shares, including the zeros, to significantly increased risk. Hargreaves Lansdown Asset Management Limited, however, continued to advertise the purpose of its SGP as the provision of only 'lower risk' investments – notwithstanding that a number of the zeros included in the SGP were of the new style. The business was predominantly execution only in nature and conducted mainly by mail.

In November 2000 the SGP's manager sought to reduce holdings in BFS Income & Growth and CGU Quarterly High Income. This proved difficult and by December 2000 the BFS managers had altered the risk rating (which was by reference to equity investments) from 'low' to 'low to medium'. No consequential change was made to the SGP brochure which continued to describe a lower risk portfolio composed only of lower risk zeros. Fresh investments were accepted into the SGP on the basis of this inaccurate brochure up to early September 2001. No attempt was made to communicate a change in risk rating to customers until the following month. The firm was accordingly found to have failed to exercise due skill, care and diligence in warning customers of the possibility of impending difficulties in the split-capital market. Further, the firm had failed to fulfil its duty to inform customers as to changes in the risk profile of the investments.

Chapter 11
Conduct Of Business

Introduction 11.1

The strength of an authorised firm's recruitment, training and competence, systems and controls and complaints handling components are put to the ultimate test at its interface with its customers. Here, compliance with the 'conduct of business' requirements will be likely to reveal weaknesses in any of the areas mentioned. This chapter will accordingly look, in broad terms, at the expectations and requirements of the conduct of business regime, concentrating first on the conduct of 'designated investment business' and then on the rules relating to sales of regulated mortgage contracts and then insurance contracts.

Designated Investment Business 11.2

Designated investment business embraces (principally) dealing in, arranging, managing and advising on investments involving life policies, shares, debentures, government and public securities, warrants, units in collective investment schemes, options, futures and contracts for differences (along with any rights or interests in any of the foregoing).

The Conduct of Business Sourcebook 11.3

The Conduct of Business Sourcebook provides the detailed regime now applying in relation to the above. In essence, it replaces the patchwork of conduct of business rules formally provided by (amongst others) the SIB, IMRO, FSA, PIA, LAUTRO and FIMBRA rules.

The Conduct of Business Sourcebook accordingly applies to all regulated activities carried on by all firms; certain of the rules, however, are excluded in relation to inter-professional business and/or do not apply save in respect of transactions with private customers. Although the rules do not as such apply to appointed representatives of authorised firms, the firm will be responsible for the acts and omissions of its appointed representatives who must accordingly comply with the regime.

11.4 Conduct Of Business

Client classification 11.4

The Conduct of Business Source book imposes an initial obligation on regulated firms to classify clients with whom it conducts or intends to carry on designated investment business. The classification options are threefold: private customers, intermediate customers and market counter-parties. Whilst, therefore, each of the foregoing will be a client to the firm it is only the first two classifications which define customers.

The purpose of the classification process 11.5

The purpose of the classification process is to determine which of the conduct of business rules apply to the client in question. Some rules are expressed to apply to clients, others to private customers and intermediate customers.

Private customers 11.6

The regime is intended to ensure an appropriate degree of regulatory protection is extended to the client in question: private customers are expected to require greater protection than market counter-parties, to take each end of the spectrum. The firm is obliged to keep the appropriateness of the initial classification under review and clients may by agreement 'step up' to a lesser degree of protection or 'step down' by asking to be treated as eg a private customer. The default position is as private customer.

Intermediate customers and market counter-parties 11.7

Broadly speaking, listed companies, corporate bodies and partnerships with called up share capital or net assets in excess of £5m will automatically qualify as intermediate customers (absent of any arrangement to step up or step down); subject to satisfying certain conditions, other firms or overseas financial institutions will automatically be regarded as market counter-parties, along with governments, central banks and local authorities. Designation as a market counter-party by the firm will not, however, obviate the need to comply with the rules on Chinese walls, personal account dealings, approval of financial promotions and safeguarding and administration of investments.

Once consequence of stepping down to the status of private customer will be that the client will be entitled to take advantage of a right to sue for any breach of the applicable conduct of business rules as a breach of statutory duty. It is a moot point whether in such an instance a client, which would otherwise be an intermediate customer, may be more vulnerable to an allegation of contributory negligence if it should seek to enforce such a right alleging losses flowing from bad advice. The better view is that such a person would probably not be so at risk for otherwise this would result in the undermining (if not deprivation) of the benefit of the protection of the private customer scope of the rules bargained for at the time of stepping down.

Conversely, if the private customer chooses to step up in the classification hierarchy then the firm may legitimately expect the elective re-designated client to take that degree of care in looking after himself as may be appropriate to eg a sophisticated (expert) investor. The risk of loss of investor protection here is guarded against by the duties imposed on firms not to accept a private customer as an intermediate customer save where it has taken reasonable care to determine that the client has sufficient knowledge and experience to waive private customer protection; it must give the customer a written warning, describing the loss of protection which will result and ensure he has had sufficient time to make an informed decision to step up. In the event of a transaction going wrong in respect of such an individual, however, disputes can be expected as to whether it was appropriate to accept the client's decision to step up. In practice, there will accordingly be a heightened risk to firms choosing to accept client reclassification of this kind.

The test for stepping up to market counter-party status from intermediate customer classification is largely identity based. To be able to make such an election to step up the intermediate customer must:

- be a limited company with a called up share capital in excess of £10m;
- have either a balance sheet total of 12.5m euros or a net turnover of 25m euros or employ an average of 250 employees in a year;
- be a partnership with net assets of more than £10m (without deducting partners loans); or
- be a trustee qualifying as an intermediate customer (ie a trustee of a small self-administered scheme or occupational pension scheme or stakeholder scheme with not fewer than 50 members and assets of at least £10m under management and/or a trustee of any other trust with cash or designated investments of at least £10m.

Even here, however, the firm must notify the intermediate customer of the intention to treat it as a market counter-party, explain in writing the loss of protection which will result and in the case of limited companies receive no objection to this course and in any other case obtain the informed consent of the client.

Terms of business and client agreements 11.8

Having appropriately classified the client, the next relevant obligation is the provision of terms of business. In relation to private customers, the firm must provide its terms of business before conducting any investment business for the customer. These must contain adequate details in relation to a number of specified matters, including a description of the services the firm will provide; how the services are to be paid for; any restrictions on the investments in which the customer wishes to invest (or a statement there are no such restrictions); and confirmation of the customer's investment objectives.

Principal Obligations

Know your customer 11.9

The requirement to 'know your customer' is engaged in relation to a firm's dealings with private customers where the firm:

- recommends a designated investment;
- arranges a pension opt-out or transfer from an occupational pension scheme; and
- acts as a discretionary investment manager.

Before making any personal recommendation to a private customer in the above context, the firm must take reasonable steps to obtain sufficient information about the customer's personal circumstances, financial position, objectives and attitude to risk so as to be able to formulate suitable proposals. Typically the information will be collated on a standardised fact find questionnaire. Non-exhaustively, key pieces of information will include the customer's:

- age, sex and marital status;
- employment details, income, assets and liabilities (including a responsibility for dependants); and
- objectives and risk profile.

Where the customer declines to provide relevant information, he must be warned that this may adversely affect the quality of any advice given or recommendations made. It would be prudent to ensure that such a warning is communicated in writing before any transaction proceeds further.

Execution-only transactions 11.10

An execution-only transaction is defined by the FSA as: 'a transaction executed by a firm upon the specific instructions of a client where the firm does not give advice on the merits of the transaction.' It follows that a customer who declines to provide full information or seeks advice only in respect of a particular aspect of a transaction will not be an execution-only client; in such cases, some advice will have been solicited and given as to how to proceed (albeit subject to a warning that the adviser has not been given a complete picture).

On the whole, customers go (self evidently) to a financial adviser for advice. Too high an incidence of execution-only business is likely to attract scepticism and regulatory concern by the FSA. Monitoring the incidents of execution-only business is one of the many key business indicators available to the Compliance Officer vigilant for early warnings as to potential non-compliance.

Product suitability 11.11

Having ascertained sufficient information about a private customer so as to be able to offer a personal recommendation by way of advice, there is a separate and distinct duty to take reasonable care not to make a recommendation to buy or sell a designated investment nor to effect a discretionary transaction 'unless the recommendation or transaction is suitable for the private customer having regard to the facts disclosed by him and other relevant facts about the private customer of which the firm is, or reasonably should be, aware.' The scope, application and fulfilment of this broad statement of duty is fact and context sensitive.

Firstly, it applies in respect of private customers where the firm:

- recommends a designated investment;
- acts as a discretionary investment manager;
- manages the assets of an occupational pension scheme or stakeholder pension scheme; or
- promotes a personal pension scheme by means of a direct offer financial promotion to a group of employees.

Secondly, in relation to packaged products, a product provider may only recommend such a product to a private customer if it can demonstrate that the recommended product is the most suitable of those available from the firm's marketing group and must decline to make any recommendation if there is no suitable package product available from the group. In the latter circumstance, the customer may be referred to an independent adviser.

So far as the independent financial adviser is concerned, he must also not make a personal recommendation for the acquisition of a package product if he ought reasonably to be aware of a generally available package product which would be more appropriate to the needs and circumstances of the particular private customer concerned. Further, if the package product he is considering recommending is provided by a connected person, it should not be recommended unless the adviser can show that it is 'demonstrably better than any other such product on the market'. The plain intention is to discourage the sale of products by connected providers in circumstances where the objectivity of any independent advice may be thereby compromised.

Understanding risk

Part of the 'fact finding' exercise will include identifying a customer's attitude to risk. This requires a degree of careful analysis by the financial adviser. A customer should not, it is suggested, be treated as having a single attitude to risk irrespective of the size of any investment transaction being considered. Thus, a customer may well be prepared to take greater risk in investing a defined proportion of funds available for investment provided the majority of the funds are protected by investment in a secure environment. Likewise, identifying a suitable product involves careful consideration of the risks attached to the investment product in question. In addition, therefore, to the foregoing cardinal requirements of good advice (know your client and recommending suitable products), there is a distinct separate duty where a firm:

- makes a personal recommendation;
- acts as a discretionary investment manager;
- arranges a deal in warrants and derivatives;
- engages in stock lending activity; or
- takes reasonable steps to ensure a private customer is made aware of and understands the nature of the risks inherent in the proposed transaction.

Suitability letter

In respect of investment transactions concerning life policies (including pension plans); income draw down schemes; collective investment schemes and investment trusts; and pension transfers or opt-outs, a private customer must be provided with a suitability letter explaining the reasons why the transaction in question was recommended. The core content of the letter is prescribed and must:

- include an explanation of the reasons for the suitability of the recommendation, taking into account the customer's personal and financial circumstances;
- summarise the main consequences and possible disadvantages of the transaction; and
- give the identity of the person in the firm authorised to advise in respect of the product.

The letter should be personalised, written in plain English and set out the connection between the personal circumstances and resources of the customer linked to the recommendation made.

Where the letter is provided in respect of a life policy or stakeholder pension scheme where the cancellation rules require notification of the right to cancel, it must be given no later than the date of issue of the post-sale notice of the cancellation right; in all other cases, the letter must be provided as soon as possible after the transaction is effected.

Cost of advice 11.14

FSA Principle 6 requires a firm to treat its customers fairly. This includes an express obligation to ensure that any charge for services provided are not excessive. Whether a charge is excessive will involve a comparison with comparable market charges, consideration as to whether the level of charge could amount to an abuse of trust of the customer and of the nature and extent of the disclosure made of the charge. The firm must, before it conducts designated investment business for a private customer, disclose in writing the basis or amount of its charges and the nature or amount of any income receivable by the firm attributable to the business. In respect of life policy business, the firm must disclose in these instances, in cash terms, any remuneration or commission received in connection with the transaction.

Key features and cancellation 11.15

Where a firm makes a personal recommendation or arranges the sale of a package product to a private customer (or to the trustees of an occupational pension scheme), proposes or arranges a variation of life policies or recommends and arranges an income draw down policy, it is a requirement that a key features document is issued; although the obligation rests on the adviser, the key features will usually be provided by the product provider in question. The document is itself a financial promotion and must accordingly satisfy the financial promotions rules. A failure to issue or the issue of an inadequate key features document represent serious examples of non-compliance.

Where cancellation rights apply, the cancellation notice must be posted by the product provider (generally) within 14 days of the conclusion of the transaction, whereafter the customer has a period of 14 days in which to exercise the right to cancel or withdraw.

Dealing and managing 11.16

The rule requirements imposed in relation to dealing in and managing customer assets will obviously be of main importance to firms carrying on stock broking and investment management activities. Much of the detail of the requirements, into which this broad overview will not attempt to go, reflect the high level Principles for Businesses, notably Principle 6 (requiring fair treatment of customers) and Principle 8 (dealing with managing conflicts of interest fairly). Thus where a firm has a material interest in a transaction with or for a customer or has a conflict or potential conflict between itself and its customer, or between one customer and another, the firm must ensure that it acts fairly as between all concerned. Such conflict management may be addressed by disclosing the firm's interest to its customer, setting up Chinese walls or, if the foregoing are not adequate as conflict management strategies, simply declining to act for the customer.

In the case of a private customer dealing with a broker fund adviser, an acknowledgement must be obtained from the customer confirming he understands the nature of the firm's dual roles as his adviser and as adviser to the operator of the relevant fund.

The firm must also take reasonable steps to ensure that any deal or switch in the customer's investments is in his best interests – both in respect of the particular transaction and in the context of earlier transactions. This is intended to deal with churning and inappropriate, frequent switches.

Best execution 11.17

So far as the execution of orders in designated investments is concerned, the principal requirements are that the firm must take reasonable care to ascertain the price which is the best available for the customer order in the relevant market at the time of the transaction of the kind and size concerned and to execute the order at a price which is no less advantageous; the order must be executed as soon as reasonably practicable. Postponing execution or effecting the transaction at a less advantageous price may only be justified if the firm can demonstrate it would be in the best interests of the customer.

Further dealing considerations 11.18

Treating customers fairly includes having in place procedures to ensure:

- a firm postpones its own account transactions when it or an associate publishes original recommendations or a piece of research or analysis in relation to a designated investment until the customers for whom the publication was intended have had a reasonable opportunity to act upon it (subject to certain exceptions, including where the information could not reasonably be expected to have a material effect on price);
- where a firm has own account and customer orders, it executes these fairly and in due turn;
- that when a firm aggregates and subsequently executes an order for a customer, together with orders on its own account or for a market counter-party, the designated investments are allocated fairly to customers; in particular, no customer order may be aggregated with a firm's own account order or that from a market counter-party unless the firm

has reasonable grounds to believe the aggregation will work to the advantage of each customer and has warned each of the risk that the effect of aggregation may not always work to their individual advantage.

Conduct of business and pension sales 11.19

In the context of a look at current conduct of business rules it is finally important to single out transactions involving personal pension plans. These were introduced in the form recognised today in 1988. The product appeared initially very successful. By mid 1994 it was estimated approximately 8.1 million employees in the UK had personal pension plans (approximately five million policyholders having also contracted out of SERPS). Concerns that not all such sales to individuals otherwise eligible to participate in pension scheme benefits already provided by occupational schemes were confirmed by a report to the Securities and Investments Board by accountants KPMG in December 1993. The investigation involved sampling a representative number of transfer transactions from occupational schemes to new style personal pension plan products. Extensive evidence of repeated failures to comply with the then conduct of business rules (in particular those of LAUTRO and FIMBRA) prompted the introduction of the formal review of pension transfers, opt-outs and non-joiner cases. Implementation of this review, which it is estimated may have resulted in at least 1.5 million investors receiving in excess of £12b of compensation has caused the FSA to be acutely sensitive to any advice to an investor to pay into a personal pension plan when otherwise eligible for benefits in an occupational scheme (whether active or deferred).

Hence, in relation to pension transfers and opt-outs detailed rules and guidance now exist to be followed by firms advising private customers on pension transfers and opt-outs. Non-exhaustively:

- Advice to transfer from an occupational scheme to a personal pension plan should be given by the firm's pension transfer specialist (or reviewed by him where the recommendation originates from a non-pension transfer specialist adviser).

- The suitability letter must explain the disadvantages (along with any advantages) of a transfer from an occupational scheme to a personal pension plan.

- Guidance given by the FSA is to the effect that the adviser should in any event assume an opt-out or transfer recommendation from an occupational scheme will not be suitable.

- In advising an investor to opt out of an occupational scheme specific consideration must be given to the loss of occupational pension scheme (OPS) benefits and the different nature of personal pension plan benefits: typical disadvantages of non-participation in a conventional defined benefit occupational scheme include the loss of an employer contribution towards the underlying fund; loss of life cover; loss of a dependant's

11.20 *Conduct Of Business*

pension; loss of ancillary benefits such as early retirement ill-health pensions; the guaranteed nature of the level of pension provided by the OPS; and the uncertain nature of the pension available from long-term investments where the annuity eventually purchased will reflect the uncertainty of such returns and the annuity rates prevailing at the time the pension is taken.

- A detailed comparison must be undertaken between deferred benefits from a defined benefit occupational scheme and the personal pension plan; the required procedures address the obtaining of information from the ceding scheme, including in particular the obtaining of a transfer value quotation.

Firms conducting such business must also provide regular information to the FSA as to the volume of pension opt-out and transfer business conducted. This is to be provided at six-monthly intervals; in addition, the FSA will require detailed quarterly of the number of:

- execution-only pension opt-outs or pension transfers arranged (if they exceed 1% of the firm's opt-out/transfer business arranged during the quarter);
- opt-outs and transfers arranged said to have proceeded against the firm's advice (if they exceed 1% of all opt-out and transfer business arranged during the quarter);
- opt-out and transfer transactions arranged on a correspondence only basis (if they exceed 1% of the opt-outs and transfers arranged by the firm during the relevant quarter).

Record keeping 11.20

The record keeping requirements in respect of designated investment advice are as follows:

- pension transfers and opt-outs – records must be kept indefinitely;
- other life and pensions business – records must be retained for six years;
- all other business – records must be retained for three years.

The FSA's sensitivity to pension transfers and opt-outs is implicit in the above record keeping requirement. That said, a firm may well be advised to arrange retention of records in all other cases for (at least) six years. This is the primary period prescribed by the *Limitation Act 1980* for bringing legal claims for mis-selling; claims may in certain circumstances still be brought outside this period. A firm, however, which has disposed of records in respect of non-life and pensions investment advice after three years may well find it is handicapped in dealing with customer complaints which arise after three years and will be disadvantaged in dealing with the Financial Ombudsman Service and/or in any litigation which comes about in respect of advice given more than three years earlier (but in respect of which complaints to the Financial Ombudsman Service and/or through the Courts remain available to investors).

Stakeholder pension schemes, group pensions and free-standing additional voluntary contributions 11.21

Consistent with the FSA's sensitivity to the whole area of pension sales, each of the above is also singled out for specific rule treatment in the Conduct of Business Sourcebook.

Stakeholder pensions 11.22

In relation to stakeholder pensions the following should be noted:

- Where a firm provides information about stakeholder pension schemes at a meeting arranged for a group of five or more employees, the information must be provided by an adviser appointed to give advice to private customers on packaged products; it does not matter that no investment advice may be given at such a meeting.

- The FSA has also published decision trees, which firms may use to talk a customer through a decision making process eg as to whether to take out a stakeholder pension. These may be used by firms in contact with a customer by telephone. It is imperative, however, that no advice is given as part of this process and that the customer is provided with a written notice that he has decided on a stakeholder pension scheme as a result of answers to the questions set out in the decision tree and not in reliance upon or as a result of advice on investments given to him by the representative of the firm.

Group personal pension plan 11.23

Where a firm chooses to promote personal pension schemes and group personal pension plans to a group of employees of a firm, it must have reasonable grounds to conclude that such a scheme 'is likely to be at least as suitable for the majority of the employees as a stakeholder pension scheme and must record why it thinks the promotion is justified.' The firm's adviser must carry out a detailed comparison between personal pension schemes and stakeholder pensions. If a scheme other than a stakeholder scheme is recommended, the suitability letter must explain the reasons for the recommendation and identify why the firm has concluded the recommended product is 'at least as suitable' as a stakeholder pension scheme.

Free-standing additional voluntary contributions 11.24

An Investor in a position to pay into an additional voluntary contribution plan may have three choices: an additional voluntary contribution (AVC) scheme offered by his employer; a stakeholder pension scheme and a free-standing AVC (FSAVC) scheme. Where an FSAVC is recommended, the adviser, in providing a suitability letter, must (as appropriate) explain why the recommendation is considered to be 'at least as suitable' as any AVC scheme otherwise available with the employer and/or 'at least as suitable' as a stakeholder pension scheme (where that option exists).

Conduct of Business and Mortgage Sales

Regulated mortgage contracts 11.25

In July 1999 the Treasury invited public consultation in respect of mortgage selling. In January the following year it published its consideration of the responses received, identifying four key areas of 'consumer detriment' in relation to mortgages: poor information given to mortgage applicants and mortgagees; disadvantageous product features; gaps in regulatory control; and unsatisfactory treatment of arrears by providers. These concerns resulted in an announcement in January 2000 that mortgage lending and administration of mortgages would be brought within regulatory control. By December 2001 these proposals had been extended to include regulatory control over advising upon and arranging mortgages.

Approximately 40% of UK households are held in mortgage. The provision of mortgage mediation services accordingly forms a significant sector of the financial market. This section, concerned with conduct of business issues, will look at the broad obligations and requirements now attaching to the mortgage selling process. The mortgages affected by the following are all 'regulated mortgage contracts' (the definition of which is considered in CHAPTER 2) entered into on or after 31 October 2004. The detailed conduct of business requirements relevant to lenders, intermediaries and those responsible for mortgage administration are to be found in the MCOB section of the FSA Handbook.

Services offered 11.26

A firm whose business includes making personal recommendations or giving personalised information to a customer about entering into or varying a regulated mortgage contract must organise its affairs so as to operate at one of three identified 'service levels. The firm must accordingly ensure the customer is aware as to whether the scope of the service offered relates to:

- the whole mortgage market;

- a limited number of members within the market; or
- a single lender.

If the level of service offered is changed, the firm must notify the customer of the change and any implications arising therefrom (eg a consequential change to any charging structure for the service given).

Advised and non-advised sales 11.27

The FSA characterises mortgage sales as either 'advised sales' or 'non-advised sales'. An advised sale covers cases where advice is given on the merits of entering into or varying a particular mortgage; non-advised sales are those representing the product of scripted questions used to narrow down the selection of mortgages so as to enable the customer to make an informed decision as to the choice of product based on the answers to questions posed. The process may be compared with that involved in the use of decision trees in respect of the sale of stakeholder pensions (see 11.22 above).

In either case, the firm must ensure the customer is made aware of the scope of the service offered ie in particular whether it relates to the whole of market or a limited number of lenders. If a whole of market service is offered then the firm must ensure it has an adequate knowledge of the mortgage market as a whole and has considered a sufficiently large number of regulated mortgage contracts generally available within the market. A whole of market service may be provided using a panel of lenders but the panel must be representative of the whole of market.

As explained earlier, advising on a regulated mortgage contract is a regulated activity; providing information about a regulated mortgage contract is not (although it may well be a step in arranging or bringing about a regulated mortgage contract). It is accordingly crucially important for firms conducting non-advised sales to ensure that the process of providing customer information does not turn into the giving of regulated advice on a particular mortgage product. Rigid adherence to scripted questions will assist in ensuring the line is not crossed between the provision of information and the giving of advice. Firms will need to ensure staff are appropriately trained in the use of scripted questions and appropriately supervised to ensure they do not stray into advising on a particular product. There is always the danger, recognised by the FSA, that the provision of generic advice and the identification of a particular regulated mortgage contract in the course of the use of scripted questions may lead the customer to believe he is being advised on how to proceed. In considering whether a resulting sale should be characterised as an advised or non-advised sale, the FSA accordingly will look at both the process and result of the scripted questions as a whole.

Relevant pointers include statements made by the mortgage intermediary as to the scope of service offered; whether any opinion has been offered rather than the provision of factual data; and whether the process was limited to helping the borrower to make a product selection himself by reference to particular product features he regards as important.

Importantly, if it is apparent that the process is leading a customer to select a mortgage which the firm knows or ought to appreciate is unsuitable then a sale should not be arranged but rather the customer recommended to seek advice ie to step up to the higher level advised sale scope of service.

Independence 11.28

Where a firm wishes to hold itself out as an independent intermediary firm, it must provide a whole of market service and permit its customer to pay a fee for the provision of that service. The fee option may be supplemented, however, with other methods of payment including a combination of fee and commission.

Initial disclosure document 11.29

A feature of the new regime is the initial disclosure document (IDD). Where contact is made with a customer so that the firm anticipates giving personalised information or advice on regulated mortgage contract, an initial disclosure document must be provided. The document headed 'Key Facts [using the FSA's key facts logo] About Our Mortgage Services' must contain the following information:

- Information as to the role of the FSA as the independent watchdog regulating financial services and the purpose of the initial disclosure document (IDD).

- Information as to the scope of the different service levels available; if the scope of service is limited to a number of lenders, the customer must be informed of his right to request a list of the lenders on whose behalf the firm offers mortgages.

- Information as to the level of service in fact being offered to the particular customer.

- Information as to whether the customer will be paying a fee or whether the transaction will be commission remunerated.

- Information as to whether any fees will be refundable.

- Information as to whether the firm is directly authorised by the FSA or acting as an appointed representative of another firm.

- Information as to how the customer may register a complaint.

- Confirmation that the Financial Services Compensation Scheme will apply to the transaction (including details as to the level of protection provided).

Where the initial contact with the customer is made by telephone, the following specific information must be provided during the course of the telephone call:

- The name of the firm and the purpose of the call if initiated by the firm.
- The scope of the different service levels available.
- If the firm is providing the 'limited number of lenders' service, the fact that the customer may request a list of lenders used.
- Whether the firm provides advice (within its identified scope of service).
- The fact that the above information will be provided in writing in the form of the IDD within five business days of the telephone call.

Conduct of business and advised sales   11.30

As noted above, advised sales involve the making of a personal recommendation to a customer to buy, sell or vary a regulated mortgage contract. There are three elements to the making of a personal recommendation. In short, the advice must

- relate to the merits of the borrower entering into or varying the terms of a regulated mortgage contract;
- relate to a specific mortgage; and
- be given to a specific person qua borrower or potential borrower.

In the case of advised sales the overarching conduct of business requirement is that the mortgage product recommended is suitable to the customer. This involves three distinct elements:

- a requirement that the mortgage is affordable to the customer;
- a requirement that the contract is appropriate to the particular customer's needs and circumstances;
- a requirement that the contract is the most suitable of those available within the firm's scope of service.

Distinct conduct of business requirements apply in relation to sales of lifetime mortgages discussed at 11.34 to 11.35 below.

Affordability 11.31

Making sure the recommended product is affordable involves advising the customer as to the current interest rates and pointing that these may rise in the future; assessing the borrower's present and future income and resources; pointing out any increase in servicing costs which may come about after the expiry of eg any initial discount period. If the borrower is proposing to consolidate other debts within the proposed mortgage, the adviser must take into account the cost to the borrower of increasing the term of any consolidated debt; in addition, the adviser should consider whether it is appropriate for the borrower to provide security for previously unsecured indebtedness and/or whether it would be more appropriate for the customer to consider negotiating some alternative arrangement with his creditors.

Appropriate to the customer's needs and circumstances 11.32

This aspect of suitability includes giving due consideration to the following:

- Eligibility criteria eg does the value of the loan offered meet the customer's need for a particular sum?

- Mortgage type ie would the customer's interests be best addressed by an interest only mortgage, a repayment mortgage, or some combination of each?

- Does the mortgage offer satisfy any identified customer preferences eg for the length of term, any initial discount period, any fixed interest period and opportunity for payment holidays?

- Does the offer meet the customer's intentions for the future eg will it permit early repayment(s) and, if so, on what terms?

Where the scope of service is not whole of market but limited to a number of lenders, the identification of a suitable product is not satisfied by offering the best nearest match from the range available. The firm will be expected to be aware of the mortgage products generally available in the market and if the only product available from a limited number of lenders in whose products it deals is not suitable then no product should be offered. Importantly, however, pricing is not necessarily the sole determinant of suitability. A mortgage adviser may make a personal recommendation based on factors other than the price eg speed and quality of service of different lenders, their individual policies on further advances, and in respect of capital repayments or other underwriting issues. Nonetheless, the adviser will still be required to be able to demonstrate that the product selected was the most suitable for the customer by reference to an objective assessment of all relevant criteria.

Key facts illustrations 11.33

Before a customer submits an application for a particular regulated mortgage contract, he must now be provided with a document entitled 'Key Features Illustration' (KFI) (unless this has already been given to him). It should be provided upon the occasion of the making of a personal recommendation (or within five days if the recommendation is made by telephone). It should also be provided on the occasion the firm either provides written information specific to the amount of the loan the customer wishes to borrow by reference to a particular regulated mortgage contract or where the customer requests written information which is specific to the amount he desires to borrow on a particular regulated mortgage contract.

The content of this prescribed disclosure document must be personalised to reflect:

- the specific mortgage contract in question;
- the amount of the borrowing;
- the price/value of the property;
- the term of the mortgage; and
- whether it is a repayment or interest only mortgage (or a combination of each).

A template is provided indicating the detailed content requirements in annex 1R to MCOB5. The purpose of the document is to facilitate comparison between products. The numerical components to the illustration must accordingly be accurate (subject to certain tolerance levels permitted in respect of certain figures). In respect of (for example) the total amount payable under the mortgage, the amount payable for every £1 borrowed and the instalment amounts the KFI must be accurate to a tolerance level of the higher of 1% and £1 below the actual figures to be charged by the lender in respect of the foregoing. The APR may not be understated by more than 0.1%. It is permissible to estimate amounts for conveyancing fees and insurance premiums. If the customer will be required to take out a tied product with the regulated mortgage contract either the KFI should contain an accurate quotation or a reasonable estimate of the premium or the adviser must furnish the customer with an accurate quotation as soon as possible after the mortgage application is submitted (and in good time before an offer is made). The customer may then exercise a right to withdraw the application within seven days of receipt of an accurate quotation.

Conduct of business and lifetime mortgages 11.34

For the purposes of this book, 'lifetime mortgages' may be taken to mean regulated mortgage contracts under which the mortgage is restricted to older

11.34 *Conduct Of Business*

customers above a specified age where the lender may or may not specify a mortgage term but will not seek full repayment of the loan until the occurrence of the death of a customer, the departure from or sale of the mortgaged home or where the lender exercises some legal right to take possession under the terms of the contract; further, whilst the customer continues to occupy the mortgaged property as his main residence, the lifetime mortgage will not require repayment of the capital advance in full.

These products are considered by the FSA to involve particular risks in that they are typically entered into by elderly persons, short of income or capital and therefore in need of a degree of consumer protection. This is particularly so given the mis-selling scandal in relation to certain equity release schemes sold in the 1980s.

Lifetime mortgages may be sold by way of advised sales and non-advised sales (see 11.27 above). Although in neither instance is the mortgage adviser required to furnish the client(s) with a suitability letter, there are strict suitability requirements which will need to be satisfied to ensure a complaint sale of such a product. The relevant stages are as follows:

- Stage 1 – An assessment of product suitability by reference to the criterion of affordability.

- Stage 2 – A consideration of the types of mortgage which would meet the customer's needs.

- Stage 3 – Recommendation of a particular mortgage that is appropriate.

In considering suitability the mortgage adviser must be satisfied that:

- The benefits to his customer of entering into a lifetime mortgage outweigh any adverse consequences (for example a loss of means tested benefits).

- Alternative methods of raising funds are less suitable than a lifetime mortgage; alternative sources of money to consider will include the provision of local authority grants and home reversion schemes; in particular, a comparison must be made with the latter form of equity release.

- The regulated lifetime contract proposed is the most suitable able to be offered within the scope of the service the mortgage adviser is able to provide (whether whole of market or limited to particular lenders).

- The product is appropriate to the needs, objectives and circumstances of the customer; this will include weighing alternative home reversion schemes against the product taking into account the amount of the borrower's need for capital, his estate planning intentions, health and life expectancy.

In relation to non-advised sales care must be taken to ensure the scripted questions assist the customer to decide for himself whether a lifetime mortgage would be suitable. This will include questions about alternative methods of raising money and whether the prospective elderly borrower has ascertained what the impact of an advance would be on his entitlement to state benefits or fiscal status.

Disclosure requirements 11.35

Similar requirements for a standardised IDD and pre-sale Key Facts Illustration document as described at 11.29 and 11.33 above apply.

Insurance: Conduct Of Business

Earlier regulation 11.36

The *Insurance Brokers (Registration) Act 1977* provided for the registration of brokers and for the regulation of professional standards. Immediately prior to FSA regulation the advising and selling standards applicable to insurance brokers were set out in a Code of Conduct approved under the 1977 Act in November 1994. The text of the Code appeared as a schedule to the *Insurance Brokers Registration Council (Code of Conduct) Approval Order 1994* (SI 1994 No. 2569). The object of the Code was expressed as being 'to establish a recognised standard of professional conduct to which all insurance brokers should, in the interests of the public and in the performance of their duties, conform.' The Code was not, however, an exhaustive or all-embracing regime. It recited in broad terms eight key high level standards comprising requirements to:

- Conduct business with utmost good faith and integrity.
- Do everything possible to satisfy the requirements of clients, including a duty to place the interests of clients 'before all other considerations' save where such a designated service to an individual client would result in a lack of proper regard for others.
- Do nothing directly or indirectly which would compromise or impair 'the good repute of insurance brokers or the insurance broking profession'.
- Make no statements in the course of advertising any product or business service which was 'misleading or extravagant'.
- Conduct their relationship with their professional body (the Insurance Brokers Registration Council) with propriety.
- 'Organise and control the internal affairs of their insurance broking business in a responsible manner and where staff are employed ensure that they are competent, suitable and under adequate day-to-day supervision by a registered insurance broker'.

- Be familiar with and mindful of guidance as to professional conduct contained in any practice notes issued or endorsed by the council.
- Conduct relevant investment business in compliance with the (then) SIB Statements of Principle.

The reader will recognise in the above collection of duties and responsibilities many concepts which now find similar expression in the Statements of Principle for Businesses and Code of Conduct for Approved Persons.

The former Code gave a number of specific examples of the application of these broad Statements of Principle. These included:

- A requirement that brokers 'shall provide advice objectively and independently in the best interests of the client'.
- Certain specific duties relating to the disclosure of commission, the identification of any conflict(s) of interest and a responsibility to ensure 'true, fair and complete' disclosure of facts material to an insurance risk on the part of their client.
- A duty to 'explain to the client the differences in and the relevant costs of the principal types of insurance, relevant investment business or, if appropriate, any other investments which in the opinion of the insurance broker would suit the client's needs ...'
- In satisfying the requirements of a client, brokers were likewise obliged to 'take care not to limit unduly the number of insurers they are able to use.'
- A responsibility to make customers aware of the Code of Conduct and the right to complain where dissatisfied with a service to the Insurance Brokers Registration Council (IBRC).

The detail of the former regime is not set out exhaustively above. The new regime governing 'advising and selling standards' is now, however, to be found in Chapter 4 of ICOB. Many of the former provisions remain but the conduct of business regime now follows closely the rules relating to advice on and sale of mortgage products discussed above.

The scheme and content of the new regime is briefly summarised below. The new rules are designed principally with a consumer protection objective in mind – both in terms of ensuring clarity as to the scope of the service being offered by an insurance intermediary and providing for appropriate disclosure of product features and securing the sale of suitable products meeting individual customers needs.

Retail customer transactions

The first key requirement relates to status disclosure. Before concluding a non-investment insurance contract the insurance intermediary must provide certain prescribed information to the customer in a 'durable medium'. The information may, however, be provided (initially) orally if the customer so requests or requires immediate insurance cover; in the case of telephone sales more limited information may be given in the course of the call providing the customer gives express consent: in either of the foregoing instances, however, the full information must be forwarded in a durable medium immediately after the conclusion of any contract.

The initial disclosure document must contain the following information:

- The name and address of the insurance intermediary.
- The insurance intermediary's statutory status.
- A statement that the name, address and status may be checked on the FSA's Register by visiting its website or contacting the FSA by telephone.
- Unless the intermediary is an insurer, details of any holding, direct or indirect, that the intermediary has which represents more than 10% of the voting rights or of the capital in an insurance undertaking.
- Unless the intermediary is an insurer, details of any holding, direct or indirect, that an insurance undertaking or parent of an insurance undertaking which represents more than 10% of the voting rights or of the capital in the insurance intermediary.
- In relation to non-investment insurance contracts, whether the intermediary has provided or will provide advice or information:

    (a)   on the basis of a fair analysis of the markets;
    (b)   from a limited number of insurance undertakings; or
    (c)   from a single insurance undertaking (in the case of (b) or (c), the intermediary must also disclose whether it is contractually obliged to conduct insurance mediation activity in this way).

- The customer must be informed that if the contract provided has not been selected on the basis of a fair analysis of the market, he can request a copy of a list of the insurance undertakings the intermediary selects from or deals with in relation to the contract provided.
- Information about how to complain to the insurance intermediary and that complaints may subsequently be referred to the Financial Ombudsman Service (or any other applicable named complaints scheme).
- That the customer may be entitled to compensation from the compensation scheme in the event that the intermediary proved unable to meet its liabilities.

It will be immediately apparent from the above that the scope of service provisions are similar to those relating to advice on and/or sale of mortgage products. Intermediaries may choose to offer advice or arrange products on the basis of a fair analysis of the market, from a limited number of insurance undertakings or from a single insurance undertaking. Where a fair analysis of the market service is offered the intermediary must ensure that he has considered a sufficiently large number of non-investment insurance contracts available in the relevant sector(s) and that such consideration as is given is based on criteria reflecting an adequate knowledge of non-investment insurance contracts in those relevant market sectors. This service may be provided by reliance on panels of insurance undertakings but the intermediary must ensure that the panels are sufficiently wide and representative as to enable him to comply with the above requirement.

Where a limited or single insurance undertaking service is provided, the intermediary must maintain and keep up to date for each type of non-investment insurance contract it deals with a list of the insurance undertakings it selects from or deals with. A copy of the list must be provided to a customer on request.

The above status disclosure requirements do not need to be complied with afresh when renewing or amending a contract of insurance provided the initial disclosure duty was complied with and the information then given remains up to date at the time of renewal.

Suitability

Where the insurance intermediary makes a personal recommendation to a customer to buy or sell a non-investment insurance contract he must take reasonable steps to ensure that the product is suitable for the customer's demands and needs based on the scope of the service disclosed in the IDD. In considering the customer's demands and needs the intermediary must:

- seek such information about the customer's circumstances and objectives as might reasonably be expected to be relevant to the identification by the intermediary of the customer's requirements;

- pay regard to any relevant details about the customer readily available and accessible to him eg in respect of other insurance contracts already advised upon;

- explain to the customer his duty to disclose all circumstances material to the insurance cover sought or being arranged and the consequences of any failure to make such disclosure: this obligation applies *before* the non-investment insurance contract commences *and* throughout the duration of the contract.

In assessing whether a particular non-investment insurance contract is suitable to meet a customer's demands and needs the intermediary is required specifically to take into account *at least* the following:

- whether the level of cover is sufficient for the risks the customer wishes to insure;
- (where relevant) the cost of the contract; and
- the relevance of any exclusions, excesses, limitations or conditions in the insurance contract.

Having enquired into and assessed the customer's needs, the intermediary is then obliged *before* the conclusion of the contract to provide to the customer a statement setting out his demands and needs, which confirms whether the intermediary has personally recommended the particular contract in question and, if a personal recommendation has been made, explaining the reasons for it. This statement must be provided in a durable medium and contain appropriate detail to reflect the complexity of the contract of insurance proposed.

Where the transaction is a non-advised sale the statement of demands and needs will be provided in a modified form reflecting the absence of a personal recommendation. Thus it would be possible to produce a demands and needs statement in the product documentation itself by identifying in the relevant documentation that the particular product would meet the particular demands and needs of those wishing to ensure that eg 'the veterinary needs of their pet are met now and in the future' to cite an example given in the guidance to ICOB.

Where a personal recommendation is made, triggering the requirement for a demands and needs statement specific to the individual in question, the statement should:

- be written in simple, plain English and avoid technical terms;
- contain a clear and concise message, explaining why the personal recommendation was regarded as suitable, having regard to the customer's demands and needs; the link between the customer's demands and needs and the reason(s) for the recommendation must accordingly be clear; and
- identify why a particular insurance undertaking has been recommended where the intermediary offers contracts from more than one provider eg because the recommended provider is keener on price.

Record keeping 11.39

In the case of retail customers the intermediary must then retain a copy of the above statement of demands and needs for a minimum period of three years from the date on which the personal recommendation is made.

Excessive charges 11.40

It is a requirement that an insurance intermediary must ensure its charges to a retail customer are not excessive. As with charges made in respect of arranging and advising on mortgage products, the question as to whether a charge is excessive must take into account:

- the amount of the charge compared with that rendered for the provision of similar services or products by others in the market;
- whether the charge in question may be viewed as an abuse of the trust the retail customer reposes in the intermediary; and
- the nature and extent of the disclosure of the charge to the customer.

The above rule does not apply to premiums but does cover fees.

Commercial customers 11.41

In respect of commercial customers the rules, obligations and duties described above are modified. Firstly, the status disclosure requirement does not apply to an insurance intermediary which is an insurer when dealing with a commercial customer; secondly, an insurance intermediary which is an insurer does not need to provide a statement of demands and needs unless the insurer makes a personal recommendation to the commercial customer; thirdly, there is a specific commission disclosure for commercial customers regime which is dis-applied where the intermediary is an insurer. Where the rule applies, however, the intermediary must before the conclusion of a non-investment insurance contract provide to any commercial customer who asks prompt disclosure of the commission he and any associate of his receives in connection with the non-investment insurance contract in question in cash terms and in a durable medium. Fourthly, the ban of unsolicited services in relation to non-investment insurance contracts that are distance contracts applicable in respect of retail customers does not apply to commercial customers.

Chapter 12
Financial Promotions

Background 12.1

Under the *Financial Services and Markets Act 2000* (*FSMA 2000*) regime there is now a unified approach to the regulation of financial promotions. The manner in which financial products are marketed represents an area of (potentially) great risk. The publication of misleading advertising material could involve a breach of Principle 7 of the Principles for Businesses, requiring firms to 'communicate information to [clients] in a way which is clear, fair and not misleading'; clients who enter into transactions on the basis of inaccurate product literature may well pursue complaints (particularly if loss results) by way of a firm's complaints machinery and/or through the Financial Ombudsman Service and/or the Courts. Further, the publication of (for example) a misleading forecast which is known to be false will involve the commission of a criminal offence. Likewise, the issuing of an unlawful financial promotion also attracts potential criminal penalties; agreements entered into as a result of such unlawful communications are also unenforceable unless a Court orders otherwise. It is accordingly important to have a basic understanding of the financial promotions regime.

General Restriction 12.2

The *FSMA 2000* imposes a blanket restriction on financial promotions, to which exceptions are then created. The starting point is that a person 'must not, in the course of business, communicate an invitation or inducement to engage in investment activity.' As noted above, a breach of this restriction amounts to a criminal offence and renders agreement entered into in pursuance of any such unlawful 'invitation or inducement' prima facie unenforceable. Given the importance of this general restriction it is appropriate to spend a few moments looking at the key ingredients.

In the course of business 12.3

To amount to a communication made 'in the course of business', it is necessary for there to be some commercial interest on the part of the communicator. The business in question, however, need not be concerned with the conduct of regulated activities. The requirement is meant to exclude eg social communications such as investment tips exchanged between friends or members of the family. Whether a communication arises in the course of business will, however, be fact sensitive in each instance. Thus, in examples given by the FSA, requests for start-up capital to get a corporate business under way may not amount to communications in the course of business; they are preparatory to setting up a business: conversely, offers to dispose of the shares in a subsidiary by a holding company will amount to a communication in the course of business notwithstanding that the purpose of the exercise is to get rid of the ownership of the business by the holding company.

Invitation or inducement? 12.4

These terms are not defined and are accordingly required to be given their ordinary and natural meaning. An 'invitation' may accordingly range from a request to positive soliciting; 'inducement' probably connotes anything between 'bringing about' a state of affairs or actively persuading a person to embark upon a particular transaction. In FSA Guidance it is suggested that an objective test must be applied ie whether the man on the top of the omnibus would consider that in all the circumstances in which the communication is made the communicator was intending that the communication 'persuade or incite' the recipient to engage in investment activity and that the communication was reasonably capable of being appropriate to persuade or incite such conduct.

Engaging in investment activity 12.5

Engaging in investment activity means entering or offering to enter into an agreement such as to amount to a controlled activity or exercising some right conferred by a controlled investment (see 12.6 below) to acquire, dispose of, underwrite or convert a controlled investment. The relevant communication, if it amounts to a financial promotion must accordingly relate in some way to a controlled investment.

Controlled investments 12.6

Controlled investments are largely similar to regulated investments but are separately defined in the *Financial Services and Markets Act 2000 (Financial Promotion) Order 2001 (SI 2001 No 2633)*. Thus, controlled investments include:

- rights under a contract of insurance;
- most kinds of shares or stock;

- instruments creating or acknowledging indebtedness such as debentures and debenture stock, loan stock, bonds and certificates of deposit; excluded from the foregoing, however, are debt instruments created in respect of borrowing to defray the cost of supply of goods or services, a cheque, bill of exchange, banker's draft or letter of credit (other than a bill of exchange accepted by a banker, a bank note, a statement showing a balance on a current, deposit or saving account, a lease or other disposition of property, a heritable security and a contract of insurance);

- loan stock, bonds and other debt instruments issued by or on behalf of a government, local authority or international organisation (with the exception of the debt instruments listed in brackets above along, in this case, instruments relating to deposits with the National Savings Bank and money raised under the *National Loans Act 1968*);

- warrants and other instruments entitling the holder to subscribe for any of the controlled investments mentioned above (subject to the exception indicated in brackets);

- certain instruments conferring contractual or property rights;

- units in collective investment schemes;

- rights under stakeholder pension schemes;

- certain categories of option;

- futures (save where the rights under the contract for the sale of the commodity or property in question is made for commercial and not investment purposes);

- certain contracts for differences;

- Lloyd's syndicate membership and the underwriting capacity of a Lloyd's syndicate;

- rights under a qualifying funeral plan contract;

- rights under an agreement for qualifying credit;

- any right to or interest in any of the above (save for interests under the trusts of an occupational pension scheme, any right or interest acquired as a result of entering into a funeral plan contract and any right to or interest in rights under an agreement for qualifying credit).

Controlled activities 12.7

Again, these largely follow the scheme of regulated activities. They are, however, separately defined in the *Financial Services and Markets Act 2000 (Financial Promotion) Order 2001 (SI 2001 No 2633)*. They include the following:

- accepting deposits;

- effecting and carrying out most kinds of insurance contracts;
- dealing in securities and contractually based investments (save where the activity comprises the acceptance of an instrument creating or acknowledging indebtedness in respect of any loan, credit, guarantee or other similar financial accommodation or assurance;
- arranging deals in investments;
- managing investments;
- safeguarding and administering investments;
- advising on investments;
- advising on syndicate participation at Lloyd's;
- providing funeral plan contracts;
- providing, arranging and advising on qualifying credit;
- agreeing to carry on any of the above 'controlled activities.'

Dis-Application of General Restriction

Having set out the blanket ban on communicating any invitation or inducement to engage in investment activity (where it relates to any controlled investment or controlled activity) the ban is dis-applied in respect of all authorised persons and in relation to the content of any communication which is approved by an authorised person for the purpose of the restriction being dis-applied. It is accordingly important that if any financial promotion is to be passed on by a recipient from an authorised person, the latter should specifically approve it for that purpose. Thus, in guidance given by the FSA, a solicitor, who is an authorised person, may approve a financial promotion from the point of view of considering its legality; that would not be sufficient of itself, however, to amount to an approval of the financial promotion for the purposes of unrestricted further dissemination.

Real time and non-real time financial promotions

The FSMA 2000 financial promotion regime also distinguishes between 'real time' and 'non-real time' financial promotions. The distinction is particularly important in relation to further exceptions from the application of the general restriction provided for in the *Financial Services and Markets Act 2000 (Financial Promotion) Order 2001 (SI 2001 No 2633)*.

A 'real time communication' is taken to refer to any communication made in the course of a personal visit, telephone conversation or other interactive dialogue. A 'non-real time communication' is then simply defined as any communication which does not fall within this definition. Certain factors are identified, however, as indicating that the relevant communication is non-real time. These are that the communication is:

- made to or directed at more than one recipient in identical terms;
- made or directed by way of a system which in the normal course constitutes or creates a record of the communication which is available to the recipient to refer to at a later time;
- made or directed by way of a system which in the normal course does not enable or require the recipient to respond immediately to it.

The definitions of 'communication' and 'communicate' are very wide. A communication may refer to anything addressed whether orally or in legible form to a particular person (whether it is contained in a telephone call or letter); 'communicate' is expressed to include 'causing a communication to be made or directed.'

Solicited and unsolicited communications 12.10

For the purposes of the FSA financial promotions regime, a real time communication is solicited if it is made in the course of a personal visit, telephone call or other interactive dialogue if the call, visit or dialogue was initiated by the recipient of the communication or takes place in response to his request for it. A person is not, however, to be treated as having requested a call, visit or dialogue simply because he fails to indicate he does not wish to receive any such approach nor merely as a result of him agreeing to standard terms that state that such visits, calls or dialogues will take place unless the person concerned has indicated clearly that he is willing for them to occur.

A real time communication is unsolicited whenever it does not fall within the above description of a solicited real time communication.

Exemptions 12.11

The *Financial Services and Markets Act 2000 (Financial Promotion) Order 2001* (SI 2001 No 2633) provides a number of general exemptions as follows:

- a customer seeking information about a controlled investment who solicits or initiates the communication;
- follow-up non-real time communications and solicited real time communications, provided these occur within 12 months of an original exempt communication;
- introductions to authorised or exempt persons provided that the introducer is not a close relative of nor a member of the same group as the person to whom the introduction is made, does not receive from anyone

other than the recipient a pecuniary reward or other benefit for making the introduction and it is clear that the recipient, in his capacity as an investor, is not seeking and has not sought advice from the introducer as to the merits of engaging in investment activity;

- communications by exempt persons;
- generic promotions;
- mere conduits ie communications in the course of a business whose principal purpose is the transmission or receipt of material provided by others in circumstances where the content of the communication is devised by another person and the nature of the service is such that he does not select, modify or otherwise exercise control over the content of the communication prior to its transmission or receipt;
- electronic commerce communications: mere conduits, caching and hosting;
- communications directed only to investment professionals;
- communications by journalists;
- incoming electronic commerce communications; and
- promotion broadcasts by company directors.

Specific exemptions 12.12

The *Financial Services and Markets Act 2000 (Financial Promotion) Order 2001 (SI 2001 No 2633), Pt V* provides certain specific exemptions in respect of deposit taking and general insurance business. *Part VI* of the Order identifies further specific exemptions in respect of particular controlled activities. Broadly, the particular exemptions apply to the controlled activities of effecting and carrying out contracts of insurance along with dealing in securities and contractually based investments, arranging and managing deals in investments, safeguarding and administering investments, advising on investments and syndicate participation at Lloyd's, providing funeral plan contracts, providing, arranging and advising on qualifying credit. With particular exceptions, the exemptions provided by *Pt VI* are as follows:

- One-off non-real time communications and solicited real time communications, one-off unsolicited real time communications provided the communicator believes on reasonable grounds the recipient understands the risks associated with engaging in the investment activity to which the communication relates and could be expected to contact the communicator in relation to the relevant investment activity.
- Certain real time communications involving introductions in connection with qualifying credit.
- Communications required or authorised by enactments.

- Solicited real time communications, non-real time and unsolicited real time communications to previously overseas customers by overseas communicators.
- Unsolicited real time communications to knowledgeable customers by overseas communicators.
- Non-real time or solicited real time communications relating to controlled investments by any government, local authority, international organisation and certain banks.
- Non-real time or solicited real time communications by industrial and provident societies relating to debentures, debenture stock, loan stock, bonds, certificates of deposit and other instruments creating or acknowledging indebtedness.
- Non-real time or solicited real time communications by nationals of EEA states other than the UK which satisfy FSA Rules relating to such communications.
- Non-real time or solicited real time communications about facilities provided by financial markets which do not identify (directly or indirectly) any particular investment or any particular person through whom transactions on the market may be effected.
- Persons in the business of placing promotional material.
- Communications by participators in joint enterprises to each other for the purpose of the enterprise.
- Non-real time or solicited real time communications between operators and participants of recognised collective investment schemes.
- Non-real time or solicited real time communications in respect of bearer instruments required or permitted by market rules.
- Non-real time or solicited real time communications between limited companies (other than an open-ended investment company) and a creditor or member of the company or undertaking in the same group relating to shares or stock, debentures, debenture stock, loan stock, bonds, certificates of deposit and other instruments creating or acknowledging indebtedness (including warrants and other instruments in respect of the foregoing and certificates or instruments conferring contractual or property rights in respect thereof);
- Non-real time or solicited real time communications by open-ended investment companies in respect of certain investments made to creditors or members of the relevant company (or otherwise entitled to certain rights in respect thereof).
- Communications between companies in the same group.
- Qualifying credit promotions to limited companies.
- Qualifying credit promotions directed at limited companies.

- Promotions communicated limited to persons reasonably believed to carry on the business of dissemination of information.

High net worth individuals, companies, unincorporated associations and sophisticated investors 12.13

The next group of exemptions is novel. First, a category of 'high net worth individuals' is created, which refers to individuals satisfying the following criteria:

- The individual in question has signed a certificate containing prescribed wording identifying himself as a 'high net worth individual'. The certificate must be verified with the signature of that person's accountant or employer.

- The individual must be certified as being in receipt of an annual income in excess of £100,000 or hold net assets to a value of £250,000 (excluding a primary residence and any rights under a qualifying contract of insurance or retirement, death and employment service termination).

- Each communication must also accompanied by an indication of prescribed factors, including that the promotion is exempt from the general restriction and has accordingly not been approved by an authorised person so that any reliance on it for the purpose of engaging in investment activity may expose the individual to a significant risk of losing all of the property.

This exemption also only applies in respect of particular categories of investment being (broadly) stocks and shares, debentures and other similar debt instruments in unlisted companies warrants and other certificates and instruments relating to the foregoing and options, futures and contracts for differences.

Secondly, a similar exemption is offered in respect of financial promotions directed at high net worth companies with a called-up share capital net assets of not less than £500,000 in the case of a company with more than 20 members or otherwise £5m; unincorporated associations or partnerships with net assets not less than £5m are included, as are trustees of high value trusts with assets exceeding £10m. In this instance the communication must also make plain that it is only directed at the foregoing category of recipient and that any other person ought not to act upon it; the communicator must also have in place proper systems and procedures to prevent recipients not falling within the following categories receiving it.

The companies, unincorporated associations and trustees of high value trusts must satisfy the above descriptions at the time of the communication; in the case of certified high net worth individuals, the recipient must likewise fall within the applicable definition at the time of the communication, but in this instance proof is available in the form of the certificate of high net worth which is valid, however, only for a 12-month period.

Thirdly, promotions are exempted to the extent of communications to 'certified sophisticated investors'. The regime here is similar to that relating to high net worth individuals. A certificate, valid for 12 months, is required to be signed by the recipient, confirming amongst other things that he accepts that the contents of any promotion may not have been approved by an authorised person and that he is aware it is open to him to seek advice from someone specialising in advising on the relevant kind of investment. He must also identify in the certificate the type of investments in respect of which an appropriate level of sophistication is claimed. The promotion, when communicated, must also be accompanied by similar indications and warnings as are required to accompany financial promotions made to high net worth individuals. So far as the sophisticated investor certificate is concerned, this must also be verified by the signature of an authorised person confirming that the investor is sufficiently knowledgeable to understand the risks associated with the description of investments to which it relates; here, the authorised persons signed endorsement is valid for a period of three years.

Finally, non-real time or solicited real time communications made to associations of the above are also exempt providing these relate only to investments which provide that a person cannot incur a liability for obligation to pay or contribute more than permitted by way of investment.

Further specific exemptions 12.14

The *Financial Services and Markets Act 2000 (Financial Promotion) Order 2001* (SI 2001 No 2633) then goes on to provide for yet further specific exemptions, which may be briefly listed as follows:

- Non-real time or solicited real time communications in respect of corporate common interest groups relating to stocks and shares, debentures and similar debt instruments.
- Financial promotions between settlors, trustees or personal representatives and fellow Trustees and personal representatives made for the purposes of the trust or Estate.
- Communications between settlors, trustees and personal representatives to beneficiaries of whose assets they have charge provided the communication relates to the management or distribution of the trust fund or estate.
- Real time communications (whether solicited or not) made by members of designated professional bodies to a recipient who has, prior to the

communication, being made, engaged the firm to provide professional services; a further exemption applies to non-real time communications made by members of such bodies setting out limited information as to a range of investment services able to be offered to clients notwithstanding the absence of FSA authorisation: here, a prescribed form of wording must be followed.

Transaction facilitation exemptions 12.15

Recognising that the circumstances in which a communication may amount to a financial promotion and the need to facilitate common administrative and other business activity, the *Financial Services and Markets Act 2000 (Financial Promotion) Order 2001 (SI 2001 No 2633)* also provides a series of exemptions which may be described under the heading of 'transaction facilitation exemptions'. Very briefly these relate to:

- Communications in respect of a report by the Parliamentary Commission for Administration.

- Communications received by a person in a publication as a result of the recipient himself placing an advertisement therein.

- Communications dealing with shares of management companies required by any person in connection with the acquisition of an interest in the managed premises.

- Subject to detailed provisions, communications by limited companies (other than an open-ended investment company) by way of the content of annual accounts and directors' reports.

- Promotions in respect of employee share schemes.

- Non-real time or solicited real time communications made by suppliers of goods and services in connection with a related sale or supply (other than qualifying contracts of insurance or units in collective investment schemes).

- Communications relating to the sale of limited companies.

- Certain communications arising in connection with the takeover of relevant unlisted companies.

- Promotions required or permitted by market rules, including any communication which a relevant EEA market requires before an investment can be admitted to trading on that market.

- Certain promotions in respect of listing applications and/or included in listing particulars and prospectus's relating to public offers of unlisted securities.

Territorial scope 12.16

Where a communication originates outside the UK, the restriction on financial promotions is dis-applied provided the communication is not 'capable of having an effect in the United Kingdom.' In the case of an unsolicited real time communication the exemption requires that it is made from a place outside the UK and for the purposes of the business carried on extra-territorially. The following communications are deemed to be regarded as directed only at persons outside the UK:

- Communications accompanied by an indication that they are directed only at persons outside the UK and that they must not be acted upon by persons in the UK; further, such communications must also not be referred to in or directly accessible from any other communication made to a person or directed at persons in the UK by or on behalf of the communicator; there must also be in place proper systems and procedures to prevent recipients in the UK engaging in the investment activity to which the communication relates with the communicator, a close relative or a member of the same group.

- Communications which are not directly referred to in or directly accessible from any other communication made to a person or directed at persons in the UK provided (again) there are in place proper systems and procedures to prevent recipients in the UK engaging in the investment activity to which the communication relates with the communicator, a close relative or a member of the same group.

Where one only of the above characteristics applies to the communication, this may afford some evidence that it was not directed at persons in the UK; in the same category are communications included in any website, newspapers, journal, magazine or periodical publication which is principally accessed in or intended for a market outside the UK; communications in the course of a radio or television broadcast or telexed service transmitted principally for reception outside the UK are treated likewise.

Promotions and conduct of investment business 12.17

Chapter 3 of the Conduct of Business Rules and Guidance sets out the FSA duties and expectations of authorised firms in making or approving financial promotions. The Rules and Guidance follow the scheme and definitions of terms discussed above. The purpose of COB3 is to reinforce Principles 6 (treating customers fairly) and 7 (communications with clients).

Non-real time financial promotions 12.18

Any firm which makes or approves a non-real time financial promotion must take reasonable steps to ensure that it is 'clear, fair and not misleading.' The emphasis is on ensuring proper consideration and documentation of any such communication or approval of a promotion. In particular, the firm must take reasonable steps to ensure amongst other things that any statement of fact, promise or prediction is clear, fair and not misleading (and any relevant assumptions behind such statements are disclosed); the firm's resources and scale of activities must not be inaccurately described nor must any indication be falsely given as to the scarcity of any particular investment or service, the subject of the financial promotion. The firm must also take reasonable steps to ensure that its promotional purpose is not disguised or misrepresented.

Solicited and unsolicited real time financial promotions 12.19

Investment firms are largely prohibited from making any unsolicited real time financial promotion (save in respect of an established customer who envisages receiving such communications). Where the financial promotion has been solicited by the customer, the firm must (obviously) ensure that anything communicated is done so in a manner which is 'clear, fair and not misleading.' Further, the communication must take place at a time which is convenient to the customer and the firm must ensure all appropriate information is given, particularly relating to polarisation and status disclosure.

Direct offer financial promotions 12.20

Certain categories of controlled investment may not be the subject of a direct offer promotion unless the firm has adequate evidence that the proposed investment is suitable for the customer to whom the promotion is directed. The prohibited types of investment are:

- investments in broker funds;
- investments in unregulated collective investment schemes;
- directives; and
- warrants.

Permitted direct offer promotions 12.21

Where the controlled investment may be the subject of a direct offer financial promotion, the firm must nonetheless ensure:

- the promotion contains a prominent statement that it is being communicated or has been approved by a firm authorised by the FSA;

- the communication contains a prominent statement advising the customer that if he is in doubt as to the suitability of the proposal, he should contact the firm for advice or an independent financial adviser if the firm does not offer advice; and
- the promotion must also contain sufficient information so as to allow a customer to make some informed assessment of the investment being promoted (including full details of any charges and expenses to be met by the customer and of any commission or remuneration payable to a third party).

General Requirements 12.22

Finally, the following general requirements in respect of financial promotions should be borne in mind:

- those which involve a potential for increase or decrease in value must contain the standard warning to the effect that investments can go up or down and that past performance is no guide to future performance;
- where the promotion relates to a life policy, it must make clear which policy benefits are fixed (and which are not);
- the fiscal consequences of an investment must be adequately summarised (with a warning that taxation provisions can change); and
- where the investment is of a kind including cancellation or withdrawal rights, these must be described.

Index

References are to paragraph numbers.

A

Abbey Life Assurance
   Company Limited   10.16
Abbey National Plc   10.20
ABM AMRO Equities (UK)
   Limited (AAE)   10.14
accepting deposits
   regulated activity, as   2.5, 6
administering investments
   regulated activity, as   2.15
administration orders   5.19
Advertising Approval Officer   10.17
advice
   cost of   11.14
   regulated activity, as   2.19
agent
   dealing in investments as   2.10
appointed representatives
   monitoring   10.25–10.27
approved persons
   customer functions   3.29
   disciplining   5.16
   generally   1.3, 3.25
   prohibition orders   5.11, 10.29
   required functions   3.26
   significant influence
      functions   3.36, 3.37
   significant management
      functions   3.28
   Statements of Principle   1.3, 3.7, 3.30–3.37
     integrity   3.31
     internal organisation   1.4
     market conduct   3.33, 7.1
     organisation of business   3.35
     relations with Regulators   3.34
     risk management   3.36

approved persons – *contd*
   Statements of Principle – *contd*
     skill, care and diligence   3.32, 3.36
   system and control functions   3.27
   withdrawal of approval   5.10
arranging deals and
   investments
   regulated activity, as   2.11
authorisation
   adequacy of resources   3.23
   application   3.38
   approved persons *see*
      approved persons
   cancellation of permission   5.9
   close links, nature of   3.22
   conflicting directorships   3.39
   deemed authorised
      firms/persons   3.3
   delegation of responsibility   3.43
   determination   3.38
     time limit   3.38
   executive directors, standard
      of care   3.40
   exempt persons   3.4
   generally   1.3, 2.2, 3.1
   handbook design and
      terminology   3.53–3.54
   head office
     location of   3.21, 3.24
     outside EEA   3.24
   holding of competing offices   3.44
   incomplete applications   3.38
   legal status of applicant   3.20
   limitations and requirements   3.46, 5.9

   EEA firms with UK
      branch   3.48

Index

authorisation – *contd*
  limitations and requirements –
    contd
    EEA and Treaty firms   3.47
    handbook design and
      terminology   3.53–3.54
    systems and controls   3.10, 3.50–3.52
    top-up permissions   3.49
  non-executive directors   3.41
  Principles for Business *see*
    Principles for Business
  professions, members of   3.5
  refusal of   3.38
  scope of Part IV permission   3.6
  Secretary of State, grant by   1.3
  shadow directors   3.42
  SIB rulebook   1.3
  SRO rulebooks   1.3
  suitability of applicant   3.24
  systems and controls   3.10, 3.50–3.52
    approved person   3.27
    key requirements of SYSC   3.51
    specific SYSC rules   3.52
  threshold conditions   3.19
    adequate resources   3.23
    close links   3.22
    legal status   3.20
    location of head office   3.21
    suitability   3.24
  time limit for determination   3.38
  top-up permissions   3.49
  variation of permissions   5.9

B

Bank of Scotland (BoS)   10.18
bankruptcy orders   5.22
body corporate
  sale of   2.28
business risks *see* risk
  assessment framework

C

cancellation notice   11.15

Carr Sheppards Crosthwaite
  Limited   10.28
certified sophisticated investors   12.13
client agreements   11.8
client classification   11.4
  intermediate customers   11.7
  market counter-parties   11.7
  private customers   11.6
  purpose   11.5
collective investment scheme
  activities
  regulated activities, as   2.17
communications
  clients, with   3.14
  'in the course of business'   12.3
  real time communications   12.9
    solicited   12.10
    unsolicited   12.10
competence *see* training and
  competence
competing offices, holding of   3.44–3.45
complaints handling   3.53
  appointed person   9.5
  breaches of duty   9.5
  closing of complaint   9.9
  compliance failures   10.24
  data protection   9.5
  dealings with the
    complainant   9.5
  definition of 'complaint'   9.4
  eligible complainants   9.2, 9.14
  final response letter   9.5, 9.6
  Friends Provident Life and
    Pensions Limited   10.24
  investigation of complaint   9.5
  professional indemnity
    insurers, notifying   9.6
  records   9.8
  regulatory requirement   9.1
  reports   9.8
  terms of the complaint,
    understanding   9.5
  time scales   9.3
  two-stage procedures   9.7

Index

complaints handling – *contd*
  see also Financial Services
    Compensation Scheme;
    Financial Services
    Ombudsman
compliance
  growth of   1.4
  origins   1.4
compliance input supervision   6.3
compliance models   6.1–6.3
compliance output supervision   6.2
conduct of business
  best execution   11.17
  cancellation notice   11.15
  client agreements   11.8
  client classification   11.4
    intermediate customers   11.7
    market counter-parties   11.7
    private customers   11.6
    purpose   11.5
  Conduct of Business
    Sourcebook   11.3
  conflicts of interest   11.16
  cost of advice   11.14
  dealing and managing   11.16
  designated investment
    business   11.2
  execution-only transactions   11.10
  generally   1.4, 11.1
  insurance
    commercial customers   11.41
    earlier regulation   11.36
    excessive charges   11.40
    record keeping   11.39
    retail customer
      transactions   11.37
    suitability statement   11.13, 11.38
  investment business   12.17
  key features document   11.15
  know your customer   11.9
  monitoring   10.28
  mortgage sales
    advised sales   11.27, 11.30
    affordability   11.31
    independent intermediary
      firms   11.28

conduct of business – *contd*
  mortgage sales – *contd*
    initial disclosure
      document   11.29
    key features illustration   11.33
    lifetime mortgages   11.34–11.35
    non-advised sales   11.27
    regulated mortgage
      contracts   11.25
    services offered   11.26
    suitability for customer's
      need and
      circumstances   11.32
  pension sales   11.19
    free-standing additional
      voluntary
      contributions   11.24
    group personal pension
      plan   11.23
    record keeping   11.20
    stakeholder pension
      schemes   11.22
    product suitability   11.11
    risk, attitudes to   11.12
  SIB rules   1.3
  suitability letter   11.13
  terms of business   11.8
conflicts of interest   3.15, 11.16
  conflicting directorships   3.39
control risks *see* risk assessment
  framework
corporate voluntary
  arrangement (CVA)
  FSA powers in   5.23
criminal offences   5.15

D

David M Aaron (Personal
  Financial Planners) Limited   10.30
DBS Financial Management
  Plc   10.17
de-materialised instructions,
  sending   2.16
dealing in investments
  agent, as   2.10
  principal, as   2.9

Index

dealing in investments – *contd*
  regulated activity, as   2.5, 2.9–2.10
Decision Notice   5.17
delegation of responsibility   3.43
Deloitte & Touche Wealth
  Management Limited
  (DTWM)   10.15
deposits, accepting
  regulated activity, as   2.5, 2.6
direct offer financial
  promotions   12.20
directors
  conflicting directorships   3.39
  delegation of responsibility   3.43
  executive directors   3.40
  holding competing offices   3.44–3.45
  non-executive directors   3.41
  shadow directors   3.42
  standard of care   3.40

E

electric money, issuing of   2.7
employee share schemes   2.29
endowment-linked mortgages   1.4, 10.16, 10.24
enforcement action   5.1
  administration orders   5.19
  bankruptcy orders   5.22
  Decision Notice   5.17
  disciplining firms and
    approved persons   5.16
  Financial Services and
    Markets Tribunal   5.25
  generally   3.37, 5.1
  injunctions   5.12
  insolvency
    administration orders   5.19
    bankruptcy orders   5.22
    voluntary arrangements,
      FSA powers in   5.23
    voluntary winding up   5.21
    winding up by the court   5.20
  investigations
    general   5.5
    obtaining information   5.3

enforcement action – *contd*
  investigations – *contd*
    powers of investigator   5.5, 5.6
    skilled person's report   5.4
    specific   5.6
  procedural issues   5.17
  prohibition orders   5.11, 10.29
  prosecution of criminal
    offences   5.15
  redress   5.14
  remedial orders   5.12
  restitutions   5.13
  restraining orders   5.12
  search and seizure   5.7
  skilled person's report   5.4
  supervisory powers   5.8–5.15
  transactions at an undervalue   5.24
  uncovering non-compliance   5.2
  variation of permissions   5.9
  voluntary arrangements, FSA
    powers in   5.23
  Warning Notice   5.17
  winding up   5.18
    by the court   5.20
    voluntary   5.21
  withdrawal of approval   5.10
Equitable Life   1.4, 10.2–10.12
  awareness of problems   10.4
  closure to new business   10.9
  growing complaints   10.5
  Hyman proceedings   10.7
  Penrose Report   10.10
  product literature   10.6
  prohibition order   10.29
  public statements   10.5
  reinsurance   10.8, 10.29
  reserves   10.11
execution-only transactions   11.10
executive directors   3.40
extra income and growth plans
  (EIGP)   10.23

F

Financial Intermediaries and
  Brokers Regulatory
  Association (FIMBRA)   1.3

Index

Financial Ombudsman Service
  award, size of   9.19
  consolidation of pre-existing
    schemes   9.20
  dealing with   9.18
  eligible complainants   9.14
  generally   6.15, 9.1, 9.5, 9.6, 9.10
  jurisdiction   9.10
    compulsory   9.12
    voluntary   9.13
  preliminary decision   9.18
  summary dismissal   9.17
  territorial scope   9.11
  time limits for referral   9.5, 9.15
    exceptions   9.15, 9.16
  see also complaints handling
financial promotions   12.1
  certified sophisticated
    investors   12.13
  communications 'in the
    course of business'   12.3
  compliance failures   10.17
  conduct of investment
    business   12.17
  controlled activities   12.7
  controlled investments   12.6
  direct offer financial
    promotions   12.20
  engaging in investment
    activity, meaning of   12.5
  extra income and growth
    plans (EIGP)   10.23
  general requirements   12.22
  general restriction   12.2–12.7
    dis-application   12.8
    exemptions   12.11–12.21
    territorial scope   12.16
  high net worth companies   12.13
  high net worth individuals   12.13
  high(er) risk products   10.30
  inducement, meaning of   12.4
  invitation, meaning of   12.4
  new product lines   10.23
  non-real time financial
    promotions   12.9, 12.18

financial promotions – *contd*
  real time communications   12.9
    solicited   12.10
    unsolicited   12.10
  real time financial
    promotions   12.9
    solicited   12.19
    unsolicited   12.19
  transaction facilitation
    exemptions   12.15
  unincorporated associations   12.13
financial prudence   3.11
Financial Services
  Compensation Scheme   9.21
  compensation limits   9.21
  eligible claimants   9.23
    dis-application of
      exclusions   9.24
    exclusions   9.23
    protected investment
      business   9.25–9.28
  pre-conditions to
    compensation   9.22
  protected investment
    business   9.25
    in default   9.28
    protected claims   9.26
    relevant persons   9.27
  quantification of claims   9.31
  rejection of claims   9.29
  replacement of pre-existing
    schemes   9.21
  reporting obligation   9.30
  see also complaints handling
Financial Services and Markets
  Tribunal   5.25
free-standing additional
  voluntary contributions   11.24
Friends Provident Life and
  Pensions Limited   10.24
FSA Handbook   1.4, 3.9
funding
  adequacy of   10.14
funeral plan contracts   2.10, 2.21, 3.6

Index

G

general prohibition	2.1, 2.2
consequences of breach	2.2
see also regulated activities; regulated products	
Gower Report	1.3
group personal pension plan	11.23
groups	
exclusion for	2.27
Head of Compliance	3.26
guaranteed annuity rate pensions	10.3–10.12

H

handbooks	
alphabetic designations	3.54
design and terminology	3.53–3.54
FSA Handbook	1.4, 3.9
Hargreaves Lansdown Asset Management Limited	10.30
head office	
location of	3.21, 3.24
outside EEA	3.24
high net worth companies	12.13
high net worth individuals	12.13
high(er) risk products	10.30
home income plans	1.4

I

information society service provided from any EEA State other than UK	2.29
initial disclosure document (IDD)	11.29, 11.35, 11.38
injunctions	5.12
insolvency	5.18
administration orders	5.19
bankruptcy orders	5.22
voluntary arrangements, FSA powers in	5.23
voluntary winding up	5.21
winding up by the court	5.20
Institute of Actuaries	1.3, 3.5
Institute of Chartered Accountants	3.5

insurance	
assisting in administration and performance of contract of	2.14
Code of Conduct	11.36
commercial customers	11.41
conduct of business	11.36–11.41
connected contracts of insurance	2.30
excessive charges	11.40
introducers	2.12
large risks contracts	2.30
Lloyd's activities	2.20
record keeping	11.39
regulated activities	2.8, 2.12, 2.14, 2.20
exclusions	2.30
retail customer transactions	11.37
suitability statement	11.13, 11.38
underinsurance	6.6
see also professional indemnity insurers	
integrity	3.8, 3.31
Interdependence Limited	10.27
introducers	2.12
Investment Management Organisation (IMRO)	1.3
Irish European Reinsurance Company Limited (IRECO)	10.29
IT systems	
adequacy of	10.18

J

J Rothschild Assurance Plc	6.8
joint enterprises	
exclusion for	2.27

K

Key Facts Illustration document	11.33, 11.35
key features document	11.15
know your customer	11.9

L

Law Society	1.3, 3.5

Life Assurance and Unit Trust
    Regulatory Organisation
    (LAUTRO) 1.3
Lloyd's activities 2.20
Lloyds TSB Bank Plc (LTSB) 10.23

M

managing investments
    regulated activity, as 2.13
market conduct 3.12, 3.33
market regulation
    Financial Service Act 1986
        regime 1.3
    generally 1.1, 1.2
money laundering
    Abbey National 10.20
    adequacy of controls 10.19–10.22
    FSA's objectives 8.1
    identification of clients 8.4, 8.10
        exceptions 8.5, 8.10
    Money Laundering
        Regulations 2003 8.1, 8.9–8.10
    Money Laundering
        Reporting Officer
        (MLRO) 3.26, 8.3
    Money Laundering Sourcebook 8.1, 8.2–8.8
    nominated officer 8.3
    Northern Bank Limited 10.21
    penalties 8.13
    Proceeds of Crime Act 2002 8.11–8.13
    record keeping 8.8, 8.10
    regulated sector offences 8.12
    reporting
        external 8.7
        internal 8.6, 8.10
        National Criminal
            Intelligence Service,
            to 8.3, 8.4, 8.7, 8.10
    Royal Bank of Scotland 10.22
    specific duties 8.3
    systems and training 8.10
mortgage sales
    advised sales 11.27, 11.30

mortgage sales – *contd*
    affordability 11.31
    conduct of business 11.25–11.35
    endowment-linked
        mortgages 1.4, 10.16, 10.24
    independent intermediary
        firms 11.28
    initial disclosure document 11.29
    key features illustration 11.33
    lifetime mortgages 11.34–11.35
    non-advised sales 11.27
    regulated mortgage contracts 2.10, 2.22, 3.6, 11.25–11.35
    services offered 11.26
    suitability for customer's
        need and circumstances 11.32

N

National Criminal Intelligence
    Service (NCIS) 8.3, 8.4, 8.7, 8.10
new product lines 10.23
nominees
    exclusion for 2.24
non-executive directors 3.41
non-real time financial
    promotions 12.9, 12.18
Northern Bank Limited 10.21

O

occupational pension schemes
    managing investments of 2.5
outsourcing of compliance 3.26
overseas persons dealing with
    authorised business in UK 2.29

P

Part IV permission *see*
    authorisation
Penrose Report 10.10
pensions
    conduct of business 11.19–11.24
    Equitable Life 10.2–10.12
    free-standing additional
        voluntary contributions 11.24

Index

pensions – *contd*
  group personal pension plan 11.23
  guaranteed annuity rate
    policies 10.3–10.12
  managing investments of
    occupational pension
    schemes 2.5
  mis-sales 1.4
  record keeping 11.20
  regulated activities 2.5, 2.18
  stakeholder pension schemes 2.18, 11.13, 11.22
Personal Investment Authority (PIA) 1.3
personal representatives
  exclusion for 2.24
Principles for Business 1.3, 3.7
  client's assets 3.17
  communication with clients 3.14
  conflicts of interest 3.15, 11.16
  customer interests 3.13, 11.16
  financial prudence 3.11
  integrity 3.8
  management and control 3.10
  market conduct 3.12
  purposes of 3.7
  relations with Regulator 3.18, 5.2
  relationship of trust 3.16
  risk management 3.10
  skill, care and diligence 3.9
professional indemnity insurers
  brokers' duties 6.12
    recent example 6.13
  cover, arranging 6.5
  dealing with 6.4–6.15
  notification 6.6
    blanket notifications 6.9
    complaints, receipt of 9.6
    failure to notify 6.6
    notifiable circumstances 6.8
    notifiable claims 6.7
    test for materiality 6.8
    timing of 6.10
  recovering costs 6.14
  Regulator, and 6.15
  renewal, arranging 6.5, 6.9

professional indemnity insurers – *contd*
  standard duties 6.11
  underinsurance 6.6
prohibition orders 5.11, 10.29
prosecutions 5.15
prudence 3.11

R

real time communications 12.9
  solicited 12.10
  unsolicited 12.10
real time financial promotions 12.9
  solicited 12.19
  unsolicited 12.19
recognised professional bodies (RPBs) 1.3, 1.4
record keeping
  insurance 11.39
  money laundering 8.8, 8.10
  pension sales 11.20
  training and competence 7.10
recruitment 7.3
redress 5.14
regulated activities 2.1, 2.5
  accepting deposits 2.5, 2.6
  administering investments 2.15
  advising on investments 2.19
  agreeing to carry on activities 2.23
  arranging deals and investments 2.11
  collective investment scheme activities 2.17
  dealing in investments as agent 2.10
  dealing in investments as principal 2.9
  definition 2.5
  electric money 2.7
  exclusions
    employee share schemes 2.29
    groups 2.27
    insurance contracts 2.30
    joint enterprises 2.27

regulated activities – *contd*
  exclusions – *contd*
    nominees   2.24
    non-investment business   2.25
    overseas persons dealing with authorised business in UK   2.29
    personal representatives   2.24
    professional business   2.25
    provision of information society service from any EEA State other than UK   2.29
    sale of body corporate   2.28
    sale of goods   2.26
    supply of services   2.26
    trustees   2.24
  funeral plan contracts   2.10, 2.21
  general prohibition   2.1, 2.2, 2.5
  insurance   2.8
    assisting in administration and performance of contract of   2.14
    exclusions   2.30
    introducers   2.12
  introducers   2.12
  Lloyd's activities   2.20
  managing investments   2.13
  occupational pension schemes, managing investments of   2.5
  regulated mortgage contracts   2.22
  safeguarding investments   2.15
  sending de-materialised instructions   2.16
  stakeholder pension schemes   2.18
regulated mortgage contracts   2.10, 2.22, 11.25–11.35
  see also mortgage sales
regulated products   2.1
  definition   2.3
  general prohibition   2.1, 2.2, 2.3–2.4
  understanding the nature of the product   2.4
relations with Regulator   3.18, 3.34, 5.2

remedial orders   5.12
restitutionary payments   5.13
restraining orders   5.12
Review of Investor Protection, A (Gower Report)   1.3
risk
  customer's attitude to   11.12
  risk assessment framework   4.1
  the 45 risk elements   4.2
  board, management and staff of firm   4.8
  business risks   4.3
  control risks   4.4–4.8
  customer profile   4.3
  distribution mechanisms   4.3
  financial soundness   4.3
  internal systems and controls, nature of   4.7
  market efficiency   4.3
  meaning of 'risk'   4.1
  operational risks   4.3
  organisation of firm, nature of   4.6
  risks to objective groups (RTOGs)   4.9
  sources of business   4.3
  treatment of customers   4.5
  types of products and services   4.3
risk management   3.10, 3.36
Royal Bank of Scotland   10.22

S

safeguarding investments regulated activity, as   2.15
St James Place Unit Trust Group   10.26
sale of body corporate   2.28
sale of goods
  exclusion for   2.26
scandals   1.4
Scottish Widows   10.23
search and seizure   5.7
Securities and Futures Association (SFA)   1.3

Index

Securities and Investment
  Board (SIB)   1.3
  rulebook   1.3
self-regulatory organisations
  (SROs)   1.3
  rulebooks   1.3, 1.4
sending de-materialised
  instructions
  regulated activity, as   2.16
Senior Management
  Arrangements, Systems and
  Controls (SYSC) *see* systems
  and controls
shadow directors   3.42
significant influence functions   3.36, 3.37
significant management
  functions   3.28
skill, care and diligence   3.9, 3.32, 3.36
skilled person's report   5.4
stakeholder pension schemes
  regulated activities   2.18
  sales of   11.22
  suitability letter   11.13
Statements of Principle for
  Approved Persons   1.3, 3.7, 3.30–3.37
  controlled functions   3.35
  integrity   3.31
  internal organisation   1.4
  market conduct   3.33, 7.1
  organisation of business   3.35
  relations with Regulator   3.34
  skill, care and diligence   3.32, 3.36
Structured Capital At Risk
  Products (SCARPs)   10.30
suitability letter   11.13
supply of services
  exclusion for   2.26
systems and controls
  adequacy of   10.16
  approved person   3.27
  authorisation, and   3.10, 3.50–3.52
  money laundering   8.10
  monitoring appointed
    representatives   10.25–10.27

systems and controls – *contd*
  risk assessment   4.7
  Senior Management
    Arrangements, Systems
    and Controls (SYSC)   3.50
  breaches   10.16
  key requirements   3.51
  specific rules   3.52

T

top-up permissions   3.49
Townsend Rayner Associates
  Limited   10.29
training and competence
  activities, meaning   7.6
  adequacy of training   10.15
  competence levels   7.4–7.5
  competent adviser status   7.5
  controls on   7.7
  core standards   7.1
  employee, meaning   7.6
  high level standards   7.2
  maintaining competence   7.8
  money laundering   8.10
  pre-competence status   7.4
  record keeping   7.10
  recruitment   7.3
  supervising employees   7.9
transactions at an undervalue   5.24
trustees
  deemed authorised   3.3
  exclusion for   2.24

U

unincorporated associations
  financial promotions, and   12.13

W

Warning Notice   5.17
winding up   5.18
  by the court   5.20
  voluntary   5.21